FLAMINGO
ESTATE

PLEASURE PRINCIPLES
An Almanac from the Garden

Richard Christiansen

CHRONICLE BOOKS
SAN FRANCISCO

Tell me, what is it you plan to do
with your one wild and precious life?

—MARY OLIVER

FLAMINGO ESTATE
LOS ANGELES, CALIFORNIA

ACKNOWLEDGMENTS

COLLABORATORS

This book is a love letter. Made with people I love and respect enormously.

All of the original photography is by Hugh Davison—my friend and collaborator for the past few years. Working with him is a great joy—chasing light, waiting for the right ideas to unfold. Wherever we are, from Melbourne to Mexico, the more we make together, the better we get. I'm grateful we've built that kind of creative relationship.

So much of the writing is because of Camila Gonzalez, who has been the voice in the back of my head at Flamingo for so long—finishing my sentences, sharpening my thoughts, and (very often) rescuing me from my own spelling. I'm so grateful for her contribution to every word here.

The recipes were created by Sandy Ho, who has become a fast friend—and someone who brings sunshine into everything she makes. We've cooked together, catered parties together, and now made a book together. Sandy is destined for fame, and she's well on her way. She was assisted by Natalie Reeves and Sienna Ricca on this project, who made good things taste great.

John Reagan painted twenty-eight oil paintings for this book. John has been part of our family for years, and his partner, Pia Riverola, has been a collaborator in so much of our storytelling.

John is a wildly creative spirit, and I'm so happy we gave ourselves the very indulgent privilege of spending a year painting flowers. One day I will sell his paintings at auction and make an obscene amount of money. I'm very happy I got in early.

The book was designed by Lauryn Alejo, Joseph Abe, and Thuyen Nguyen—three remarkable designers who practice their craft with real care, and bring that excellence to everything they touch. I'm grateful for their eye, their patience, and their obsession with making things the very best they can.

A great debt is also owed to Jack Campbell, Jennifer Miller, Sam Bilinkas, Alexandrea Vizcarra, Taylor Kirby, and Ella Murphy, who worked incredibly hard to move things onward and upward—with enthusiasm, steadiness, and a little magic.

All of this would be a lie without the Flamingo Garden team who actually get their hands dirty: Valentino Del Toro, Katelyn Luevano, and Hank Jenkins. This book is an inadequate record of the enormous contribution they give to all of us.

And finally, if this book is a love letter, the person who deserves the most love is my partner, Aaron Harvey. He makes everything bigger, bolder, brighter—and somehow more possible. Harvey designs everything we make. He is the best Creative Director I know. Flamingo would never have happened without him by my side, at work and at home. The garden gave me flowers, but Harvey made them bloom. He is my great love.

THE FLAMINGO ESTATE FUND

All author profits from this book will go to supporting the Flamingo Estate Fund. The Flamingo Estate Fund is dedicated to the two causes we care about most: the environment and protecting the animals who call it home. As our business grows, a share of what we earn will flow into this fund, so any success we have is shared with the planet that makes it possible. You can read more about the Flamingo Estate Fund and the projects it supports on our website.

A NOTE ON CAPITALIZATION

We've always said that Mother Nature is the last great luxury house. At Flamingo Estate, we hold deep reverence for every plant and tree, every fruit, vegetable, and flower. As a gesture of that respect, throughout this book we capitalize the names of all plants, trees, and ingredients—the way you might honor a person or a place you love. Camellias, Cacti, Citrus—all of them are as important to us as anyone in our family. If they grow here, we treat them with the utmost care.

DEDICATION

My mother taught me the name of every plant I love. Her garden was a magical place for my imagination to take flight. This book is a thank you to her. x

Library of Congress Cataloging-in-Publication Data available.

ISBN 978-1-7972-4458-7

Manufactured in China.

MIX
Paper | Supporting responsible forestry
FSC™ C169962

WORDS BY Richard Christiansen and Camila Andrea Gonzalez.
CREATIVE DIRECTION BY Aaron Harvey.
DESIGN BY Joseph Abe, Lauryn Alejo, and Thuyen Nguyen.
PROJECT DIRECTION BY Sam Bilinkas.
EDITING BY Jack Campbell.
PHOTOGRAPHS BY Hugh Davison.
ARTWORK BY John Reagan.
IMAGE RESEARCH BY Jennifer Miller.
RECIPES AND FOOD STYLING BY Sandy Ho.
RECIPE DEVELOPMENT BY Ella Murphy.
FOOD STYLING ASSISTANCE FROM Natalie Reeves and Sienna Ricca.
RESEARCH BY Madeleine O'Sullivan Stearns.
COPYWRITTEN BY Shawnee Elliot.
TYPESET IN Exposure, Maison Mono, and Maison Neue.

Chronicle books and gifts are available at special quantity discounts to corporations, professional associations, literacy programs, and other organizations. For details and discount information, please contact our premiums department at corporatesales@chroniclebooks.com or at 1-800-759-0190.

CHRONICLE BOOKS LLC
680 Second Street
San Francisco, California 94107
www.chroniclebooks.com

CONTENTS

INTRODUCTION

↑
A propaganda poster was launched by the British government, shortly after the outbreak of World War II. Featuring a close-up of a boot treading a spade into the earth, the image served as a powerful call to action for civilians to transform every available space—from private lawns to public parks—into Victory Gardens.

←
Me with buckets of Protea in the Goat Shed. Photographed by Sean Hazen, 2025.

THE WAR ON TERROIR

This book was originally about Victory Gardens. I spent months researching the phenomenon of these gardens during World War I and World War II—the panic to win the war, the way families tore up lawns and vacant lots and planted food on every scrap of soil they could find. The propaganda machine asked every citizen to garden as if their lives depended on it. One World War I poster declared: "Every garden a munition plant." A shovel was a rifle. A seed packet, a magazine clip.

By the mid-1940s there were close to twenty million Victory Gardens in the United States alone—tiny patches of Tomatoes and Beans and Chard that ended up producing as much as 40 percent of the country's vegetables. At the urging of the government, they were planted on rooftops and in backyards, in city parks and on school grounds, in oil drums and window boxes. It was ordinary people with dirty hands, quietly deciding that growing something was a way to feed the country, feed the troops, and defeat the enemy.

What fascinates me now is the brilliance (and deceptiveness) of the idea—how it galvanized an entire country. Gardening became a wartime campaign. When the United States joined the war in April 1917, the government recruited big public voices—botanist Luther Burbank among them—and made a clean, almost militaristic ask: you grow vegetables at home so commercial farms can push more grain, meat, and sugar to soldiers and allies. Citizens were called "soldiers of the soil," and the nation got drafted into the war machine. President Woodrow Wilson said, "Food will win the war." It was a clever way to make people feel afraid and unify them at the same time.

The truth is, America was never in danger of running out of food in the way Europe was. Nevertheless, by the end of 1917, Americans had planted about 3 million new gardens; in 1918, roughly 5.2 million. The US School Garden Army enrolled 2.5 million children and produced crops valued (then) at $48 million—more than a billion dollars today. It was social media before social media: millions of children connected by the desire to garden.

When I first started this book, I kept asking myself: if we were to have a Victory Garden today, what would we be fighting? Not Germany. Not Japan. The enemy now is slipperier. It's the numbness that comes from scrolling all day. It's the convenience that makes us forget where anything comes from. It's our worship of speed and efficiency at the expense of smell, touch, and taste.

And maybe that's the real war now—not on food itself, but on the time to discover its character. On the subtle differences between things you can only discover by eating, drinking, making, or doing. The French call it terroir: the taste of place. The hillside in the glass. The summer in a Tomato. The way a Peach can taste completely different depending on where it grew. Convenience has made the whole world faster. And that has a way of sanding those edges down until everything is quicker to swallow—and harder to feel.

Most of us now spend four to five hours a day on our phone—an entire day every week, or more than two months of every year, staring into a small backlit rectangle. We say we don't have time to plant a tree, but we somehow have time for twelve years of our lives on a screen. Big Tech and AI (and the deregulation and cheerleading around both) were all in my head. I was deep in research about this, and about the equivalents of Victory Gardens in different cultures.

Then, as I was writing an early draft, two things happened in quick succession. First, my friend Jane Goodall died. She crossed over at ninety-one, after a life spent listening to forests and living alongside chimpanzees, teaching the rest of us that animals have families, grief, and joy just as we do. At her memorial service, people spoke about how time in nature for her was almost a religious experience—a kind of patient prayer. She believed every individual could make a difference, no matter how small, just by doing something, anything. Sitting there, I realized that the "quiet revolution" I'd been trying to write about was exactly the kind of thing she'd been asking of us in our everyday lives.

Days later, the news announced yet another attempt by Donald Trump to weaken environmental protections—chipping away at the Endangered Species Act and at the Clean Water Act through rules that stripped protections from countless streams and wetlands that feed our rivers and our drinking water. It felt like watching the guardrails being unscrewed in real time. I was furious. And, like many of us, I felt angry in the face of a government seemingly committed to breaking the very rules that keep us alive.

So I started again.

Instead of writing a book about an enemy "out there"—a politician, a policy, an algorithm—I decided to make a workbook: an exploration of the plants and ideas from the grounds of Flamingo Estate, and the small revolution each of us can have with the green world that is still right here. With the pots on our balconies. The little seedlings on our windowsills. The food we grow and eat. It's a Victory Garden—yes—but not to fight an enemy. To declare peace.

What I'm after now isn't a clean victory. It's dirty work. Something harder, slower, and (in the long run) far more radical: taking the time to work with the living world. It's why we named the workbook you're holding PLEASURE PRINCIPLES. Pleasure learned by making, cooking, tasting, and smelling.

Right now we hardly agree on anything. We don't agree on politics. We don't agree on pronouns. We don't agree on immigration or religion. We don't agree on the environment, or how to end a war, or how to start one. But I have a quiet suspicion that there is one thing we can still meet around: our senses. We all know what it's like to be hijacked by a scent, or a taste.

A Victory Garden in the heart of New York, 1944. The image illustrates the massive scale of the civilian war effort during World War II. Urban residents transformed vacant lots, parks, and rooftops into productive agricultural spaces to supplement their food rations and boost domestic supply.

Published in 1919, the "marching vegetables" (Potatoes, Carrots, and Beets) symbolize the mobilization of the entire country—even the soil—toward a common goal of global stability.

To catch the smell of Garlic sizzling in a pan and, without warning, you're back in your grandmother's kitchen. To take a bite of a sun-warmed Stone Fruit and let the juice dribble down your arm, and suddenly remember a summer you thought you'd forgotten. To press your face into your dog's fur and feel your shoulders drop and your heart open. To pass a neighbor's Jasmine at night and slow down, just for a heartbeat, because the air has turned almost indecently sweet.

That's what this book is about. I wanted a workbook of sorts. An almanac of twelve months of the Flamingo Estate garden, my favorite plants, and the things I do with them. A month-by-month guide to falling back in love with nature in the most ordinary, sensual ways: how we grow things, how we smell them, how we eat them, how we share them.

While I was writing this book I was inspired to significantly expand my own garden. I purchased my neighbor's property to demolish the house and build a greenhouse. I used the new property to create a giant Camellia Garden, and a new Rose Garden. The research in this book motivated me to plant a new Sage Garden, plus a Spice Garden and expand our Medicine Garden. I invested in a more extensive collection of night-blooming plants, and built a new Lavender Garden. I see all my little gardens within the Estate as tiny acts of resistance. They reclaim my attention from my phone and from the tech companies that profit off our numbness. These gardens bring me back to life. And the dirty work of building them is a joy.

But you don't need an estate or acres of land. You can start with a windowsill. A single pot of Basil. A hot frying pan. The work is simply this: to pay attention. To smell, to taste, to listen. To let these small, daily encounters with the living world rearrange your priorities. If the old Victory Gardens helped feed soldiers at war, maybe our new gardens can help feed a different kind of army—a generation of people awake to their senses, fiercely protective of the land that feeds them, unwilling to let it be poisoned or paved over.

My hope is that these pages will make you want to plant something, cook something, make something. That they'll give you a few tools, a few recipes, a few experiments—and maybe a few jolts of beauty—to help you start your own dirty work, wherever you are.

—Richard Christiansen

THE GARDEN

The word "paradise" comes from an old Persian word for "walled garden." That feels right to me. Flamingo Estate has always felt like that: a secret, high-walled garden wrapped around a pink house in the middle of a city that forgot it was there. Los Angeles grew up and out in every direction, and somehow this place stayed tucked behind its hedges, hiding in plain sight for decades.

When I first discovered Flamingo, it was obvious that someone had once loved this garden. You could see it in the old stone paths and the way a few stubborn Oleanders still bloomed in the wrong places. The house and grounds had been neglected, but there were tender fingerprints everywhere. Someone had really tried to once build something beautiful. The soil was parched and lifeless, the irrigation systems long rusted. But the bones were there: walkways where rows of plants once stood, and long trellises that had clearly supported Grapes at some point in their lives.

When we began adding new structures and renovating the house, I was lucky enough to work with my friends Karl Fournier and Olivier Marty, the founders of Studio KO in Paris. They had designed extraordinary projects all over the world, but never in the United States. From their studios in Paris and Marrakesh, we started talking about California and Morocco—two sun-drenched, bone-dry landscapes punctuated by pockets of oasis. Both were made for indoor-outdoor living. We began to imagine a series of pavilions stitched together by a garden, and a garden broken into smaller rooms.

Karl and Olivier introduced me to Arnaud Casaus, an extraordinarily talented landscape architect living in France who had a deep curiosity for hot-weather gardens. Arnaud flew to Los Angeles, and we walked every inch of the hillside together and visited all the other great gardens in LA. We threw out my early ideas for fussy, over-organized "garden rooms" and instead listened to what the land was asking for: one giant Mediterranean garden, with a series of spaces that would hug the hill-side and flow into each other.

←
My friend Jeremy Liebman came to photograph the Estate just after I purchased it and every few months following. Clearly, someone had loved the garden deeply once upon a time, but it had fallen into disrepair. The structure above would later be demolished to become the music room. Below is part of the property that I flattened with a Bobcat; it later became the Cactus Garden.

Together we embarked on a years-long process that transformed the property from a dusty series of slopes into a sprawling botanical garden filled with hundreds of plants, trees, and rare species. The plan was to design a kind of Noah's Ark in the middle of the city, planting hundreds of varietals from around the world that could survive amid California's water shortages.

Slowly we began replanting, buying hundreds of new trees, including rare Cycads, Cactus, and fruit trees. We rebuilt the sandy soil and coaxed it back to life, so it could support everything from Papayas, Zucchini, Grapes, Pomegranates, Apples, Macadamia nuts, Figs, Apricots—and much, much more. We planted, and then we waited for everything to sync up.

A garden is a giant orchestra tuning up. All these new plants needed time to learn each other's rhythms, to find the right key. Every season they grow taller, stronger, stranger—more themselves. As the trees have matured, they've carved out new alcoves and shadowy nooks that now belong to the birds and animals living high in their branches. If you sit in the garden at night, when the owls glide overhead and the crickets start their chorus, you realize the garden has become the new nightclub—wildly alive, crowded, and pulsing with color and energy.

Like all of us, the garden keeps changing shape. I bought the neighboring properties on two sides and pushed the borders outward, planting an expansive Camellia Garden, a bright Azalea slope, and moving the Rose Garden so it could stretch its legs and become the riot of blooms it always wanted to be.

None of this would exist without the people who tend it every day—Hank, Val, and Katelyn. Gardening is an ongoing conversation between you and Mother Nature, and it's written by the hands that show up with pruners and muddy knees, season after season. I am endlessly grateful to Hank and his team for helping to turn this place into our own small paradise.

Looking up the staircase from the Spice Garden.

Beehives in the Cycad Garden.

THE GOAT SHED

The Goat Shed is the beating heart of Flamingo Estate. It sits at the bottom of the orchard, just above the Macadamia trees and below the Vegetable Garden on the hillside. The whole area where we now live was once a goat farm, with animals roaming the entire valley. This little wooden house was one of the earliest structures built up here, and in some photographs from the turn of the last century, you can see a family standing barefoot around a simple building—no stairs, no terraces, no fruit trees, just a shack and a handful of goats. That little house was the original shepherd's hut, accessible from the street only by a narrow path that wound up and over the hill to the nearest road.

Curiously, there's a deep cave next to the Goat Shed carved into the slope. We assume it was once used to store goat milk and cheese before refrigeration—a cool, earthen pantry where someone, a hundred years ago, checked on crocks of milk the way we now check emails. When I was digging a hole for an Olive tree, we also found a rusty gun buried just in front of the cave. So, this place has clearly lived a few lives.

Over the years, Los Angeles forgot that any of this was here. The city built itself up and over and around it. By the time I discovered the property, the Goat Shed was almost a teardown: sagging roof, peeling paint, and a few stubborn boards holding on precariously. But the minute I walked inside, I knew it had to stay. It was the perfect distance from the main house—far enough that it could have its own identity, yet close enough that you could get there at sunrise with a cup of coffee.

We took out some walls and opened up the interior, then salvaged the original cast-iron bathtub from inside and dragged it out onto the terrace—a garden soaking tub with a view of the whole valley. A couple of times a year, I manage to escape long enough to sit in that tub and watch the sun disappear behind the Macadamias, listening to the owls clock in for their shift.

Truthfully, the Goat Shed is my favorite place on the whole property. It's the best place to sit on the small porch and watch the birds dart around the orchard, or to see the last light slide over the hills with my own goats bleating somewhere below. When the Macadamias and Olives are in leaf and the Wisteria is growing like mad above, it feels like you are sitting in a lost paradise.

In the early days of Flamingo, the Goat Shed was our entire factory. We made all of our soaps in that little building, along with our tinctures and a few uncertain experiments that never saw the light of day. It's hard to believe now that those four walls were the genesis of what has become a large brand, but it's true: it all started here. In one corner, there is still a small apothecary, shelves full of jars and tins—seeds and herbs collected over the years, dried petals, bits of bark, and sample essential oils from as far away as Japan that we fell in love with.

Around the table is where we would dream up new candle fragrances or new pantry staples. Every one of our original products was born in that room. We met farmers here. We broke bread here. We sat up too late here, with wax on our hands and notebooks full of ideas. We made magic mushroom tea here and dried armfuls of flowers from the ceiling. It was also here that I wrote my last book, spending six months with my head down until late in the night.

Today, it's still the most important place on the Estate. It's the center of all the action and all the glory that's happening in the garden. Under the stewardship of Hank Jenkins, our lead gardener, and the entire team, the Goat Shed has become the control room for a kind of slow, gentle revolution—one where we all get to become shepherds again. Not of goats anymore, but of plants, bees, soil, and people. We plan plantings from here. We stand on the porch with mud on our boots and try to coax everyone, ourselves included, toward a life that is a little happier, a little healthier, and a lot more green.

→
In the early 1900s, the Estate was a huge goat farm. This was the shepherd's house, and one of the earliest in the area. When I purchased the property, it was abandoned. We restored it to become the Goat Shed, the heart of the garden. This image was taken after we planted an orchard of small Macadamia trees around the building. Today, these trees tower high above the roofline. Our Vegetable Garden is now located on the hill above the Goat Shed, and our goats live down below.

↑
The interior of the Goat Shed, the heartbeat of the garden. The Estate crew meets here every day. The walls were hand-painted by de Gournay, showcasing the flora and fauna of the Estate.

←
Winter flowers drying from the Goat Shed ceiling. This room is where we made our first soaps and body products when we started the business.

→
Apothecary jars with seeds and herbs from the garden.

January is about faith. Not the Jesus kind. But the faith in knowing that change is coming. The garden looks naked and lifeless—all branches and roots, except for the absurd generosity of Camellia flowers and Torch Aloe hanging like lanterns in the cold. This is when we tuck bare-root Roses, fruit trees, and berries into the earth, sow Sweet Peas and Poppies we won't see for months, and lace the beds with

JANUARY

compost and mulch like extra warm blankets. While the world is still insisting it's winter, we're slipping Kale, Fennel, Lettuce, Pea, and Broccoli seeds into trays and trusting they know what to do. January asks us to believe in what we've buried—to know that somewhere under the cold, small green shoots are already rising, rehearsing for a spring the rest of the city hasn't quite dreamed of yet. We have faith.

Coco Chanel adopted the Camellia early. She first pinned a white one to her belt in 1913; by the early 1920s, it had moved from a personal emblem into her work—embroidered on blouses and pinned to chiffon dresses. She loved it for its graphic symmetry and winter-blooming purity, and because it had no thorns and no scent—a flower that wouldn't snag a dress or clash with the perfume a woman chose to wear. In a house built on restraint, the Camellia became the code for quiet power.

Camellias often remind me of the porcelain-faced Geishas in Japanese paintings. They don't like the sun, they're incredibly fragile, and they face the world with perfect white, shocking red, and sensual pinks—yet most carry only the faintest, greenest scent, as if they've turned the volume down to speak in powerful whispers.

In Japan, the Camellia is known as Tsubaki, literally "the tree with shining leaves." Those glossy, lacquered leaves reminded people of the sacred bronze mirrors used in Shinto shrines—one side polished to a high shine, the other carved with birds and butterflies. The flower itself has always been complicated there. Tsubaki symbolizes love, devotion, elegance, and the ephemeral nature of life, but it is also associated with death. Unlike a Rose, which sheds petal by petal, a Camellia often drops its whole head at once, flower and stamens intact. For the Samurai, that single, heavy fall looked too much like a beheading—the head tipped from the body in one clean stroke. Some called it the Samurai flower, a symbol of noble, sudden death. To this day, it is considered bad luck in parts of Japan to bring red Camellias to someone in the hospital.

The flower found other uses, too. Oil pressed from Camellia seeds—Tsubaki oil—was used to gloss Geisha hair, to protect swords and knives from rust, and to preserve wood. A quiet, invisible function: protecting steel, feeding hair, never announcing itself. Again, beauty working offstage.

Two maiko (apprentice geisha) tending to Camellias in their garden, Japan, 1910.

French model Inès de la Fressange, wearing a Chanel Camellia, poses in Coco Chanel's apartment, Paris, 1986.

A Satsuma Kurenai Camellia from our collection at Flamingo, photographed by Hugh Davison, 2025.

When I was a little boy, none of this history was available to me. All I knew was that my mother had planted long lines of Camellias in the narrow strip between our house and garage in rural Australia. It was probably the only place on the entire farm where they could thrive—protected on both sides by high walls, with just enough sky above to catch gentle light. Those trees grew strong and tall, and my childhood is punctuated with memories of the Rose-like flowers in bright magenta, deep red, soft pink, and brilliant white. Their fluffy, pollen-rich centers were blinding yellow; their leaves so shiny they looked freshly polished.

I have such happy memories of watching my mother water them in the cool of night, with the crickets singing and mosquitoes biting. As I grew older, I would water them too, knowing how much she loved them. I would pick buckets of the flowers and place them around the house: tight ivory blooms floating in bowls, big reds balanced on saucers. I am sure this is when my father realized I did not want to play football. My head was in the flowers. While other boys were tackling each other in the field, I was arranging Camellias on the kitchen table.

Today, when I type "Camellia" into my iPhone, it brings up hundreds of photos I've taken in the garden. But the AI filter often can't discern the difference between a Rose and a Camellia. Perhaps this confusion predates our lazy technology. For centuries people have called Camellias "Winter Roses" or "Chinese Roses." In many ways it's a shame, because the Rose has become a ubiquitous workhorse of pageantry—corsages, bridal bouquets, red-carpet arrangements—while the Camellia has mostly stayed in the shadows as the more regal of the two. The Rose is prom queen; the Camellia is the unfussed woman in the corner watching quietly and missing nothing.

It might be why some are surprised when smelling the Camellia. It does not offer the loud, perfumed shout of the Rose. Instead, most prefer a much more quiet fragrance, leaning toward the green, the dewy, the clean—or, in many cases, almost nothing at all. Chanel loved that; she wanted a flower that wouldn't compete with N°5. But one cannot make aromatic generalities, because every variety offers its own quirks. For this, we have people like Dr. Robert K. Cutter to thank. A pioneer in Camellia research from Berkeley, California, he committed himself in the 1960s to developing fragrant varieties from the species *C. lutchuensis*—introducing backcross hybrids like 'Alice K. Cutter' and 'Virginia W. Cutter.' These flowers aired notes reminiscent of Apple Blossoms, Olive Groves, and Green Tea, laying the groundwork for successors like Kenneth Hallstone ('Scented Sun') and Toichi Domoto ('Scented Gem' in 1983).

Freshly painted Camellia accessories for the 1992 Chanel Fall Runway Show.

Coco Chanel, with Camellias pinned to her jacket, shares a cigarette with Salvador Dalí in 1938.

Part of the aromatic mystique of the Camellia is that it cannot be captured. There is no true Camellia essential oil; the flowers yield almost no volatile oil at all. In perfumery, a "Camellia note" is always a fantasy accord—a blend of Green Tea, Peony, watery florals, Jasmine, and sometimes even a whisper of Violet and musk. Only a master perfumer can evoke its essence, and even then, nothing ever quite compares to the fresh bud on the tree: that strange, almost silent presence of scent, sitting somewhere between leaf and petal.

In Europe, the Camellia took on a completely different kind of fame. In 1848, Alexandre Dumas *fils* published *La Dame aux Camélias*—"The Lady of the Camellias"—based on his love affair with the courtesan Marie Duplessis. The heroine, Marguerite Gautier, wears Camellias as a kind of coded language: a red one in her corsage when she is unavailable to her lovers, a white one when she is "free." Verdi turned the novel into the opera *La Traviata*, and for years actresses and sopranos fluttered across European stages trailed by Camellias. A flower that had once symbolized Samurai death and Shinto mirrors became, in Paris, a symbol of a very different kind of transaction—love, money, illness, sacrifice—and eventually, tragic redemption.

So by the time a Camellia appears on a Chanel jacket, or in my mother's narrow garden, it is already carrying an enormous amount of luggage: Samurai and Geishas and courtesans and opera and couture and tea ceremonies and hair oil and sword oil and my father's confusion about football. Not many flowers are this busy.

The Camellia's popularity in California was largely fueled by Japanese American gardeners. Before World War II, many Japanese families owned farms and nurseries in Southern California. As I mentioned elsewhere in this book, Japanese farmers once provided most of the produce in California and were instrumental in cultivating and introducing species, including rare Camellias. When these families were forced into internment camps, many had to sell their nurseries and plant collections for a fraction of their value.

E. Manchester Boddy, a newspaper publisher and horticulturalist, purchased a significant number of these plants, which formed the foundation of the now-famous Camellia collection at Descanso Gardens in Los Angeles. Modern-day research has revealed that the "fair price" he was said to have paid was not accurate; Descanso is now working to acknowledge this history and honor the Japanese American growers who built their collection without ever having their names on the plaques.

Descanso Gardens aside, today Los Angeles is a tough place for this delicate flower. It's rare to see Camellias thriving here, given the sunshine, the heat, and their insatiable thirst for year-round water. They have not evolved to survive everywhere. They remind us to find our own protected place where we can truly bloom, rather than trying to endure in harsh environments that are not made for us. Just like me not wanting to play football as a kid. The Camellias were a signal that it's okay to bloom where others don't.

I was determined to plant Camellias at Flamingo Estate as a reminder of my mother and the joy she got from hers. Previously, we had planted a handful under the arms of my vast Jacaranda tree. Her wide limbs and ample shade were not enough to protect them. I moved them to the base of the giant concrete Bathhouse at the bottom of the garden, where I thought they would thrive in its shadow. No luck. Los Angeles is not made for Camellias.

And yet, the most famous Camellia nursery in America is in the City of Angels. Nuccio's Nurseries, a ninety-year-old Altadena nursery specializing in breeding and growing rare Camellias and Azaleas. Martha Stewart was the first to tell me about Nuccio's, in a tone that made me feel like it was a luxury brand I had somehow missed. She was here filming a TV commercial and asked me to accompany her to pick out some varieties to fly back to her house in Connecticut. When we arrived, I was struck by the vast collection of these incredibly beautiful things, literally ten minutes from my home. She strapped them into the seats of a private jet and flew them east. The following year, I sent her a dozen varieties for her birthday, like sending little pieces of a lost garden.

In January 2025, Los Angeles fell victim to massive fires in different corners of the city, including the Eaton Fire not far from the Estate. It swept into the neighborhood sometime early on January 8, leapfrogging some homes and gutting others. Nuccio's old family home burned to the ground, as did several wooden outbuildings. Somehow, the fire spared thousands of Camellias and Azaleas arranged under a wood-lath structure covered with shade cloth, but

Camellias at Nuccio's Nurseries in Altadena, California. Dania Maxwell / © 2023. *Los Angeles Times*.

Our head gardener, Hank Jenkins, at Nuccio's Nurseries, selecting Camellias to bring back to the Estate in fall 2025. Photo by Valentino Del Toro.

destroyed the infrastructure needed to water and care for them.

Martha called me the night of the fire. Her first question was about my home. Her second was about Nuccio's—so legendary is that nursery in the imaginations of all of us who love the garden. Though many of the plants survived the fire, without easy access to water the nursery's future is now at risk. After almost a century of breeding rare Camellias and Azaleas, Nuccio's Nurseries may close its doors. By the time you are reading this, it may already be gone.

As I wrote earlier in this book, I recently purchased my neighbors' home and property. The house doesn't interest me at all (it was demolished to become a greenhouse). But the garden, covered in a canopy of mature Oaks and the tallest Pine trees, was traditionally considered a lost cause. There's almost no direct sunlight, so at ground level it had become a wasteland. For years I thought it was a Camellia paradise waiting to happen. Truthfully, I purchased the whole place so I could plant them. And not just a few. When Nuccio's announced they were closing, I knew I wanted to be the guardian of as many Camellias as possible—170 in total. They would thrive in the shade and under the care of the Flamingo Garden team. A place for their aromatic ghost to finally come home—fleeting and elusive, almost transparent, always there.

My Camellia Garden is now settling nicely, soon to be awash with Geisha-faced flowers. Some say that the scent of Camellias is the sound of silence made fragrant. I like that. I hope to finally return to the quiet nights when I can water them all under a bright, starry sky, listen to the crickets, and get bitten by the mosquitoes. To stand between the Camellias—guarded by a flower that has always known how to be a code for quiet power.

←
A collection of our Camellia flowers from the garden, winter 2025. Photographed by Sean Hazen.

→
Our living room at Flamingo Estate, with Camellias in the center. On the coffee table is a collection of our candle named Blooming Camellia, which launched in fall 2025 with Monica Lewinsky, with all proceeds going to anti-bullying charities around the world.

[GROUNDING] : A MAP OF PLEASURE FROM THE GARDEN

THE SAGE GARDEN

34°08' N / 118°12' W LOS ANGELES, CALIFORNIA

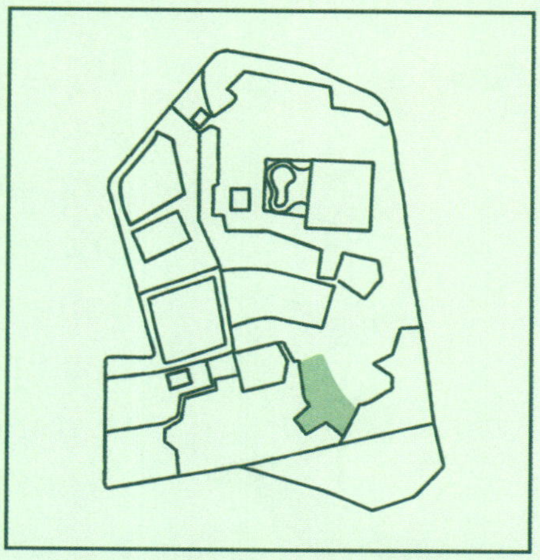

If Flamingo Estate had an official fragrance, it would be Sage.

On certain days, the whole hillside smells sharp and green—the scent of sun-warmed Sage lifting off the slope. It's a camphorous, earthy fragrance that's not just my favorite scent, but my favorite attitude. Sage, cliché or not, feels like change to me—a clearing of energy, a way of moving on. For centuries, people have burned its leaves to shift heavy energy away and welcome in the bright and new. I'm all for that.

Sage—particularly White Sage (*Salvia apiana*)—has deep roots in many cultures, especially among Indigenous peoples of North America. Its use for clearing energy is often called "smudging," a sacred ritual with profound spiritual significance. As it has moved into mainstream Western culture, it has raised important conversations about appropriation and respect. For many Native American and Indigenous nations, particularly those in Southern California and northern Baja, White Sage is considered a sacred medicine. It is not just an herb to be burned; it is a gift from the land, lovingly referred to by some as "grandmother." This plant carries stories much older than any of us.

Garden Sage (*Salvia officinalis*) by Nicolas François Regnault, from his influential work *La Botanique mise à la portée de tout le monde ou collection des plantes d'usage dans la médecine, dans les alimens et dans les arts* (Botany Made Accessible to Everyone, or a Collection of Plants Used in Medicine, Food, and the Arts), published in Paris starting around 1774.

↘

Images from a project using Sage from the Estate, by artist Jeremy Kost, summer 2019.

Herbalist Sebastian Kneipp once said that growing Sage in your garden is like having your own pharmacy at hand. Research suggests it supports cognitive function, memory, and attention. In England, folklore held that Sage strengthened memory; hence a "sage" (wise person) was someone with a long memory. Its powerful free-radical scavenging properties also play a role in bolstering the body's defenses against aging. Even its name hints at its reputation: the botanical *Salvia* comes from the Latin *salvere*, "to be saved."

There are over nine hundred species of Sage worldwide, with nineteen native to California. They grow along the Pacific Coast, cross valleys, and thread their way up our mountain slopes. The *Los Angeles Times* once wrote that Sage is to the West what Lavender (*Lavandula*) is to France. Among these native species are Hummingbird Sage (*Salvia spathacea*), Pitcher Sage (*Lepechinia fragrans*), Black Sage (*Salvia mellifera*), Purple Sage (*Salvia leucophylla*), Mexican Bush Sage (*Salvia leucantha*), and White Sage (*Salvia apiana*)—all currently growing wild at the Estate after a good winter rain.

Until recently, Sage grew just about everywhere on our Estate: under the Macadamia trees in the orchard, along the Olive walkways, and all the way down the hillside. We had many varieties, but never all of them gathered in one place. None of them need fertilizer, and they need very little water, so they punctuated the Estate wherever there was a gap.

Then last summer, Harvey and I went to the dry Balearic Islands of Spain. Here we discovered the island's long history with the plant. Ibizan Wild Sage (*Salvia officinalis subsp. lavandulifolia*) is a naturally growing variant with a sweet, earthy aroma—less sharp than our White Sage, more like a mix of Thyme and dry Lemon peel. We stayed at a farmhouse with a beautiful vegetable and herb garden, where Ibizan Wild Sage and Balkan Clary Sage (*Salvia sclarea*) grew together in a kind of fragrant tangle. Most impressive of all was the Clary Sage that sent up pink-purple

Each of them has its own accent. HUMMINGBIRD SAGE holds the title of Miss California in the garden, reigning supreme in the southern half of our state. It commonly colors the understory of Oaks in bold fuchsias and magentas, spiking into the air with firework-like flowers. It seduces Hummingbirds with a fragrance that's floral, minty, and just a touch spicy—warmer, sweeter, and more approachable than other native Sages, which are sharper by nature.

WHITE SAGE on a hot afternoon smells like hot stones and resin—sharp, pungent, almost silvery. When you rub a leaf between your fingers, the oils shoot into the air: medicinal, smoky, and strangely comforting. You can see why people feel it "clears" things. Today, its wild populations have declined due to overharvesting for commercial use. At the Estate, we counter this by planting it everywhere, paying it a visit when in need to breathe a little lighter.

PITCHER SAGE leans more toward camphor and Eucalyptus, like someone cleaned the house with herbs. PURPLE SAGE is warm and resinous, with a hint of Honey and dust. MEXICAN BUSH SAGE smells a bit like Lavender that's spent too much time in the sun—soft, woody, a little purple even in the nose. And CLEVELAND SAGE (*Salvia clevelandii*), with its brilliant blue flowers surging skyward, leads with one of the most intense aromas of all—camphor, Eucalyptus, Rosemary, and Mint—so potent it can even repel deer and pests.

My favorite is BLACK SAGE. If we could bottle the smell of California, we would begin and end with it. In this incredibly tough, drought-tolerant California native, there's an enthralling will to live. It thrives in some of the poorest soils, goes dormant during severe drought, and at the first drop of rain springs back to life as if nothing happened—changing the color of its leaves from nearly black (hence its name) to a rich, deep green. In its rough leaves, you'll find its oil: deeply resinous, alarmingly camphorous, and peppery with a hint of salinity. Honeybees have their own love affair with the plant's perfume, following it religiously, swooning at its nectar. Once it's found, they collect it eagerly to make the deeply herbal, warm, and wild Honey California is known for. I love Black Sage so much that we created a line of products with it: a Black Sage Soap, Candle, Hydrosol Spray, and Salts. We source our Essential Oil from White Buffalo Land Trust, based at Jalama Canyon Ranch, a 1,000-acre living laboratory in Santa Barbara. Here they harvest Black Sage in abundance and distill the most powerful version of the oil that we have ever smelled.

Colored lithograph of seven (out of nine hundred) Sages in bloom, nineteenth century.

flower spikes that drew pollinators like magnets. Its smell is oily, nutty, almost like Amber and Tea.

Like the Damask is to the Rose, the Clary is to the Sage. Among the hundreds of species of Sage worldwide, Clary Sage is the only one that reigns supreme in the world of luxury perfumery. This is due to its versatility—at once cool, mineral, and astringent—opening bright and green, evolving into a sweet floral, and drying down to an amber finish. It acts as a bridge between florals, herbs, and musk, and it fixes them into place, allowing them to last longer on the skin. Part of that is its high concentration of the diterpene alcohol sclareol, which helps other fragrance notes evaporate more slowly. But the other secret is time: the scent is much deeper when the Sage is left to wilt before distilling. If cut and distilled while still green, it will not offer the depth that gives it its indispensable role in perfumery.

Anyway, standing in the Balearic Islands, surrounded by bees in that cloud of scent, I began to imagine a dedicated garden—a place where every kind of Sage we love could grow side by side. So, our head gardener, Hank, and the team began carving out a section of the hillside to plant a proper Sage HQ. Now, when you walk into our Sage Garden, it feels like stepping into a game of fragrance Whac-A-Mole. Black Sage, White Sage, Clary, Hummingbird, Purple, Mexican Bush—each one popping up with its own scent. One moment you get a hit of something sharp and cleansing; the next a waft of something sweet and almost floral; then a deep, smoky undercurrent.

For me, the Sage Garden is a model of what Flamingo Estate is trying to be: rooted in place, generous to its history, and grounded in folklore but stretching toward the future. A place to let the old energy go, smell the wildness on your own hillside, and feel a little clearer, a little more ready for whatever comes next.

Bundles of dried Sage, Eucalyptus, and Rosemary from the orchard. We make these throughout the year and burn them to shift the energy and fill the home with fragrance. Photographed by Hugh Davison in winter 2025.

INSIDE THE SAGE GARDEN AT FLAMINGO ESTATE:

CLARY SAGE [*SALVIA SCLAREA*]

WHITE SAGE [*SALVIA APIANA*]

BLACK SAGE [*SALVIA MELLIFERA*]

HUMMINGBIRD SAGE [*SALVIA SPATHACEA*]

MEXICAN BUSH SAGE [*SALVIA LEUCANTHA* 'MIDNIGHT']

COMMON SAGE [*SALVIA OFFICINALIS*]

PINEAPPLE SAGE [*SALVIA ELEGANS*]

SPANISH SAGE [*SALVIA OFFICINALIS SUBSP. LAVANDULIFOLIA*]

GREEK SAGE [*SALVIA FRUTICOSA*]

BLUE SAGE [*SALVIA AZUREA*]

TRICOLOR SAGE [*SALVIA OFFICINALIS* 'TRICOLOR']

SONOMA SAGE OR CREEPING SAGE [*SALVIA SONOMENSIS*]

WAVERLY SAGE [*SALVIA* 'WAVERLY']

SANTA ROSA ISLAND SAGE [*SALVIA BRANDEGEEI* 'SANTA ROSA ISLAND']

BRAZILIAN SAGE [*SALVIA GUARANITICA*]

BOLIVIAN SAGE [*SALVIA OXYPHORA*]

NODDING SAGE [*SALVIA NUTANS*]

LIMELIGHT SAGE [*SALVIA MEXICANA* 'LIMELIGHT']

PINE MOUNTAIN SAGE [*SALVIA SEMIATRATA*]

SILVER SAGE [*SALVIA ARGENTEA*]

JERUSALEM SAGE [*SALVIA HIEROSOLYMITANA*]

GUATEMALAN LEAF SAGE [*SALVIA CACALIIFOLIA*]

[3]

YOU NEED
WILLIAM FARNUM
AMERICA'S MOST POPULAR ACTOR
NOW ON THE PINNACLE OF SUCCESS
PROFIT FROM HIS DRAWING POWER
BOOK THIS PRODUCTION NOW!
STANDARD PICTURES
FOX
FILM CORPORATION
WILLIAM FOX PRESENTS
RIDERS OF THE PURPLE SAGE
A WILLAM FARNUM DE LUXE PRODUCTION — DIRECTED BY FRANK LLOYD
DRAMATIZED FROM THE ZANE GREY NOVEL
FILMED AMID THE SCENIC GRANDEUR OF THE GRAND CANYON OF ARIZONA

[5]

[2]

[4]

[1]

[6]

[7]

[8]

[1] Harvesting our Black Sage at White Buffalo Land Trust on Jalama Canyon Ranch.

[2] A Sage smudge stick is lit and held by a hand during a Native American ceremony. The rising smoke is believed to cleanse the spirit.

[3] Garden Sage from the garden, photographed by Phillip Huynh for the 2022 launch of our Sage candle and body products.

[4] A bundle of Purple Sage (*Salvia leucophylla*) from the garden.

[5] *Riders of the Purple Sage*, an American silent Western film directed by Frank Lloyd in 1918.

[6] Drying Sage in the Goat Shed at the bottom of the garden.

[7] Sage growing on the native hillside near our beehives.

[8] A Wild Sage engraving from 1833, France.

[1] JANUARY WINTER	# DIRTY WORK	*"Do the best you can until you know better. Then when you know better, do better."* —MAYA ANGELOU

GARDEN TASKS:

Plant bare-root Roses, fruit trees, and berries.	☐	Deadhead Marigolds and Calendula to extend flowering.	☐
Lightly prune Olives to shape and encourage spring growth.	☐	Harvest in-season Citrus.	☐
Mulch tree bases with organic compost to protect roots (keep it off the trunks).	☐	Sow Sweet Peas and Poppies for spring blooms.	☐
Harvest winter herbs: Rosemary, Thyme, Parsley, and Oregano are at their peak.	☐	Turn compost piles and mix in greenpruning waste.	☐
Plant cool-season crops: Fennel, Kale, Lettuces, Arugula, Peas, Radishes, and Broccoli.	☐	Cut back shrubs to encourage spring growth.	☐
Feed soil with mild compost tea or fish emulsion.	☐	Test soil pH if plants look yellow; treat alkaline soil with Cottonseed meal to acidify.	☐
Protect tender seedlings from cold nights with row covers or cloches.	☐	Treat yellowing Citrus leaves (chlorosis) with chelated iron.	☐

TASK

MAKE A SAGE TINCTURE

<u>WHAT IT DOES</u>:

Aids digestion, soothes stress, and helps balance hormones.

<u>YOU'LL NEED</u>:

Fresh Sage

High-proof alcohol (vodka is perfect)

A clean glass jar with a tight lid

A dark glass dropper bottle for storage

<u>TO MAKE</u>:

Gently chop the Sage to wake it up, then loosely fill your jar halfway. Cover completely with vodka. Seal, shake, and store in a cool, dark place for 4-6 weeks. Shake it every few days—don't let it get lonely in the dark. When ready, strain through cheesecloth, squeezing out every last drop, and decant into the dropper bottle.

<u>TO USE</u>:

Add a few drops to tea or water, dab onto temples or wrists, or add to a room spray.

TASK

HELP BUILD A BIRD'S NEST

You can help them out every January, before the spring building rush. Place a small open basket in a quiet corner of the yard and fill it with a simple, safe mix of dry grass, small twigs, a pinch of straw, and dried Moss—that's plenty to get started.

If possible, add a shallow dish of muddy water nearby, since some birds use mud like cement. In Los Angeles, the nesting scramble hits February through April, so setting materials out early gives them a head start. Keep it natural and skip anything that tangles or turns to mush: no yarn, string, dryer lint, hair, plastic, or paper towels.

TASK ☐

MIX KATELYN'S BIRD SEED

This recipe was created by Katelyn Luevano, Flamingo Estate's resident animal whisperer, who knows exactly what our feathered neighbors crave.

WHAT IT DOES: Provides extra fat and protein when food is scarce, keeping birds warm. Tailored for Western native species, this mix encourages bright melodies and a bug-free garden in spring.

YOU'LL NEED:

- 2 parts white proso Millet
- 1 part cracked Corn
- 1 part black oil Sunflower seeds
- 1 part Canola seed
- ½ part Thistle (Nyjer) seed
- ½ part Safflower seed
- ½ part unsalted nuts (Peanuts, Walnuts, Pistachios; roughly chopped)
- ½ part dried fruit (Cranberries, Blueberries)

TO MAKE: Measure all ingredients using the same vessel (a cup, scoop, or jar). Combine in a large bowl or bucket and mix until evenly distributed. Store in an airtight container in a cool, dry place.

TO USE: Fill feeders or bowls in the garden as needed throughout winter. You can also sprinkle a small handful directly on the ground or a low platform for ground-feeding birds.

TASK ☐

FIND BURIED TREASURE

Every December, return your crystals to the earth. Since they were born in the ground, putting them back in the soil recharges their energy. Leave them buried for at least one full-moon cycle. I like to dig mine up on January 1. It is a symbolic start, but symbols matter. The calendar flips, the garden is quiet, and you reach into the cold soil to retrieve what you want to carry into the new year. A healer once told Harvey and me to bury ours together to set intentions. We did, and when we dug them up, they felt like relics, newly claimed.

TASK ☐

TAKE UP SMOKING

Sage your space. It's an ancient way of telling bad energy to grab its coat and see itself out. Light a bundle of dried Sage (or a pinch of loose leaf) over a fireproof bowl and let it smolder. Give the house a slow, smoky bath—wafting the smoke into corners, doorways, and anywhere the mood feels stuck. I like to add dried Lavender, Rosemary, or Mugwort for a softer, more complex scent. Crack a window to give the unwanted an exit. When you're done, snuff the ember (no heroic last puffs) and let the whole place exhale.

TASK

GO GREEN

Olio Nuovo is Olive oil at its most alive: pressed once a year at the start of harvest, when the Olives are still bright green and bursting with energy. We mill the fruit within hours of picking, bottle it unfiltered, and leave every microscopic bit of Olive flesh intact. Those living enzymes and polyphenols give it that electric green color, sky-high antioxidants, and a wild, grassy, peppery bite. But because it's truly alive, it doesn't last. So here's the sprint: open the bottle the day it arrives, write the date on the label, put it on the counter (never in the back of the pantry), and promise to finish it within three months—on bread, beans, soup, eggs, Tomatoes, fish, and anything that needs a little green lightning. No hoarding. This is the special occasion.

TASK

GET SCRUBBED

SAGE CAMELLIA MUD

Find a clean patch of earth away from roads or pets. Dig a few inches down for the finer soil, sun-dry it, then crush and sift through a fine kitchen strainer to remove any grit.

Next, prepare the botanical elements. Finely chop fresh Sage leaves and crush them with the back of a spoon to release their oils. In a small bowl, muddle fresh Camellia petals into Jojoba or Olive oil until they bruise and surrender their essence. Mix the sifted earth, crushed Sage, and floral oil together to form a thick, fragrant paste.

In the shower, massage the mud in slow circles over your whole body—from neck to heels—spending extra time on elbows and knees. Let it sit for a quiet minute, then rinse. Finish with a final slick of oil on damp skin so you step out polished, calm, and new.

RECIPE

SAGE PASTA WITH POACHED EGG

PASTA SHEETS:

- 3 cups all-purpose flour
- 4 large eggs
- 1 pinch Salt
- Semolina flour for dusting
- 1 bunch small Sage leaves, picked

[1] Measure 3 cups of flour onto a clean working surface and create a mound.

[2] Make a well in the center of the mound and crack in 4 eggs with a pinch of salt.

[3] Using a fork, carefully whisk the eggs to break the yolks and mix while using your free hand to gently push in a little flour at a time. Continue until it is no longer easy to use the fork and using both hands, incorporate the remaining flour into the dough.

[4] Knead by pushing down with the heel of your hand and turning the dough each time. Continue for 7–10 minutes.

[5] Wrap the pasta dough in plastic wrap and leave to rest for 30 minutes.

[6] Working with ¼ of the dough at a time, leaving the rest covered so it doesn't dry out, roll out the dough on the widest setting of a pasta roller, 3–4 times, each time folding it onto itself.

[7] Continue rolling the dough through; however, each subsequent time, turn the dial to a thinner setting until you reach setting 5.

[8] Cut the pasta sheet in half. Arrange sage leaves over one sheet, then place the second sheet on top. Flatten gently with a rolling pin, then trim the edges with a knife.

[9] Feed through the pasta machine once more, rolling to setting 6.

[10] Repeat steps 6–9 with the other three segments of dough.

[11] Cut the pasta sheets down to squares. Dust with semolina, cover, and set aside until ready to cook.

SAUCE:

- 4 Tbsp Flamingo Estate Tuscan White Truffle Oil
- Reserved pasta water
- 4 Tbsp unsalted butter
- Salt and pepper to taste
- Parmigiano-Reggiano
- Poached eggs for serving

[1] Bring a pot of salted water to a heavy boil.

[2] Add the pasta and cook until al dente, about 90 seconds. Strain, reserving ⅔ cup of the cooking water.

[3] Place a sauté pan over high heat. Bring white truffle oil and the reserved pasta water to a simmer, then add the pasta sheets and butter, plus salt and pepper to taste. Toss vigorously until a silky sauce forms.

[4] Serve garnished with lots of freshly grated Parmigiano and a poached egg.

RECIPE

Dreaming Broth

This dreaming broth was created for us by Chef Ella Murphy. Built on a mineral-rich umami base of vegetables and mushrooms, it offers a sense of grounding and nourishment that allows the nervous system to feel held. Taken in the evening, this broth becomes a quiet ritual.

INGREDIENTS:

- 1 Tbsp Olive oil or ghee
- 2 Leeks, chopped
- 2 Carrots, chopped
- 2 Celery stalks, chopped
- 2 small Shallots, cut in half
- 4 cloves Garlic, lightly crushed
- Sea Salt, to taste
- 2 cups sliced Shiitake Mushrooms (or ½ cup dried)
- 2–3 dried Reishi Mushroom slices
- 2 small strips Kombu
- 1 tsp Coriander seed
- ½ tsp Fennel seed
- 6–8 whole black Peppercorns
- 2 Bay leaves
- 2 slices fresh Ginger
- 2 Tbsp dried blue Lotus petals
- 10 cups filtered water
- 2 Tbsp dried Skullcap
- Optional: 2 tsp white or Chickpea Miso

PREPARATION:

[1] Warm oil or ghee in a pot over low-medium heat. Add leek, carrot, celery, shallot, and garlic with a pinch of salt. Cook slowly, stirring, until everything is very soft and aromatic, about 10 minutes. This step builds sweetness and prevents blandness.

[2] Add shiitake mushrooms and cook another 3–5 minutes, allowing them to release their juices.

[3] Add reishi mushrooms, kombu, coriander, fennel, peppercorns, bay leaves, ginger, blue lotus, and water. Bring to a gentle simmer. Lower heat and simmer covered for 1 hour.

[4] Turn off heat. Add skullcap, cover, and steep for 30 minutes.

[5] Strain. If using miso, whisk it into the warm (not hot) broth just before serving. Adjust salt to taste.

JAN.

FEB.

MAR.

APR.

MAY.

JUN.

JUL.

AUG.

SEP.

OCT.

NOV.

DEC.

NOSE DIVE
[I]

PETRICHOR

JAN.

The storms come to Los Angeles in January. Petrichor is the smell of the earth after that rain. The word comes from the Greek *petra*, meaning "stone," and *ichor*—the blood of the gods. And honestly, it deserves a name that epic: raw, primal, a little bit holy. The sky has just taken a bath. The old, the no-longer-necessary, gets washed away. The air turns clean and electric. The world has been reset.

For years, scientists couldn't quite agree on what we were actually smelling—or why we love it so much. Some thought it was rain meeting clay. Others blamed plant oils. Then two Australian scientists, Isabel Bear and Richard Thomas, began to decode the mystery. They found that during dry spells, aromatic molecules accumulate on the ground—trapping remnants of plants, microbes, and fungi. Day after day, the scent is there, but too faint for us to notice. Until the rain arrives. Then everything wakes up.

Rain of the Fifth Month by Utagawa Kunisada. An example of ukiyo-e storytelling about seasonal rains, circa 1832 in Japan.

[PAGE 50] Our Petrichor candle, photographed by Pia Riverola in the orchard, during the storms of December 2025.

Hegel's Holiday, 1958, by René Magritte.

Here's the magic trick: falling drops trap tiny air bubbles in the soil. Those bubbles rocket upward through the droplet and burst into the air as a fine mist of aerosols—carrying the earth's perfume with them. At the same time, the soil releases geosmin: an earthy-smelling compound made by certain bacteria (like Streptomyces). The human nose is astonishingly sensitive to it—so sensitive we can detect it in near-impossible traces (a trait we share with Camels, who use it as a clue to find water). And gentler rain—slower drops—tends to create more of those aromatic aerosols, which is why Petrichor often feels strongest after a light shower.

JAN.

The Arrival of Spring, David Hockney.
One of our favorites from his iPad series.

Running through the orchard at Flamingo Estate during the first winter storms. Photographed by Hugh Davison, December 2025.

After the big storms of winter 2021, we formulated an entire range devoted to this scent and released it on January 1—our small ritual of renewal. To mimic the smell of rain at Flamingo, we blended Kelp, Camellia seed, Sandalwood, Spirulina, Myrrh, Eucalyptus, Amber, Vetiver root, Cedarwood, Spikenard, and Tulsi. It sold out immediately, and it's still our most requested scent.

Paulo Coelho once said that not all storms come to disrupt your life—some come to clear your path. That's what Petrichor means to me.

Pray for rain.

To capture the scent of Petrichor, we carefully sourced Chaga Mushrooms, Kelp, Sage, Eucalyptus, Myrrh, and Vetiver. These botanicals are gently infused into our Olive oil and Brazilian Babassu oil. Our Babassu is sustainably harvested by Indigenous communities in the Amazon who protect the trees as an alternative to logging.

February is about tough love. If January is for dreaming, February is for discipline. The garden asks us to be ruthless in service of beauty—taking sharp shears to the Citrus, Figs, and Pomegranates, opening their canopies to the air. We cut back Sage and Lavender hard, removing old wood to make way for the new. It feels counterintuitive to cut so deeply just as life returns, but this is the secret language of growth: you have to make

FEBRUARY

space for the light. While trees get their winter haircut, we steel ourselves with fiery shots of Ginger and Jalapeño to ground ourselves. Under our feet Anemones and Poppies break the surface, and Jasmine swells on the vine, holding its breath before the bloom. We feed hungry soil with compost and worm castings, replacing what rains washed away. It is a time of preparation, a clearing of the throat before the full song of spring begins.

Fresh winter rain on Blue Gum Eucalyptus *(Eucalyptus globulus)*, harvested and distilled in our apothecary for its cool and bracing essential oil. Photographed by Phillip Huynh.

Outside the Bathhouse window at Flamingo Estate, there are a few giant Eucalyptus trees that have no business being in Los Angeles, and yet here we all are together. I sit in the tub and watch them move. Their trunks rise in blue-gray columns, taller than the house, higher than the power lines, higher than anything in the neighborhood. The bark hangs in long ribbons and peels in curls, like Parmesan shaved with a knife. When the Santa Ana winds come, the whole canopy shivers, and the garden fills with the sound and smell of Australia.

These are trees from my childhood, from the other side of the planet, planted here a century ago for reasons that had nothing to do with me. We are all immigrants on this hillside—me, the Eucalyptus, the Olive, the Rosemary—trying to behave as if we've always been here. I heard once that Eucalyptus trees have roots as long as the trees are tall, spearing straight down into the center of the Earth. I loved that idea: a 100-foot tree holding hands with the underworld. The truth is less dramatic and more interesting. Most of their roots spread out near the surface, fanning sideways rather than drilling down—more like a net than a spear. But still, when I soak in the tub and look up at those tall, pale trunks, I can't help imagining a matching ghost of roots below, feeling for water under the foundations, trying to make a home here.

The leaves outside my window are the long, sickle-shaped ones, hanging on the branch like green curved knives. They don't sit flat and broad like a Maple's; they turn themselves sideways, presenting the narrowest possible edge to the midday sun, dodging the worst of its glare. As the day moves, the leaves seem to rotate in place, following the light and avoiding it at the same time. Before a storm, they flick and show their paler undersides, not because they can tell the future, but because the air thickens and the wind arrives from a different angle. From the bath, watching steam and foliage together, it feels like the trees are signaling: something is coming.

Eucalyptus was the wallpaper of my childhood. The smell of Gum trees after the rain is one of my favorite scents. On our farm, the paddocks were edged with windbreaks of Blue Gum and Sugar Gum, long straight rows marching uphill. Forest Red Gum and Spotted Gum would punctuate the property. Koalas slept in their crooks like small, disgruntled pillows. Their flowers were like fireworks in slow motion—tight caps of green popping off to reveal froths of cream and scarlet stamens, bees drunk in the blossom, and later the hard little Gumnuts left behind like coins in a fountain.

Eucalyptus blossoms and seed pods, California, 1925.

And then there were the stories. In Australia, Eucalyptus doesn't just stand at the edge of the paddock; it walks into our early imaginations. A famous Australian author named May Gibbs

↑
Gum-Blossom Babies and Gumnut Babies, 1916.
May Gibbs's iconic Gumnut Babies are cherished Australian bush fairy characters designed to foster a love for nature, often featuring in stories alongside Snugglepot and Cuddlepie. These whimsical characters nestled in Eucalyptus blossoms promote conservation and are staples of Australian children's literature.

→
Two men demonstrate the scale of a 25-year-old Blue Gum Eucalyptus at Sunny Slope Ranch, San Gabriel, circa 1900.

5550

The Eucalyptus as seen from the Bathhouse window at the Estate. Painted by John Reagan, winter 2025.

took the nuts and blossoms and turned them into *Snugglepot and Cuddlepie*, the Gumnut Babies—two small children in Eucalyptus caps who have been wandering through Australian childhoods for more than a century. Their hats are young Gumnuts, their skirts are Gum Blossoms, their world is a forest of trunks and Banksia Men. Those books teach you early that a Eucalyptus branch isn't just wood and leaves; it's a village. Every nut a baby, every knot a face. Every child in Australia knows the stories, and maybe that's why we see the Eucalyptus trees as our friends.

The trees outside my bath are a long way from that world. They arrived in California in the mid-1800s, in seed packets and nursery pots, tucked into the pockets of sea captains and gold-rush hopefuls who thought they were bringing over a miracle. The state was worried about running out of timber. Hillsides were stripped for mines and railroads, and here came this gift from the Southern Hemisphere: a tree that shot up quickly, made dense wood, needed almost no water, and seemed to eat bad air for breakfast. Doctors called it the "Fever Tree" and believed its sharp, menthol breath could disinfect swamps and chase away malaria. Railroad men dreamed of endless railroad ties and telegraph poles grown in straight blue rows along the tracks. Speculators promised fortunes to anyone who would plant enough of them.

So they did. Whole hillsides along the coast were planted to Blue Gum (*Eucalyptus globulus*), sometimes by the hundreds of thousands at a time. The Southern Pacific Railroad alone experimented with vast plantations for ties and poles.

Advertisements promised "forests while you wait," a kind of botanical get-rich-quick scheme: plant today, harvest hardwood tomorrow. By the early 1900s, Eucalyptus had become a boom in itself—not just a tree, but an investment product.

Then, like after so many booms, the bust arrived.

The young wood turned out to be a carpenter's nightmare. When the trunks were sawn and dried, the timber was too soft. It warped and twisted, split and spat out nails. Fence posts rotted early. Railroad spikes worked loose. The iron rails wobbled. California farm journals filled up with disappointment: *these trees are no good.* The real hardwood Eucalyptus of Australian legend came from trees that were 70, 80, 100 years old. No one wanted to wait that long. The Eucalyptus timber dream collapsed. Investors were left with fast-growing trees they couldn't easily turn into money, and the trees, indifferent to the whole drama, simply kept growing.

In California now, Eucalyptus is a kind of immigrant celebrity who has long outstayed their welcome—perhaps a bit like Mel Gibson: once idolized by Americans, then fallen from grace and cast as a villain. Planted in their millions for fast timber and railroad ties that mostly split and failed, the trees stayed anyway, seeding the coastal hills with blue-green groves that some people now love like natives. Ecologists call them invasive, fire crews call them kindling, and still there are people who will chain themselves to the trunks when the chainsaws arrive. It is a tree as hated as it is loved.

Some of the fear is justified. Eucalyptus groves shed everything they don't need. Bark peels off in long, papery strips that dangle and then fall, building shaggy skirts of fuel at the base. I wrote about this at length in my past book, *The Guide to Becoming Alive*. This is the tree detoxifying itself, shedding layers clogged with salt and soot and insects and whatever didn't work, so the new skin underneath can breathe. Leaves drop in drifts for the same reason. Anything tired or inefficient is let go. I suggested in my book that we can learn a lot from the Eucalyptus about shedding the things (and people) we no longer need in our lives.

Nevertheless, the oils that make the trees smell like a clean bathroom also make them burn hot; the litter can carry flames up into the canopy and throw embers far ahead of a fire front. In the Oakland Hills fires, Blue Gums were accused of behaving like open filing cabinets for fire. Once you've seen a Eucalyptus stand after a burn—trunks blackened, leaves gone, new shoots quickly pushing from the base—you realize they didn't just evolve with fire. They expect it. Many Eucalypts only really get their chance when fire comes through; the heat cracks open hard seed capsules that grow high in the canopy, showering fresh seed onto blackened, fertilized ground, and the trees themselves re-shoot from hidden buds under the bark.

Illustration of *Eucalyptus pulverulenta*, 1930. Known as the "powdery" Eucalyptus, this rare species is a botanical anomaly—it never "grows up," retaining its silver-blue juvenile foliage throughout its entire life. In the 1930s, such illustrations were vital for documenting these rare Australian natives found only in the high country of New South Wales.

This sort of behavior is what makes them so stubbornly useful. They grow fast, throw shade quickly, hold a slope, break the wind. In bare landscapes, they draw a line in the sky. In Australia, whole communities of birds, insects, and mammals depend on the nectar and shelter they provide. In California, hawks and owls roost in them, monarch butterflies cluster in the branches in winter, and bees work the winter blossoms when not much else is in flower. They drink deeply, yes, their roots spreading wide through the topsoil, but they also hold the earth in place and stand up to the kind of dry, bright weather that exhausts other species.

And then there is the smell.

If you pick a leaf from the tree outside my window and roll it between your fingers, it resists at first—tough, leathery, designed to last in sun and drought. Then the skin breaks, and the air fills with that unmistakable, medicinal sweetness. It rushes up your nose and down into your chest, a cold ribbon of scent. There is menthol in it, but also Pine, and something almost like rubbed Sage. Sharp, camphorous, clean, like opening a hospital cupboard and a mountain path at the same time. Underneath the first shock, there's a faint honeyed note and a ghost of smoke, as if the tree remembers every bushfire it has ever stood through.

Eucalyptus Drive, Baldwin's Ranch, Arcadia, California, 1931. A vintage postcard capturing the towering windbreaks that defined the landscape of the San Gabriel Valley during the early twentieth century.

The oil that carries that smell, rich in Eucalyptol, is the reason Eucalyptus made the jump from the paddock to the medicine cabinet. Distilled from leaves in farm stills, it went into cough syrups and throat lozenges, chest rubs and steam inhalations. Mothers rubbed it on children's ribs in winter. People poured it into saunas and hot baths. It showed up in mouthwash and antiseptics and floor cleaners. It's a smell that had begun as a trick of survival—a cocktail of compounds to deter insects, protect leaves, and manage water—and was repurposed as a global symbol of cleanliness, skin health, and fresh breath. At Flamingo, Eucalyptus was the ingredient in our first Body Wash and Hand Soap—together with Sage and Rosemary. And it's still the best-selling fragrance, a medley of green leaves.

Up close, Eucalyptus isn't just "green." It's a whole library of greens. The leaves outside my window are blue-green, the color of old glass bottles left in the sea. Some are a flat, chalky Sage, edged in a cooler, almost silvery line. Others are darker, bottle-green and glossy, catching the light like nail polish. New growth comes in soft bronze and apple-lime, before it settles down into something more restrained. On dull days they read as smoke; on bright days they go bright turquoise—as if the tree is constantly repainting itself to keep up with the weather. All these greens became the inspiration for the stripes painted on the walls of my living room. I wanted to bring the Eucalyptus inside.

Back in the Bathhouse, with my elbows tucked over the rim and the Eucalyptus outside drawing slow, invisible water up its trunk, I can smell the faintest trace of it through the windows. And then again in the soap that's full of its essential oils. It's like sharing a room with another immigrant. The tree and I, both from a dry island continent, both anchored shallowly and spread wide in this improbable city, both occasionally accused of taking up too much space. But both working hard to make ourselves useful.

To live with Eucalyptus is to live with contradiction. I think of Snugglepot and Cuddlepie, the Gumnut Babies, and how their whole world was painted in Eucalyptus greens. I think of Californian environmentalists chaining themselves to trunks in foggy dawns, fighting off the bulldozers. And others who call it an invasive weed. I think of fire crews eyeing the same trees like loaded guns. I think of the hospital floors cleaned with its scent, and the icy-cold Eucalyptus towels gifted at Equinox after an expensive yoga class. I think of those roots—not spearing deep but roaming outward, as far as the branches reach, making a kind of horizontal claim on the soil. The Eucalyptus has taught me that belonging is not always the same as being welcomed, and that roots don't have to be deep to hold on. In a city that loves Palm Trees and hates them, that plants lawns in a desert and calls it normal, perhaps a Eucalyptus from another hemisphere is not the strangest thing of all.

There is room on this hillside for everyone. And everyone is welcome.

[TOP] Workers inside a Eucalyptus sawmill in the Berkeley Hills, 1911. Between 1904 and 1912, millions of Eucalyptus trees were planted across California under the belief they would solve the nation's looming "timber famine." This mill represents the height of that speculation. However, the industry soon discovered a fatal flaw: the wood from these young trees was so stressed and moisture-heavy that it warped, twisted, and cracked almost immediately after being sawn. By the time this photo was taken, the "miracle timber" was already being relegated to firewood and railroad ties, forever changing the skyline of the East Bay. [BOTTOM] Melrose Avenue, looking west from Western Avenue, Los Angeles, 1905. Photographer Charles C. Pierce captures a dense canopy of Eucalyptus trees arching over the roadway, with a lone automobile appearing in the distance. Though they defined the landscape at the turn of the century, these historic trees were entirely removed by 1923 to make way for city expansion.

[GROUNDING] : A MAP OF PLEASURE FROM THE GARDEN

THE CITRUS GARDEN

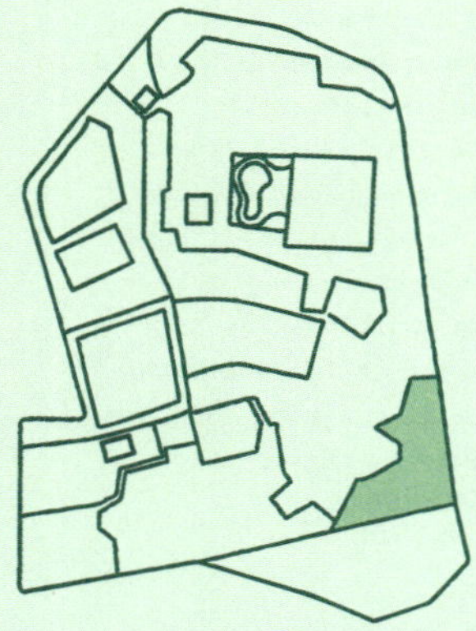

34°08' N / 118°12' W LOS ANGELES, CALIFORNIA

Long before Flamingo Estate was overrun with Roses, Tomatoes, and too many dinner guests, these hillsides were Citrus country. The slope we stand on now was once part of a quilt of orchards that wrapped around Los Angeles from mission to mission, all the way to the Mexican border.

Citrus first came here in the late 1700s with the Spanish padres, who planted the earliest recorded Orange Trees at the San Gabriel Mission. By 1841, a man named William Wolfskill had put in the first commercial Orange grove near what's now downtown Los Angeles, just a short drive from Flamingo. His fruit found its way to hungry Gold Rush miners, who tasted California sunshine and just enough vitamin C to keep scurvy at bay.

Then came the real turning point—and a woman at the center of it. In 1873, the US Department of Agriculture sent two small cuttings of a seedless Orange from Brazil to Eliza Tibbets in Riverside. She planted them in her yard and nursed them along with kitchen dishwater. The trees adored

[PAGE 66] Picking Oranges, circa 1900. Originally published by the Detroit Photographic Company, this image is a photochrom—a colorized print created from a black-and-white negative. It depicts a harvester kneeling beside an Orange tree heavy with fruit and blossoms, a scene typical of the Southern California Citrus boom that transformed the region into a global agricultural hub.

the climate and soil. Soon they were dripping with sweet, seedless, glowing fruit unlike anything else. The Washington Navel became a national sensation, and almost every Washington Navel tree in California today descends from those two original plants in Eliza's garden. One woman, two cuttings, and suddenly the whole state was being redrawn in groves: Riverside boomed, rail lines chased the blossom, and Orange County was born.

→ *Palace of Versailles: View of the Orangerie* by Jean-Baptiste Martin, circa 1695. This painting illustrates the orangerie as the height of French Baroque luxury, showcasing the architectural masterpiece designed by Jules Hardouin-Mansart to house King Louis XIV's vast collection of Citrus and exotic trees. The scene depicts the meticulously manicured parterres and the massive vaulted galleries that protected more than a thousand Orange and Lemon trees during the harsh winter months. By the time of this painting, the orangerie was not only a botanical feat but a symbol of the king's absolute power over nature, with many of the trees sourced from royal houses across Europe to fill the sun-drenched terrace. Source: Palace of Versailles.

In Europe there was the orangerie—glass palaces built in England and France just to house Citrus trees. There was a tax on windows, so flaunting a building made almost entirely of glass was an act of insolent wealth. To sit in an orangerie in midwinter, surrounded by glossy leaves and hanging fruit, was to declare that you had bent the climate—and the taxman—to your will. Simon Barnes writes about this in his book *The History of the World in 100 Plants*, and it always makes me laugh: Citrus as the ultimate bragging rights.

Today, most of those great commercial groves have been pushed aside by freeways and stucco, but Citrus still clings to the hills—including ours. At Flamingo we tuck trees wherever we can: Bergamot and Bitter Orange, Blood Orange, Lemon,

Grapefruit, Yuzu, Mandarin, Kumquat, Key Lime, and more. We pick their fruit, peel, leaves, and blossoms and turn them into oils and soaps, so that when you step into the shower you're standing inside a small fragrant echo of California's Citrus history—from the padres, to Eliza's backyard, to this hillside. The real story is the smell.

Perfumers call it the top note—the first thing you smell when you spray a scent, the impulse that makes your lungs expand. It's clean and bitter and sweet and green all at once. The moment you tear open a Lemon or crush a Bergamot leaf in your hand, the volatile oils in the peel explode into the air. That little mist is really a weather event: a burst of limonene, linalool, citral, and hundreds of other molecules your nose reads as sunlight, clarity, and the desire to stay alive.

All Citrus does this, but each one has its own personality.

→
The Parent Washington Navel Orange Tree, pictured in 1902 at its current location in Riverside, stands as one of the most significant botanical artifacts in California history. This tree was one of two original specimens received by the US Department of Agriculture from Brazil and sent to Eliza Tibbets in 1873. Originally planted at the Tibbets homestead, it was the parent tree for a multi-billion dollar California Citrus industry. By the time of this photograph, the tree had already sparked a "Second Gold Rush" leading to the vast Citrus groves that came to define the Southern California landscape.

LEMON (*Citrus × limon*) is the universal passport. No matter where you go, a Lemon smells like itself. It might have started somewhere between India and China, but it has made itself at home everywhere—Amalfi balconies, Japanese kitchens, street stalls in Marrakesh, backyard trees in Los Angeles. The scent is a luminous union of juice and zest: sharp, sparkling, almost antiseptic, and yet somehow completely domestic.

SWEET ORANGE (*Citrus × sinensis*) is gentler, rounder, more childlike. Before people had a word for the color orange, they called it red-yellow, or saffron. Now when you say "orange," the mind instantly supplies the smell. Sweet Orange oil—pressed from the peel—is creamy and sunny and uncomplicated. It doesn't snap like Lemon; it smiles. You smell it and think of breakfast, of hands sticky from peeling, of the small pleasure of pressing a thumbnail into the rind and watching the oils spray out like tiny fireworks.

BLOOD ORANGE (*Citrus × sinensis*) is Orange that has decided to tell secrets. The flesh is ruby, edged with purple, and the scent is richer, sweeter, with a berry-like depth and a faint rosy shadow. It smells like an Orange crossed with a Strawberry and a glass of red wine. I had my first Blood Oranges in Rome, on the Spanish Steps, buying them from an old woman at the market who told me only to share them with people I loved, because they were symbolic of blood pumping through our hearts.

GRAPEFRUIT (*Citrus × paradisi*) is a slap in the face you end up thanking. Cut one in half and the oils mist into the air—a clean, bitter, slightly sulfurous brightness that makes your eyes open wider. The rind oil is heavy on limonene but laced with a green sharpness that's less sugary than Orange, less sour than Lemon. It smells like getting your act together. Grapefruit in a perfume wakes the composition up the way a cold shower does for a human: whatever was drowsy is now paying attention.

BERGAMOT (*Citrus bergamia*) is the dandy of the family. The fruit itself is almost inedible, sour and bitter in all the wrong ways, but the oil in the peel is one of perfumery's greatest tricks. It smells like Earl Grey tea in a linen cupboard: herbal and citric all at once, with a green, slightly floral sophistication. Jacques Cavallier-Belletrud, the nose for Louis Vuitton, talks about the sensuality of crushing a Bergamot in your hand, an intimate ordeal that's green and bitter and light. It's in almost every classic *Eau de Cologne*; it's what makes them feel crisp and clean and expensive rather than just lemony. Bergamot is the suit-and-tie version of Citrus.

BITTER ORANGE or Neroli (*Citrus × aurantium*) is a whole perfume by itself. The tree gives three different oils. There is NEROLI from the blossoms—high, sparkling, almost metallic-white floral, like Orange Blossom dressed for Versailles. There is PETITGRAIN from the leaves and twigs—green, woody, slightly smoky, the smell of shade under the tree. And then BITTER ORANGE from the rind—sharper, more complex than Sweet Orange, with a spicy edge. Smell all three and you realize one plant can do an entire fragrance pyramid without help: top, heart, base. Anne-Marie de la Tremoille, the Princess of Nerola, supposedly soaked her gloves and bathed in the blossom oil in the seventeenth century, which is where Neroli gets its name. All she was really doing was turning herself into a walking Bitter Orange tree.

CITRON (*Citrus medica*) is Citrus as antique. Huge, gnarled, more rind than flesh, it smells warmer and more resinous than Lemon—like someone mixed fresh peel with Cedarwood and Honey. In Italy, *Cedro* is candied and tucked into Panettone and Cassata; in perfumery, its oil feels like an older, slower Lemon, less about cleaning the kitchen, more about sitting in a stone courtyard somewhere in the Eastern Mediterranean and deciding not to do anything for an hour.

[1] Postcard from 1913 of Orange packing in California. [2] Pickers cutting Orange stem, circa 1910, from the University of Southern California Libraries, California Historical Society. [3] The terrace at Flamingo during Citrus season, photographed by Pia Riverola. [4] Portrait of Miss Jerry Wood, "Queen of the Orange Crop," at the Los Angeles County Fair in Pomona, circa 1932. Source: California Historical Society. [5] Citrus at Flamingo Estate, photographed by Hugh Davison, 2024. [6] Mission Orange tire cover, Southern California, 1926. [7] In the Flamingo Estate Citrus orchard, photographed by Sean Hazen, 2025. [8] National Orange Show, Southern California, 1927. [9] Our Bergamot Orange flowers, photographed by Phillip Huynh.

[1]

979 Orange Packing

[2]

[3]

[4]

[5]

[6]

DRINK
Mission
Orange
Its Real Juice

[7]

[8]

LOS ANGELES COUNTY
LOS ANGELES COUNTY

[9]

The Citrus Garden painted by John Reagan, winter 2025.

MANDARIN (*Citrus reticulata*) is the talkative one. It's one of the original Citrus species—along with Pomelo and Citron—and you can smell its DNA in almost all the others. Unpeeling one releases a cloud that has bits of everyone in it: Orange Blossom, Lemon, Grapefruit. Perfumers harvest green Mandarin in October for a sharp mineral oil; yellow in November for something softer and fruitier; and red in February for a sweet, almost syrupy note. To me, Mandarin always smells like children and Lunar New Year—pockets full of puffy-skinned fruit, the satisfying pop as you break a segment free.

TANGERINE (*Citrus × tangerina*) and CLEMENTINE (*Citrus × clementina*) are Mandarin's cousins who stayed out too late at the candy shop. Their oils are sweeter, juicier, more sherbet. If Sweet Orange is breakfast juice, Tangerine and Clementine are dessert, or the good sweets at the bottom of a grandmother's handbag.

KEY LIME (*Citrus × aurantiifolia*) is mischief in a green jacket. The whole fruit—rind and juice—smells fizzy, almost electric. There's a sharp, piercing brightness that makes your jaw twinge before you even taste it. We squeeze Key Limes over grilled fish, over Tarragon syrups for poolside drinks, over fruit salad; every time the aroma comes up like a joke you've heard a hundred times and still find funny.

KUMQUAT (*Citrus japonica*) is Citrus turned inside out. You eat the peel and discard the inner pith if you're smart. The skin is sweet, floral, almost creamy; the flesh is sharp and sour. The scent is fizzy—like Orange soda bubbles on your nose—with a delicate, candied edge. The fact that Kumquats can handle frost means their oils carry a memory of cold; there's always a tiny metallic glint under the sweetness.

And then there are the oddballs: Grapefruit crossed with Tangerine into TANGELO (*Citrus × tangelo*); POMELO (*Citrus maxima*) that smells like an enormous, gentle Grapefruit without bitterness; little CALAMONDINS (*Citrus × microcarpa*) that smell like Oranges turned up to eleven.

Finally, the mighty YUZU (*Citrus junos*)—the truffle of Citrus. Rough, knobbly, more seed than flesh, but the oil in the peel is the greatest of all Citrus fragrance: bright, floral, with a slightly metallic edge that cuts through everything. A few drops in a broth or a salad and the whole dish sits up. In Japan, they float it in hot baths at Winter Solstice, the steam carrying that strange, hopeful smell—somewhere between Grapefruit, Mandarin, and Pine—into cold houses. Up here on the hill we shave it into Honey, into Turmeric Sea Salt, into sauces; every time it feels a little wilder than the rest, the *wabi-sabi* Citrus that refuses to be round or reasonable.

A vintage postcard featuring a lush Redlands orchard heavy with fruit, December 26, 1905. This era represents the peak of California's "Second Gold Rush," a period of explosive growth fueled by the Citrus industry that transformed the Southern California landscape into a Mediterranean ideal. Postcards like this served as vital marketing tools, showcasing the state's agricultural abundance and year-round sunshine to lure new residents and tourists from the East Coast. The handwritten message on the card highlights the personal connections fostered by these scenic views, which documented the rapid transition of the California frontier into a global agricultural powerhouse.

Citrus season at Flamingo Estate,
in the garden fountain.

↙
The photograph depicts a Los Angeles County exhibit at the National Orange Show in San Bernardino around 1930. These fairs were not just agricultural competitions; they were elaborate theatrical productions designed to brand Southern California as a Mediterranean paradise of health, wealth, and eternal sunshine. Notice the figures in the background dressed in Spanish-style attire. Boosters often used "Mission-era" imagery to give the region a romantic, European-influenced history that appealed to tourists.

At Flamingo, all of this is happening at once. Walk the garden in late winter and the air is chaos: Lemon and Orange and Grapefruit blossom, bees drunk, leaves exhaling, the ghosts of the old groves wrapping themselves around the hill. Crush a Bergamot leaf in your palm. Strip a little Yuzu zest into your pocket. Snap a Kumquat off a branch and eat it whole. You start to understand why entire religions chose Citrus trees for their gardens, and why the smell of an Orange sliced open on a cutting board can reset your whole day.

The Citrus section of the Estate is a living orangerie without walls, full of fruit that doesn't care what month the supermarket flyer says it is. We use the peel in soaps and oils, in candles and cleaning products, but at heart what we're really bottling is this feeling: bright, bitter, electric, alive.

Roses might be the language of love, but Citrus is the language of wakefulness. It's the garden slapping you lightly on the cheek and saying: you're here, you're alive, pay attention.

INSIDE THE CITRUS GARDEN AT FLAMINGO ESTATE:

BERGAMOT [*CITRUS BERGAMIA*]
BITTER ORANGE / NEROLI [*CITRUS × AURANTIUM*]
BLOOD ORANGE [*CITRUS × SINENSIS*]
BUDDHA'S HAND CITRON [*CITRUS MEDICA VAR. SARCODACTYLIS*]
CALAMANSI / CALAMONDIN [*CITRUS × MICROCARPA*]
CLEMENTINE [*CITRUS × CLEMENTINA*]
CITRON [*CITRUS MEDICA*]
FINGER LIME [*CITRUS AUSTRALASICA*]
GRAPEFRUIT [*CITRUS × PARADISI*]
KEY LIME [*CITRUS × AURANTIIFOLIA*]
KUMQUAT [*CITRUS JAPONICA*]
LEMON [*CITRUS × LIMON*]
LIMEQUAT [*CITRUS × FLORIDANA*]
MAKRUT LIME [*CITRUS HYSTRIX*]
MANDARIN [*CITRUS RETICULATA*]
MELOGOLD [*CITRUS GRANDIS × CITRUS PARADISI*]
MEYER LEMON [*CITRUS × MEYERI*]
OROBLANCO [*CITRUS GRANDIS × CITRUS PARADISI*]
PERSIAN LIME / TAHITI LIME [*CITRUS × LATIFOLIA*]
POMELO / PUMMELO [*CITRUS MAXIMA*]
RANGPUR LIME [*CITRUS × LIMONIA*]
SATSUMA MANDARIN [*CITRUS UNSHIU*]
SWEET ORANGE [*CITRUS × SINENSIS*]
TANGELO [*CITRUS × TANGELO*]
TANGERINE [*CITRUS × TANGERINA*]
YUZU [*CITRUS JUNOS*]

[II] FEBRUARY

WINTER

DIRTYWORK

"In the coldest February, as in every other month in every other year, the best thing to hold on to in this world is each other."
—LINDA ELLERBEE

GARDEN TASKS:

- [ ] Lightly prune Citrus after peak fruiting: remove crossing branches and open the canopy for airflow.
- [ ] Keep harvesting Rosemary, Thyme, and Parsley—they thrive now.
- [ ] Mulch Orchard beds with composted leaves and straw to lock in winter moisture.
- [ ] Feed Citrus with organic Citrus fertilizer or compost tea to replace nutrients leached by winter rains.
- [ ] Prune deciduous fruit trees (Fig, Pomegranate, Apple, Pear) before buds break.
- [ ] Cut back Sage and Lavender by one-third for dense spring regrowth.
- [ ] Sow early spring herbs and greens: Cilantro, Dill, Sorrel, Chervil, Spinach.
- [ ] Plant Brassicas and Peas; add worm castings or a handful of compost to each bed as you plant.
- [ ] Prune and train Jasmine as it buds—shape it onto trellises.
- [ ] Keep Anemones, Ranunculus, and Poppies evenly watered as they emerge.
- [ ] Start vegetable and flower seeds indoors or in trays for next month's transplanting.
- [ ] Feed Roses with compost or fish emulsion before new leaves unfurl.

TASK

Scent Your Firewood ☐

When the cold hits Los Angeles, we keep the fireplace going every night. We don't like synthetic fire logs, so we started scenting our own wood with essential oils. It makes the fire light faster and fills the house with fragrance even before the match is struck. Growing up on a farm, we burned Eucalyptus that grew wild on the property—that smell still feels like home to me. To recreate it, I pour camphor oil over our firewood and let it soak for a couple of weeks, usually in the bathtub in the orchard or on a large tarp. Once the wood absorbs the oil, it perfumes the whole room, and the first logs burn beautifully. I now make a batch every winter—usually camphor, sometimes mixed with Cedarwood, Pine, or Rosemary—just to witness how the fragrance shifts when it meets the flame.

TASK

TAKE A SHOT

An immunity shot defends against public door handles, mouth breathers, and those who don't cough into their elbow. Fill a jar with Ginger, Turmeric, Garlic, Jalapeño, Rosemary, and Peppercorns. Cover with Apple cider vinegar and Lemon, top with Honey, and shake well. Let it steep overnight if you're impatient, or a few days if you're committed. Strain, pour into a little bottle, and take a shot when the world feels germy.

TASK

LEARN TO GRAFT A CITRUS TREE

Late winter is ideal for quiet garden surgery. Choose a healthy Citrus tree (or rootstock) and one pencil-thick scion from a variety you want more of. Make clean, matching cuts, align the cambium, wrap firmly, and label. Then, practice patience. If it takes, you've made living abundance with your hands.

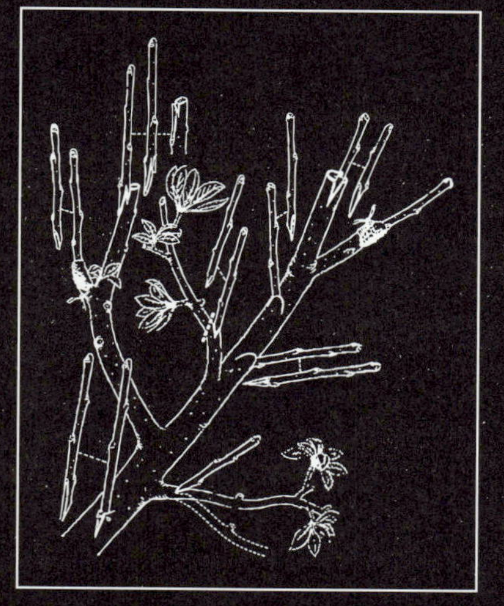

TASK

Make Florida Water

INGREDIENTS:

Peel of 2 Oranges (no white pith)
Peel of 1 Lemon (no white pith)
Peel of 1 Lime (no white pith)
Peel of ½ Grapefruit (optional)
1 small sprig fresh Rosemary
1 tsp dried Lavender
½ Cinnamon stick
2-3 whole Cloves
Small pinch freshly grated Nutmeg
2 cups high-proof Vodka or perfumer's alcohol
8-10 drops Bergamot essential oil (optional)
4-6 drops Sweet Orange essential oil
2-3 drops Neroli or Petitgrain essential oil

METHOD:

[1] STERILIZE THE JAR: Wash a glass jar or bottle with a tight-fitting lid, rinse well, and let it dry completely. [2] PEEL THE CITRUS: Use a vegetable peeler to remove only the colored zest (avoiding the bitter white pith). [3] BUILD THE INFUSION: Add all Citrus peels to the jar, then add Rosemary, Lavender, Cinnamon, Cloves, and Nutmeg. [4] ADD ALCOHOL + OILS: Pour in the vodka to cover everything. Add essential oils drop by drop until it smells bright and sunny—more Citrus than spice. [5] INFUSE: Seal and store in a cool, dark place for 2-4 weeks, shaking whenever you remember. [6] STRAIN + BOTTLE: Strain through a coffee filter or fine cloth into a clean bottle. Label and date it.

TASK

BUILD AN OWL A HOME

Build (or buy) a simple wooden nest box from untreated exterior plywood—think sturdy, weatherproof, and plain. Add a sheltered entry, a few small drainage holes, and a rough patch inside so chicks can climb. Mount it high on a tree or pole in a quiet spot with a clear "runway" to fly in and out. Keep it hands-off once it's up. If you want the best odds, choose a box style that matches the owls in your area (local Audubon or wildlife groups usually share the right size).

FLAMINGO ESTATE

Citrus Sorbets

Three steps, four different types of Citrus for you to enjoy.

RECIPE

Lemon Sorbet
1 cup lemon juice
½ cup agave or maple syrup
Zest of 2 lemons
1 cup fine cane sugar
2 cups water

Lime Sorbet
1 cup lime juice
½ cup agave or maple syrup
Zest of 2 lemons
1 cup fine cane sugar
2 cups water

Orange Sorbet
2 cups orange juice
¾ cup fine cane sugar
⅓ cup agave or maple syrup
1 cup of water

Grapefruit Sorbet
2 cups grapefruit juice
¾ cup fine cane sugar
⅓ cup agave or maple syrup
1 cup water

★ ★ ★

[1.] For each of the above flavors, bring sugar, syrup, and water (and zest if stated) to a boil to dissolve sugar. Turn off heat and leave to cool. [2.] Add juice to the sugar syrup and churn in a prepared ice cream machine to manufacturer's instructions. [3.] Place in an airtight container and freeze until ready to serve. We like to serve them right out of their own citrus cups by scooping out the insides.

★ ★ ★

TASK

MAKE TURMERIC GINGER YUZU SALT

This was made by Blanca Carreño, who runs the Flamingo kitchen department, and it's a total knockout—nothing we've ever made compares to this Salt. On a Margarita rim or a whole fish, it's like Blanca discovered a new kind of umami. Zest a few Yuzu (just the yellow peel) and rub the zest into flaky Sea Salt until the whole bowl smells like a Citrus grove. Spread it on a tray and dry it completely (overnight is perfect, or use the lowest oven setting with the door cracked) until it's crisp. Finally, blitz it in a spice grinder and finish with a small spoonful of ground Ginger and ground Turmeric (black Turmeric if you can find it) until it tastes bright, warm, and a little electric. Jar it and start using it on absolutely everything.

RECIPE

EUCALYPTUS TOFFEE LOLLIPOPS

INGREDIENTS:

- 3 Tbsp Flamingo Estate Manuka Honey
- 1 cup sugar
- 6 Tbsp unsalted butter
- 4 drops of food-grade Eucalyptus oil
- 8–10 wooden skewers

METHOD:

[1] Line a half baking sheet with parchment paper and lay out the skewers 3 inches apart.

[2] In a saucepan, combine the honey, sugar, and butter. Stir over low heat until the sugar dissolves.

[3] Bring the mixture to a boil and cook for 10 minutes, or until a little toffee dropped into cold water forms a hard ball.

[4] Add the eucalyptus oil and stir to combine.

[5] Carefully spoon 1–2 tablespoons of the toffee onto the ends of each prepared skewer. Leave to set.

TASK

RUN A YUZU BATH

This is a classic winter ritual in Japan—a way to warm the body, relax the mind, and make your whole house smell like bright, expensive sunshine. Yuzu is sometimes called the "Truffle of Citrus" because the peel is so intensely aromatic that even a little goes a long way. This bath is basically the most indulgent way to enjoy that scent.

YUZU
"Truffle of Citrus"

[STEP 1]
Rinse a few Yuzu well; keep them whole.

[STEP 2]
Lightly score the rinds with a few shallow cuts to release the oils.

[STEP 3]
Drop them into a hot bath (or tie them in a mesh bag if you want things tidy).

[STEP 4]
Soak for 15-30 minutes while the Citrus steam does its work.

JAN.

FEB.

MAR.

APR.

MAY.

JUN.

JUL.

AUG.

SEP.

OCT.

NOV.

DEC.

NOSE DIVE
[II]

FIRE AND STEAM

FEB.

The Bathhouse at Flamingo Estate, located at the end of the Cactus Garden, was the first structure we built on the property. Designed by Studio KO in Paris, the lower underground level features a hammam, and the upper level is the bath. Photographed by Drew Escrivá.

[PAGE 82] In the Bathhouse. Photographed by Pia Riverola, 2025.

The Bathhouse at the end of the Cactus Garden was the first space we built at the Estate. It was inspired by the Alamut fortress in ancient Persia, a stone stronghold where soldiers would gather to bathe, recover, and search for a glimpse of heaven before returning to battle. We built ours entirely out of concrete, with no other materials to clutter the mind. It is a three-story monolith: a poured-concrete tub oriented toward the sunrise, giant stained glass casement windows, and a fireplace raised high enough to watch from the bath. Downstairs, a concrete steam room has peek-a-boo windows—just enough to remind you the world is still growing outside.

When you enter, you hear it before you smell it: the quiet crackle and hiss of heat working on water and wood. Then scent arrives in layers.

Steam is technically odorless—but it's one of the great transport systems of smell. Heat lifts aromatic molecules off skin, soap, and stone, and humidity keeps them suspended, giving fragrance more time to bloom instead of vanishing. Warm, wet air also sharpens perception by hydrating the nasal lining, helping odorants reach receptors more efficiently. Steam doesn't smell—it makes smelling possible. In the tub, hot water volatilizes the soap's oils and throws them into the air in fine, fragrant spirals.

Smoke is ancient information. Once we learned to control fire roughly half a million years ago, smoke became the scent of nourishment and safety—the signal for food, warmth, and a protected circle. Before a log "burns," it dries; the crackling is steam escaping. Then heat begins pyrolysis—breaking cellulose and lignin into vapors and volatile molecules. The flame you see is not the wood itself, but those gases igniting. As temperatures change, the perfume changes too: brighter, resinous top notes early on; sharper acids and aldehydes as heat builds; then deeper phenolic smoke as the fire drops into ember—leather, ash, sweetness, shadow.

Each wood has its own signature. Cedar burns dark and resinous. California Bay Laurel burns sweeter—almost spiced. In winter, we dress the kindling with essential oils so the opening notes bloom before the fire gets too fierce: Lavender for calm, Sage for clarity, Rosemary for thrill.

FEB.

That's the Bathhouse's
real ritual

Smoke for structure,
steam for reach.

And when the air is thick
with it: wood, soap, wet stone, garden . . .

You catch a fragrant
glimpse of heaven.

Just enough to carry with you when
you return to battle again.

Images from the Flamingo Estate Bathhouse over the years,
by Pia Riverola, Drew Escrivá, and Francois Halard

March is a fever dream at Flamingo. If February was about the discipline of the blade, March is about the intoxication of the bloom. The garden is no longer holding its breath; it is exhaling, filling the night air with the heavy, narcotic perfume of Jasmine and Tuberose. We trade our shears for shovels, planting the first warm-season lovers—Tomatoes, Basil, and Zucchini—into soil that is finally waking

MARCH

up. Beneath our feet, the compost is cooking, a dark alchemy turning death into life, while we feed the Citrus trees to thank them for their winter bounty. This is the month of the "moonstruck," where we learn that nature doesn't sleep when we do. We build homes for owls, listen for the biorhythms of the trees, and walk the path by moonlight. March is not just a transition; it is a seduction.

American filmmaker David Lynch poses for a portrait sitting in a Packard in Los Angeles, California, circa 1986.

Los Angeles's most iconic filmmaker, David Lynch, died in January 2025. On his gravestone there are only three words etched: NIGHT-BLOOMING JASMINE. No dates. No list of his films. Just the name of a flower.

It makes perfect sense. Lynch once described driving through Los Angeles at night with the windows down, catching that narcotic waft from a hedge somewhere in the dark, and feeling the ghosts of old Hollywood climb into the car with him—Clark Gable in the passenger seat, Gloria Swanson in the back. For him, Night-Blooming Jasmine was not a plant, it was a portal. A scent that proved the past was still shimmering inside the present, that the city was beautiful and haunted at the same time. If you were going to reduce his whole universe—the dreamy surface, the menace underneath, the way one smell can tip you sideways into another world—into a single phrase on stone, you could not do better.

Her name is already a little spell. "Jasmine" comes from the Persian *yasmin*, "gift from God." In ancient Persia she was the King of Flowers, a symbol of absolute, divine love. In India, one old story says that Jasmine was once a woman loved by the sun god. When he left her for another, she threw herself into his fire. Her ashes turned into sweet-smelling white flowers that only release their perfume at night, when they think he might be watching. It's melodramatic and completely believable: a flower that saves everything for the dark.

Cleopatra supposedly understood the power of that darkness. One version of her meeting with Mark Antony has her soaking the sails of her royal barge in Jasmine oil, so that the scent arrived at his senses before she did. Whether that detail is historical or just excellent PR, it fixed Jasmine forever in the imagination as an accomplice in seduction. You smell it before you see the face. By the time you realize what's happening, you're already in trouble.

The plant, of course, has its own agenda. What Jasmine really loves are moths.

Most Jasmines keep their true voice for after sunset. They time their scent to when their pollinators are awake—hawk moths, those hummingbird impersonators with long tongues and excellent noses. They're not doing anything mystical; they're doing logistics. Why waste perfume on bees when your real lovers don't clock in until dark? We drape Jasmine over balconies for romance; she pumps out molecules designed for the night shift.

David Lynch's grave, Los Angeles, 2026. The grave is surrounded by tributes that reference his famous daily rituals—most notably Coca-Cola cans and cigarettes—alongside the epitaph for his favorite fragrance, Night-Blooming Jasmine.

Those molecules are little contradictions. On paper, Jasmine is built from clean, pretty notes—hints of Citrus and green leaf, a soapy clarity—sitting on a base that's frankly animal. One of the key components, indole, in high concentration smells like something decaying; in trace amounts it's what makes white flowers like Jasmine and Orange blossom smell fleshy and alive, a bit like warm skin. Perfumers talk about Jasmine as "both virginal and filthy." That's exactly why she sits in the heart of so many great perfumes: she keeps them from being too polite.

↑

White Jasmine (*Jasminum polyanthum*), a prolific evergreen climber with dense clusters of buds that open into star-shaped, snowy white flowers.

→

Night-Blooming Jasmine growing around the wall of the Goat Shed and the outdoor tub. Painted by John Reagan in November 2025.

The labor behind that is spectacularly unpolite. It takes millions of hand-picked flowers—sometimes five million or more—to produce a single kilo of Jasmine absolute. Women in fields in India, Egypt, Morocco, picking before dawn, filling baskets that will never become bouquets, only go straight into solvent and stills. All of that work to make a liquid that will sit quietly in a tiny brown bottle, waiting to be measured in drops into a formula. You can smell that density. Even cheap Jasmine oils feel expensive in the nose.

At Flamingo Estate, Night-Blooming Jasmine erupts in waves from late spring through fall, with the big, operatic bloom in May and June. I've planted it all around the house, but especially under the bathroom window. On hot nights I lean out of the tub and grab handfuls of it, hang the branches over the hot plumbing in the shower, and let the steam coax the scent out. That bathroom—fogged mirror, tile, Eucalyptus outside, a cloud of Jasmine—became the template for our Jasmine and Damask Rose Body Wash, Hand Soap, Rich Cream, and Candle. The "brief" was simply: make it smell like this room at 11 p.m.

The scent is nothing short of narcotic. There are studies showing that inhaling Jasmine can measurably calm the nervous system—shifting brain waves, nudging people toward the same sort of relaxation some sedatives deliver—but you don't need an EEG to understand it. Stand under a hedge in full bloom and you can feel your muscles lose their armor. It's not a wellness-influencer calm; it's something older and stranger, a mix of comfort and slight disorientation, like being both held and undone at the same time.

Los Angeles knows this. When Jasmine arrives, the whole city smells it. As the first pink buds open into white stars, they let rip with a perfume that refuses to be upstaged by anything else in the air: exhaust, smoke, Bougainvillea, even the strange scorched-rubber smell of summer asphalt. On those first warm nights, a thin fog of Jasmine drifts over neighborhoods in Silver Lake, Hancock Park, Glendale, Hollywood. You can be stopped at a red light and, without warning, you're back in some other country, or at a party you shouldn't have left, or in love with someone you haven't met yet.

Emily Green wrote in the *Los Angeles Times* that Jasmine "seduces us back into a state where we are capable of wonder at the pulses of the natural world," reminding us there are "profound mysteries unfolding nightly in our own backyards." She's right.

One moment you're thinking about emails; the next you're thinking about pollinators, childhood, desire, and the fact that a shrub in front of a bungalow can overpower an entire freeway.

Jasmine is quintessentially an LA flower not because she belongs here botanically (she doesn't; she's from the Himalayan region of India and China), but because she has threaded herself into the city's private mythology. For a lot of us, the smell of Jasmine is the smell of a choice. It's the night you first arrived. The night you decided to stay. The night you realized you couldn't keep living the life you had planned.

Joan Didion, writing about leaving New York for Los Angeles, described seeing the moon on the Pacific and smelling Jasmine all around and knowing, in that moment, that the apartment in New York no longer made sense. Jasmine has a way of doing that: it keeps insisting that here and now, in this messy garden, in this messy city, might actually be enough.

What I love most is that she does all this mischief in an extremely inefficient way. By three in the afternoon she looks tired, a bit limp. By five she's practically invisible behind the Tomatoes and the Roses. Then the light drops, the air cools, and she starts again—molecule by molecule—to rewrite the night.

Maybe that's why Lynch wanted her on his stone. She is the smell of the scene just before something happens: the drive through Mulholland before the plot twist, the walk up a path at Flamingo before you see who is waiting there, the moment you step outside and remember you have both a past and a future. Love is love, yes. But Jasmine is what it smells like when the city—and the garden—decide to show you just how strange and beautiful that can be.

←

Jasmine from the Flamingo garden, photographed by Hugh Davison.

→

Harvesting of Jasmine flowers near Reggio Calabria, Calabria, Italy, 1965.

Narcissus flowers from the garden, photographed in March 2022
by Drew Escrivá for the launch of our White Flower Soap.

[GROUNDING] : A MAP OF PLEASURE FROM THE GARDEN

THE NIGHT-BLOOMING GARDEN

34°08' N / 118°12' W

LOS ANGELES, CALIFORNIA

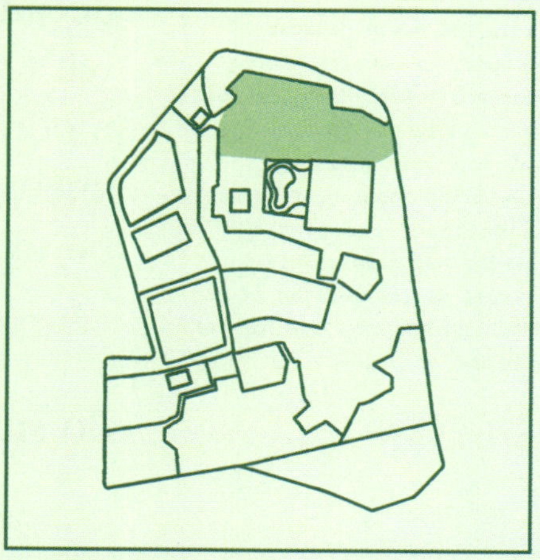

Moonstruck. The moon has always been blamed for the things we can't explain about ourselves.

When people behave oddly, we say it must be the full moon. When someone is jittery, restless, a bit unhinged, we say they're "moonstruck." Police departments and hospitals will quietly tell you that full-moon nights feel different—more fights, more odd calls, more drama. The data is messy, but the stories are consistent. For thousands of years, we've suspected that the white disc in the sky reaches down and pulls on more than just the tides.

Cinema understood this long before science did.

In 1902, Georges Méliès made *Le Voyage dans la Lune* in a glass-roofed studio outside Paris—a greenhouse for dreams. He painted the moon as a round, powdered face with kohl-rimmed eyes, then shoved a cardboard rocket into its cheek by hand. That single image—the moon, wounded and slightly offended, tolerating our nonsense—became one of the first icons of film. In those early

↓
Diana, the Roman goddess of the hunt, as seen in Pierre Blanchard's 1803 *Mythology of Youth*. While she is famously depicted with her bow, arrows, and loyal hunting dog, the delicate crescent moon crowning her head signifies her role as the goddess of the moon, lighting the way for her nocturnal mischief.

decades of cinema, you can feel directors falling hopelessly in love with her. Silent films couldn't depend on dialogue, so a shot of the moon did enormous work. If the camera cut to a full moon, you knew exactly where you were: somewhere you probably shouldn't be, at a time when you probably shouldn't be there.

The moon turned up whenever somebody was about to do something they'd regret.

In *Nosferatu* and those first werewolf films of the 1920s, the moon is not just scenery; it's a trigger. The cutaway to the rising disc is the moment your stomach drops. *Here we go.* Bodies will change, demons will rise, appetites will wake up, rules will lose their grip. In *Fantasia*, Walt Disney and his animators imagine what nature gets up to when we're asleep: fairies slipping out at night to frost leaves and lay dew on spiderwebs, flowers waltzing in blue-black water. Plants become mischievous in the dark, waltzing for their own amusement.

By 1987, the moon had become a full-blown relationship counselor. In *Moonstruck*, Cher's character, Loretta, is engaged to a man she doesn't love and is pulled toward one she absolutely shouldn't be kissing. The giant full moon hanging over Brooklyn is treated like a character: it keeps dropping into frame as if to say, *Of course you're acting crazy. Look at me.* The moon is blamed for making men fall in love, for making old men howl at the sky, for loosening everyone's grip on their good intentions. "It makes things happen," one character says, shrugging, as if that explains it—and maybe it does.

And it's not just movies. Long before the camera, the moon was doing this job in myth and gossip.

Every culture seems to have turned it into a person at some point: a goddess with a bow (Artemis,

Diana), a pale god in a chariot (Chandra), a woman stranded forever with a rabbit at her feet (Chang'e). Men were warned not to trust the inconstant moon. The word *lunatic* comes from the old suspicion that too much moonlight could tilt the mind. Witches were said to fly on full-moon nights; wolves were said to remember they weren't supposed to be tame.

View of a full moon above the Flamingo Estate terrace on Monday, February 2, 2026.

In Yucatán, my friends talk about the Alux—tiny spirit people who come out at night to guard fields and play tricks, especially under a bright moon. In Europe, there were will-o'-the-wisps leading travelers off paths; in Japan, fox spirits and yōkai playing their games at the forest edge; in the Middle East, jinn in ruined gardens, very busy after dark. The moon gives us permission to take risks, and for others to do the same.

Remember this: Romeo does not climb Juliet's balcony at lunchtime. He slips into the orchard after dark, stumbles through the trees, and stands under her window swearing by the moon—until she tells him not to, because the moon changes too much. Secret meetings in hedged-in gardens, trysts in orangerie courts, monsters in Rose alleys: night gardens are where deals are struck, where people become a little less sensible, where desire and danger step a little closer together.

The moon, in other words, is a universal excuse for mischief.

It pulls the ocean up and down twice a day. It pulls our hormones into rhythms we still don't fully understand. It certainly pulls our stories into strange shapes. And it absolutely pulls at the garden.

[1]

[2]

[3]

[9]

[7]

[8]

[1] The official poster for the 1987 romantic classic *Moonstruck*, featuring Cher against a massive, glowing full moon. The artwork mirrors the film's central theme: the chaotic, transformative power that a "moon over Brooklyn" can have on the human heart. [2] A rainy sunrise over LA with Palm trees. [3] An animation still from Disney's *Fantasia* (1940). In the world of *Fantasia*, the garden truly comes alive once the sun sets and the moonlight takes over. [4] 1922 German classic *Nosferatu: A Symphony of Horror*. In the world of silent horror, the moon acts as a silent witness to the encroaching dread. [5] Elliott and E.T. soar across the face of a massive, glowing moon in Steven Spielberg's 1982 masterpiece, *E.T. the Extra-Terrestrial*. [6] This woodblock print by Takahashi Bihō, titled *Bat in Moon*, circa 1890–1930, captures a

[4]

[5]

[6]

[11]

[10]

moment of quiet suspense. Bihō focuses entirely on the intersection of the celestial and the nocturnal, creating a sense of a world frozen in moonlight. [7] Fozzie Bear, Kermit the Frog, Miss Piggy, Rizzo the Rat, Gonzo, and Animal shoot for the stars in the 1999 film *Muppets from Space*. [8] Buzz Aldrin's boot print from the Apollo 11 moon landing, 1969. [9] Romeo and Juliet always find love under the full moon. A kiss between the two lovers, Germany, 1902. [10] Georges Méliès, 1902. A surreal moment from *A Trip to the Moon* that defines early cinematic suspense and fascination with the lunar landscape. [11] Henri Rousseau's *The Snake Charmer*, 1907, presents an exotic, mysterious garden illuminated by a glowing full moon. The moonlit silhouette of the charmer plays her flute, drawing serpents from the dense, oversized foliage.

Narcissus papyraceus blooming around the fountain at the bottom of the garden. Photographed by Drew Escrivá.

An 1870 engraving by Émile-Antoine Bayard for Jules Verne's science fiction novel *From the Earth to the Moon*. The caption below, *"Rien ne pouvait égaler la splendeur . . ."* ("Nothing could equal the splendor . . ."), underscores the awe-inspiring nature of the moon as seen through the eyes of Verne's nineteenth-century explorers. The image depicts the moon as a vast, detailed orb suspended in a sea of countless stars, capturing the "splendor" described in the text.

Night at Flamingo Estate feels like the moment the director calls "Cut" on the daytime show and the understudies take the stage. The bees clock off. The gardeners coil hoses. The paths empty. The sensible plants close up shop. And then, as the sky deepens and the first white light slides over the hillside, a different cast steps out.

Jasmine, Gardenia, Tuberose, Moonflower, Night Phlox, Honeysuckle—all the daytime wallflowers—suddenly decide it's time to perform. During the day they look almost modest, hiding behind foliage. At night they become the loudest things in the room. Most of them are pale—white or cream or the palest lemon—because they didn't evolve to seduce our eyes. Their lovers are moths and bats and other creatures with mediocre color vision and spectacular noses. So they bloom when we go to bed and flood the air with scent.

The animals follow the same script. Moths do lazy, intoxicated circuits around the Moonflowers and Brugmansias, powdered in pollen like tipsy guests leaving a party. Spiders reset their webs across the path, stringing up invisible tripwires for anyone who forgot a torch. Bats flick through the air in fast little arcs, catching the insects that came for the flowers. Owls sit in the Eucalyptus like disapproving ushers, watching it all. Opossums, raccoons, the odd skunk or fox slide along the fence line, hoovering up fallen fruit. It's the same hillside, but the energy is completely different: less calendar, more carnival. Like Cher, we all become moonstruck.

Many of the night-blooming flowers up here are literally wired to the dark. They have internal clocks that tell them when to open and when to release scent. They know when the moon is up and when the moths are hungry. They time their perfume like a director timing a cue.

So the Night-Blooming Garden up here is not just a collection of plants; it's a little stage where the moon gets to direct. It turns up, fat and pale, and everyone behaves a bit strangely: flowers open at unreasonable hours, moths go into overtime, owls come in for their shift, and we all act a little strange. Maybe that's why we keep putting her in our stories. Méliès gave the moon a face and let us stab it with a rocket. Disney gave her choreography and a cast of dancing flowers. Shakespeare made her the unreliable witness to teenage lust. Cher gave her a Brooklyn accent in *Moonstruck* and let her take the blame when people did the mad, necessary thing instead of the sensible one.

We talk about being "moonstruck" as if it were a weakness, but I think it's permission. The moon gives us cover to be bold, to sneak through orchards and fall for the wrong person and plant Jasmine where we have no business planting Jasmine. Cher sings, "If I could turn back time," but the moon doesn't turn anything back; she just keeps pulling the tide forward through her phases, dragging us with her. The best we can do is meet her halfway—out in the garden at night, where the flowers have already decided to misbehave, and let ourselves be a little bit crazy too.

Jimson Weed, 1936-37 by Georgia O'Keeffe.

Jupiter above the Flamingo Estate
terrace on February 2, 2026.

The Night Blooming Garden

Night-Blooming Jasmine
[*Cestrum nocturnum*]

Jasmine is the first whisper. In daytime, it smells like nice soap. At night, the white blossoms turn their faces upward and the scent drops an octave. It gets heavier, sweeter, a little indecent—the glamorous, slightly dirty Jasmine that perfumers put at the heart of the big brand perfumes. It's the smell of someone who has stayed out too late and is absolutely going to stay out later.

Gardenia
[*Gardenia jasminoides*]

Gardenia is moodier. On hot nights, when the air feels like soup, the waxy white blooms smell like cream and Coconut and rubbed pencils—lush and tropical and faintly nostalgic. But the deeper you smell, the stranger it gets: hints of mushroom and Blue Cheese funk appear, a heavy, funky North Star for pollinators who rely on scent rather than color. On cold nights, she says almost nothing. There is something wonderfully temperamental about that.

Moonflower
[*Ipomoea alba*]

Moonflower is more innocent, but no less dramatic. The big white trumpets of *Ipomoea* open right on cue at dusk, unfurling rapidly in just one to two minutes. You can sit there with a drink and actually watch them open, one petal at a time, like slow fireworks. They last for only one precious night, smelling green and slightly sweet, like Cucumber and Vanilla and rainwater. If you were a Hawk Moth, you would probably compose love songs about them.

Night Phlox
[*Zaluzianskya capensis*]

Night Phlox is a small surprise. By day it's unremarkable, curled up in tight burgundy balls. At night its little stars open to smell like Honey, Marzipan, and warm Chocolate Cake. It is impossible to sit next to it for long and not feel suddenly hungry for dessert.

Honeysuckle
[*Lonicera spp.*]

Honeysuckle, the childhood vine, doesn't really wait for night, but darkness amplifies it. The same sharp, sugary, slightly feral smell you remember from sucking the nectar out of blossoms as a kid, but now it fills the path, hangs in the air in long ribbons, and makes you walk slower without quite knowing why.

Tuberose
[*Agave amica*]

Tuberose is not temperamental; she is unhinged. In Victorian times, young girls were actually forbidden from smelling it, fearing it might awaken "erotic urges." It's easy to see why. By midnight, the air around it is thick with what perfume people call "narcotic white floral": creamy, rubbery, almost overwhelming. French perfumers use Tuberose to say, "This is not a nice girl." It's the note in scents like Fracas and Carnal Flower that makes people either swoon or run away. Under a full moon, standing too close to a clump of Tuberose is said to make you look for trouble and not look away.

White Angel's Trumpet
[*Brugmansia spp.*]

And then there is Brugmansia, the Angel's Trumpet, hanging at the edge of the night garden like the most magnificent warning sign. Every part of the plant is poisonous, which feels exactly right: of course, the most persuasive smell in the garden belongs to something you shouldn't touch too much.

[III] MARCH **SPRING**	# DIRTY WORK	*"No winter lasts forever; no spring skips its turn."* —HAL BORLAND

GARDEN TASKS:

- [ ] Feed Citrus after harvest with compost, worm castings, and a balanced organic fertilizer.
- [ ] Thin fruit on overloaded branches to prevent breakage.
- [ ] Shape and train Figs, Olives, and Pomegranates as new shoots appear.
- [ ] Plant warm-season crops by mid-month: Tomatoes, Peppers, Eggplant, Zucchini, Basil, and Cucumbers.
- [ ] Plant flowers in kitchen beds; transplant seedlings and starts into the ground.
- [ ] Harvest the last winter greens (Kale, Arugula, Chard) before they bolt.
- [ ] Succession sow Lettuces and Radishes for steady harvests.
- [ ] Plant perennials and tropicals.
- [ ] Cut back woody herbs (Thyme, Sage, Lavender) for fresh spring growth.
- [ ] Pinch Basil and Mint tips to keep plants compact and flavorful.
- [ ] Brew and apply compost tea to boost soil biology.
- [ ] Deadhead Jasmine, Freesia, and Narcissus to extend bloom.
- [ ] Plant summer flowers: Dahlias, Cosmos, Marigolds, Zinnias, and Nasturtiums.
- [ ] Feed flowering plants with Seaweed or compost extract to support buds.
- [ ] Divide and replant clumping perennials (Mint, Daylilies, Irises).
- [ ] Turn compost piles; mix in pruning waste and Citrus rinds.
- [ ] Watch for gophers and aphids; plant insectary flowers (Alyssum, Borage, Calendula).
- [ ] Start monthly fertilizing (March-October).

A Moon Mist captures the energy of the night garden—pale flowers that release their perfume at dusk. It borrows from the ritual of "moon water," where water is left under moonlight to charge. To make it, place a heatproof bowl in the center of a large pot and scatter fresh Jasmine (or Tuberose or Magnolia) around the bowl. Add water to the pot—enough to cover the flowers but not float the bowl—and cover with the lid flipped upside down. Pile ice on top of the inverted lid and simmer gently. As the steam rises, hits the cold lid, and condenses, it will drip into the bowl as pure flower water. Blend this with a splash of Orange Blossom water or Neroli hydrosol. Pour into a clean spray bottle and leave it outside or on a windowsill overnight under the moon. Mist it over your sheets or into the air whenever you need a little magic.

TASK ☐

GIVE A JASMINE LEI

We first received these when we visited a hotel in the Mexican jungle—it was the most fragrant, thoughtful welcome gift we'd ever been given. Now we make them for events at the Estate so everyone arrives with a lush strand of flowers around their neck, and it's always the favorite party gift. Just thread fresh Jasmine blossoms onto string (a needle makes it wildly easier), keep the lei cool until guests arrive, then place it on them like a little ceremony.

TASK ☐

SIT IN A JASMINE BATH

Scatter a generous handful of fresh Jasmine flowers into a warm bath. Swirl the water once to wake up the scent—that deep, narcotic perfume that usually belongs to the night. If you want to make it a proper ritual, add a big handful of epsom Salts for the body and a spoonful of raw Honey (or a splash of Oat milk) to soften the water. You can anchor the fragrance with a few drops of Jojoba or sweet Almond oil, or brighten it with a fresh strip of Citrus peel or a sprig of Lavender. Then simply sink in and soak until you feel brand new.

TASK ☐

Make a Perfume

Capture Jasmine's soul in a solid perfume. It's one of the most beautiful things you can make from the garden, using the ancient technique of enfleurage. Spread a thin, even layer of odorless fat (vegetable shortening or refined Coconut oil) in a shallow dish. Lay fresh Jasmine blossoms on top in a single layer. Cover and let it sit for 24 hours somewhere cool and away from direct sun, allowing the fat to absorb the exhaling scent. Remove the spent petals—they will look tired, having given up their ghosts—and replace with fresh blossoms. Repeat this daily ritual for 3-5 days, until the fat smells completely intoxicating. Scrape the scented fat into a clean jar—this is your Jasmine pomade.

TASK

Make Honeysuckle Honey

It is a magical taste. Use only edible, unsprayed Honeysuckle flowers (no leaves, no berries). Pick a small bowl of fragrant blossoms and pull off any green parts, then let them sit on a clean towel for an hour so they dry and soften a little. Fill a clean jar halfway with the blossoms and pour in mild, runny Honey until the flowers are fully covered. Close the lid and leave it in a cool, dark place for 1-2 weeks, turning it upside down now and then. Strain out the flowers if you like (or leave a few in for drama), then drizzle over yogurt, toast, or fruit, or stir into warm tea.

NOTE: *Never give Honey to children under one year old.*

TASK

RECORD A MOONLIGHT SOUNDTRACK

In the late 1970s, the Damanhur community in northern Italy developed a device that turned a plant's electromagnetic signals into music. Founded by Oberto Airaudi, Damanhur is home to scientists, mystics, and artists who study nature as a living, intelligent force. They wired leaves and roots to little synthesizers, translating tiny changes in bioelectric activity into melody. The belief was simple and enormous: music is the most universal way for a plant to speak to a human. A few years ago, the Damanhur team actually traveled from Italy to Los Angeles to wire up the garden at Flamingo Estate, turning the biorhythms of our trees into a living soundtrack.

We now know plants don't just sit there quietly. They send chemical messages through the air when they're stressed. They share sugars and information through fungal networks under the soil. A tree being cut down can change the behavior of trees meters away. It's not a Snow White fantasy; it's biology wearing a very beautiful dress.

If you can't fly the Damanhur team out from Italy, the good news is that today it's much easier to listen in. You can buy a little machine, like PlantWave or PlantsPlay, that uses electrodes to translate a plant's electrical signals into sound. Clip the sensors to a leaf, open an app on your phone, and suddenly your Fiddle-Leaf Fig or Rosemary bush is playing ambient music through your headphones. The Ritual: Pick one plant you love, attach the sensors, and sit still for ten minutes while it plays. Don't touch your phone. Just listen, and see what part of you starts to answer back.

TASK

START SPRING CLEANING

For those who find joy in spring cleaning, here's a simple, fragrant, chemical-free solution. Simply fill a clean jar loosely with fresh Jasmine blossoms and a few strips of Lemon peel, then cover completely with white vinegar. Seal it tight and leave it in a sunny spot for 10-14 days, giving it a gentle shake whenever you remember. When it's ready, strain into a fresh bottle, dilute 1:1 with water, and use on sinks, tiles, mirrors, and counters—basically anywhere that wants to sparkle.

Jasmine-Infused Cleaning Vinegar

RECIPE

The Best Late Night Grilled Cheese

The best grilled cheese is meant to be something you can pull together with little fuss when those late-night cravings hit. In my opinion, the best grilled cheese is made with low-quality cheese and high-quality butter! The cheese should be easy to melt and sharp, while the butter should be craveable enough to eat by the spoonful.

INGREDIENTS:

- 2 slices of white bread
- 2 slices of American cheese
- 1 slice of Pepper Jack cheese
- 2 Tbsp French-quality butter, room temperature

METHOD:

[1] Heat a 9-inch griddle over medium-low heat.

[2] Assemble your sandwich as follows: bread, American cheese, Pepper Jack, American cheese, bread. For advanced grilled cheese-making, leave the corners of the cheese to poke out the sides of the sandwich; this makes for a great cheese lace!

[3] Spread 1 tablespoon of butter on each outward-facing side of your sandwich.

[4] Place the sandwich on the griddle and allow to slowly sizzle and caramelize, 3 minutes.

[5] Flip and allow to caramelize the other side.

TASK

GET STARSTRUCK

☐

Last year, Harvey and I took his parents stargazing in a remote corner of the Utah desert, where there was no light for miles. We all sat covered in blankets, looking into telescopes and trying to spot the greats. Here's our challenge to you:

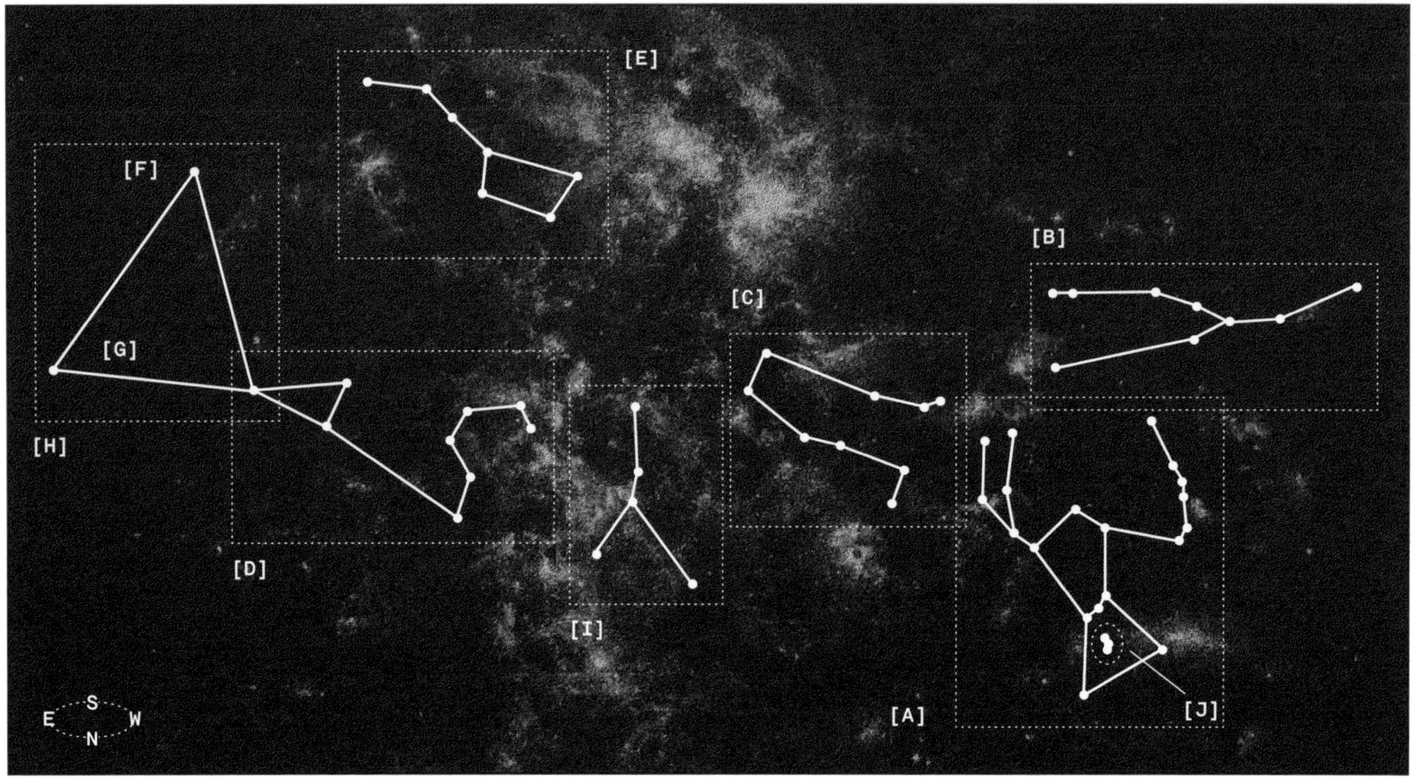

[A] ORION (EARLY EVENING): Look for the three-star belt, then trace the big hourglass of the Hunter as it slides toward the west.

[B] TAURUS (EARLY EVENING): Spot the Pleiades (that tiny glitter cluster) and bright Aldebaran nearby, then watch them follow Orion down.

[C] GEMINI: Find the "twin headlights," Castor and Pollux, and trace the simple stick-figure twins.

[D] LEO: Look east/southeast for the "backward question mark" (the Sickle) and bright Regulus.

[E] THE BIG DIPPER: Catch it high in the northeast, then use it like a handle to guide your eyes around the sky.

[F] ARCTURUS: Follow the curve of the Big Dipper's handle—"arc to Arcturus"—and land on a bright orange star.

[G] SPICA: Keep going—"speed on to Spica"—and find the bright star in Virgo below Arcturus.

[H] THE SPRING TRIANGLE: Connect Arcturus, Spica, and Regulus—a big, satisfying shape that basically announces spring.

[I] CANCER (BONUS): Between Gemini and Leo lies a faint constellation; try to spot it on a darker night just for the challenge.

[J] THE ORION NEBULA (BONUS, EARLY EVENING): In Orion's "sword," look for a soft cloudy smudge before he sets.

TASK
HAVE A FULL MOON PARTY

RECIPE

Jasmine Pavlova

INGREDIENTS:

MERINGUE:

- 6 large egg whites, room temperature
- 1½ cups granulated sugar
- 2 tsp cornstarch
- ½ Tbsp Lemon juice
- ½ Tbsp Vanilla extract

WHIPPED CREAM:

- 1½ cups heavy whipping cream (very cold)
- 4 Tbsp powdered sugar
- 1 Tbsp Jasmine syrup

METHOD:

[1] Preheat your oven to 300°F and prepare a half sheet tray lined with parchment paper. Set aside.

[2] Add egg whites to the clean bowl of a stand mixer and begin mixing on medium speed.

[3] Add the sugar 1 tablespoon at a time, leaving 1–2 seconds in between for the sugar to incorporate.

[4] Turn the mixer up to high and beat for 4 minutes until the egg whites are stiff, pale, and glossy, and a small amount of the mixture rubbed between your fingers shows no granules of sugar left to dissolve.

[5] Turn the mixer down to medium, and add the cornstarch, lemon juice, and vanilla. Continue mixing until combined.

[6] Using a spatula, scoop out the meringue mixture and form a dome shape on the parchment. You can use your spatula to create a vertical pattern along the outside of the dome.

[7] Bake for 1 hour, then turn off the oven, leaving the door closed, and allow the meringue to cool completely in the oven.

[8] Combine the cream, powdered sugar, and jasmine syrup and whip until you get just-stiff peaks; the tip of the cream's peak should fold on itself when a small dollop is made.

[9] To assemble, pipe whipped cream over the pavlova to your liking and top with your favorite fruit.

JAN.

FEB.

MAR.

APR.

MAY.

JUN.

JUL.

AUG.

SEP.

OCT.

NOV.

DEC.

NOSE DIVE
[III]

COMPOST

MAR.

Compost Is the Scent of Earth Cooking

It's the scent of the earth cooking. Just as a chef caramelizes sugar or ferments dough, soil organisms cook four essentials—carbon, nitrogen, water, and oxygen—into something living: darker, richer, almost luxurious. As everything cooks, smell becomes the spokesperson. In simple terms: if it smells like rotten garbage, something is wrong. Most often, it's a lack of oxygen—nature's reminder that all things need to breathe.

At the beginning, compost smells mild and fresh. Nitrogen-rich "greens" meet carbon-rich "browns." We add water, and we turn for air. Soft fruit and vegetable scraps mingle with musty leaves and resinous sawdust. Microbes arrive fast, and if the balance is right, they work so hard the center of the pile can heat to temperatures hot enough to kill weed seeds and pathogens. It's a living oven.

Then the pile goes feral—in the best way. Inside, the microbial universe enters a frenzy, metabolizing everything. When it's properly aerated and evenly moist, the scent starts to mimic baking and fermenting at once: warm, mineral, slightly sweet.

Turn the pile and the heat blooms outward, releasing a complicated cloud—funk, stone, wet forest, humus. It can smell truffle-like, almost umami. A scent bomb that mirrors the invisible intensity inside.

This is where smell becomes a diagnostic tool. If it smells rotten or septic, the pile is too wet and oxygen-starved—anaerobic. If it smells sharply ammoniacal, there's too much nitrogen and not enough carbon. If it smells sour, it's compacted and needs air. The fixes are usually the same ones that save most things: add browns, add oxygen, loosen it up, and give it time.

As the pile leaves its adolescent chaos behind, it cools and stabilizes. Decomposition slows, fungi become more prominent, and the scent quiets into something deeper and cleaner.

Finished compost smells like fertile earth—moist, mild, unmistakably alive. Like a forest after rain. Harmony. Full circle. Ready to go back into the ground and start the next cycle.

[PAGE 114] Taken on July 15, 1993, this photo captures a worker named Adrian Carrick at the Elf Mushroom Farm in Mulgrave, New South Wales, Australia. The image provides a glimpse into the industrial-scale production of compost required for mushroom cultivation.

Our infamous 2022 Mother's Day Compost remains a legend at the Estate. A bespoke, nutrient-dense blend of free-range goat, horse, chicken, and cow manure, this batch was meticulously tended by our own gardeners to ensure peak biological richness. We cheekily dubbed it "the finest poop in LA"—and our community agreed, as it sold out almost instantly.

MAR.

April is about alchemy. The wild rush of winter is over and the garden is stable enough for us to tend the things that will later tend to us. This is the month of transformation: compost turning into soil, sunlight turning into sugar, and roots turning into medicine. We feed the fruit trees and Citrus, dose the soil with compost and seaweed, and slip Tomatoes, Basil, Peppers, Squash, and Eggplants into their summer beds like

APRIL

patients being settled under fresh sheets. Ladybirds are released like tiny nurses onto the Roses, and the worms pull our offerings down into the dark like mad scientists. We mulch the beds to hold the heat and harvest the last cool herbs, knowing that everything we touch is in the process of becoming something else. Something stronger. April asks us to treat the garden like a living medicine cabinet.

Mugwort at the Estate, painted by John Reagan, January 2026.

On a winter night in Anglo-Saxon England, if you were bitten by something you couldn't name or struck by a fever that wouldn't break, you didn't call a doctor. You called the woman at the edge of the village. She would arrive with her apron full of leaves and roots, her head full of prayers and half-remembered spells, and she would stand over the bed and begin to chant. Some of what she said sounded like church Latin, some of it like an angry nursery rhyme, and some of it like a dare aimed at the darkness itself. Then she would take a bundle of bitter, gray-green Mugwort (*Artemisia vulgaris*), crush it with animal fat and ash, and press it against the skin.

Around the same time—about eleven hundred years ago—someone in a monastery sat down to write a version of that work in ink. The result is an Old English manuscript now kept in the British Library known as the *Lacnunga* (Remedies). It's a strange collection of medical texts and spells, including a piece we now call the Nine Herbs Charm. In it, you name each herb, praise its powers, then explain how to use it to cure wounds, infections, "flying venom," and unknown dark evils.

At the very top of that list—the first herb you call by name—is Mugwort. The charm addresses it as the oldest of herbs, the one with power "against three and against thirty." Long before anyone called it a weed, it was the herb of first resort, the senior witch in the medicine garden. Botanically, it belongs to the genus *Artemisia*, named after Artemis, the Greek goddess of wild things, childbirth, the moon, and every edge where one thing turns into another: forest to field, girl to woman, living to dead. It makes sense that her plant is not a neat little shrub but a knee-high, unruly roadside sorceress that refuses to stay in garden beds and insists on growing at the edge of everything.

An image from the *Omne Bonum*, a massive encyclopedia compiled by James le Palmer in London between 1360 and 1375. It depicts a figure providing remedies to a patient suffering from leprosy.

On Midsummer's Eve in parts of what is today Germany, the Netherlands, and Belgium, people once tied belts of Mugwort around their waists before they went out to the bonfires. They danced, drank, sinned, and jumped the

↓
A Tlingit shaman performing a healing ceremony for a patient in Alaska (c. 1906), where native species of Mugwort, such as *Artemisia tilesii*, were vital to both medicinal and spiritual practices. The leaves were often prepared as a poultice or a strong tea to treat skin ailments and infections, a practice that mirrors the "cleansing" properties frequently described in European herbal texts. Beyond physical medicine, shamans utilized the plant to facilitate "spirit travel" and ward off negative influences during sessions, reinforcing Mugwort's global reputation as a "protector" plant used to purify sacred healing spaces through ritual smoke.

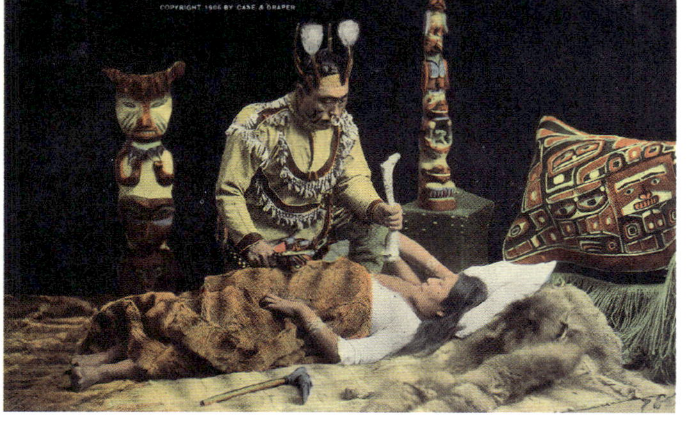

↑
A woodblock print by Okumura Masanobu (1686-1764) depicting a courtesan treating a woman with moxibustion. The treatment involves burning moxa—a substance derived from dried and processed Mugwort leaves—directly on the skin to stimulate healing and circulation.

→
A fifteenth-century botanical illustration of Mugwort (*Artemisia*) from the Italian manuscript of the *Herbarium of Pseudo*.

flames. Just before dawn, they took the Mugwort off and threw it into the fire, believing that whatever illness, bad luck, or witchcraft had clung to them during the year would burn away with it. Some legends say John the Baptist himself wore a belt of Mugwort in the wilderness, which is why the plant picked up the nickname "St. John's Plant."

In English custom, it was tied into "witches' garlands" hung in stables and over doors. Roman soldiers supposedly put it in their sandals to ward off fatigue on the march. In China, mothers stitched it into little cloth sachets for children to wear against summer fevers. In Japan, it was slipped into hot baths and steam rooms to warm the blood and soothe the womb. In Korea, it was an ingredient for postpartum baths, a plant for women recovering from hard childbirth. In India, a slightly different variety of Mugwort (*Artemisia indica*) was used to wake up digestion, clear toxins, and help with liver complaints. In Nepal, it's used as an eyewash for burning eyes and applied as a paste to wounds.

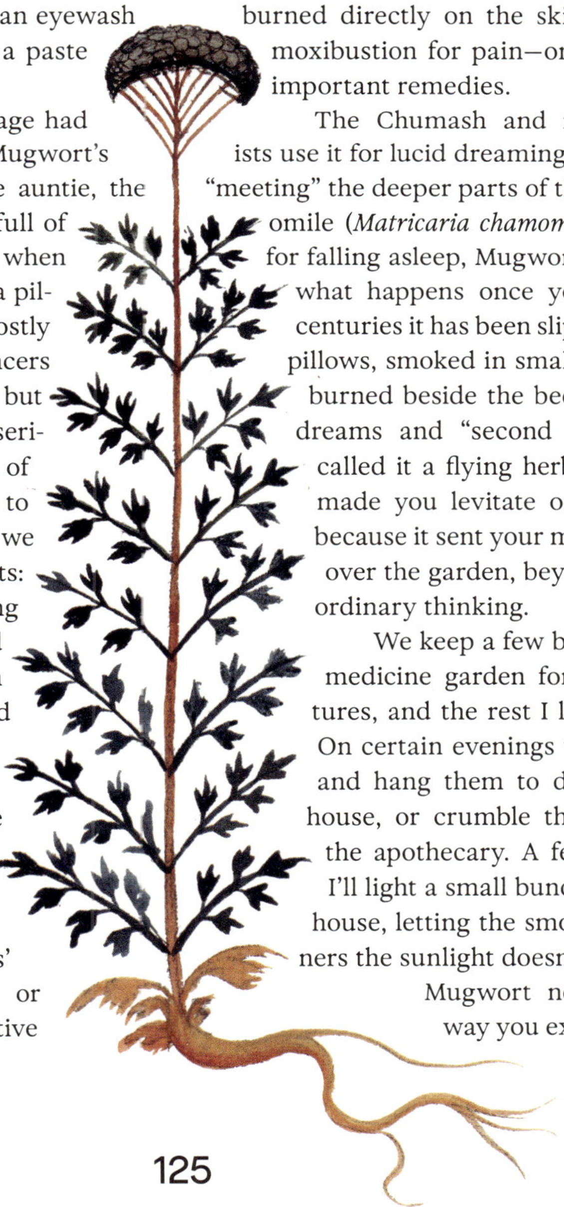

Around the world, every village had at least one person who knew Mugwort's moods—the cunning woman, the auntie, the midwife with her apron pockets full of leaves. She knew when to boil it, when to burn it, when to tuck it under a pillow. In our time, that job has mostly been handed to wellness influencers and pharmaceutical companies, but somewhere in the back of every serious garden there is still a clump of Mugwort waiting for someone to ask the right question. Today we also know some of the hard limits: pregnant women, or those trying to become pregnant, should avoid Mugwort completely, since it can stimulate uterine contractions and menstrual bleeding.

Flamingo Estate is hardcore Mugwort country. The native Mugwort here is *Artemisia douglasiana*—a very close sibling to the one in Europe and Asia, sometimes called Douglas' Sagewort, California Mugwort, or simply the dream plant. It's native all along the Los Angeles Basin and the rivers that cut through it, including the LA River and the Arroyo Seco that run very near the Estate. When I first moved here it was growing like a weed everywhere. It loves poor soil (which was the entire Estate until we fixed it). It's tough, drought-resistant, and almost impossible to get rid of, acting like an invasive weed if not managed—a kind of vegetal curse of "I will be here whether you want me or not," like the craziest ex-boyfriend you've ever had.

For the Indigenous peoples whose land we're on—the Gabrielino-Tongva communities—and their neighbors the Chumash, Miwok, Luiseño, and others, Mugwort wasn't a weed; it was a core medicine. California tribes used it as a women's herb, for joint pain and headaches, for stomach aches and "nervous affections," for rashes and poison oak, even as a wash for wounds. Its leaves were put into bathwater to soothe aching bones; cones of dried leaf were burned directly on the skin as a form of moxibustion for pain—one of their most important remedies.

The Chumash and modern herbalists use it for lucid dreaming and as a way of "meeting" the deeper parts of the self. If Chamomile (*Matricaria chamomilla*) is the herb for falling asleep, Mugwort is the herb for what happens once you're there. For centuries it has been slipped into dream pillows, smoked in small, bitter rolls, or burned beside the bed to invite vivid dreams and "second sight." Witches called it a flying herb not because it made you levitate on a broom, but because it sent your mind elsewhere—over the garden, beyond the fence of ordinary thinking.

We keep a few big clumps in the medicine garden for teas and tinctures, and the rest I let be a bit wild. On certain evenings we cut handfuls and hang them to dry in the Bathhouse, or crumble them into jars in the apothecary. A few times a year I'll light a small bundle and walk the house, letting the smoke find the corners the sunlight doesn't reach.

Mugwort never smells the way you expect a medicine

plant to smell. When you crush a fresh leaf between your fingers, it smells like something wild that has just brushed past your leg on a walk—sharp, green, and bitter. There's Sage in there, and Wormwood, and a hint of crushed Chrysanthemum.

As the leaves dry, the scent deepens. The bright green top note softens into something more smoky and medicinal. Dried Mugwort smells of old paper and dry hay, with little sparks of camphor and Mint running through it—a bit dusty, a bit bitter, but strangely comforting once you lean in. It's not a "nice" smell in the conventional way; it's a smell that asks you to pay attention. You catch a whiff of it when you brush past the plant in the garden and some part of your nervous system sits up straighter.

This 1497 woodcut of Mugwort from the *Hortus Sanitatis* represents the birth of the printed medical guide. It was designed to show that God created the natural world specifically to heal humans. The book was one of the most expensive things a person could own. If you lived in 1500, having this book on your shelf would have been the ultimate status symbol. It considered Mugwort a vital remedy for everything from exhaustion to supernatural protection.

Burn it, and Mugwort shows you her witch face. When you burn a tight little bundle, the leaves give off a thin, ghostly smoke that smells like a cross between Sagebrush, Tea Tree, and something almost sweet, like dried Orange peel that's been left on the dashboard too long. In a small room, the smoke wraps itself around the ceiling, then slides down into the corners, as if it's deliberately looking for things that don't belong there. The scent feels like an old grandmother standing guard at the door, making sure nothing unwelcome comes in.

In dream pillows Mugwort loosens its grip and becomes almost friendly. I love to mix it with Lavender in a little cloth sachet and give it to friends who come to the Estate. I especially love to put those sachets under my pillow when I take a long flight. I'd rather have lucid dreams than jet lag.

Mugwort in the bath smells like water in a vase after the flowers have been sitting in it for a week—a little funky, a little floral, very alive. It's that moment when the bouquet is past its prime but somehow more interesting: stems, sap, a whisper of decay, all the sweetness dragged a little closer to the soil.

In fragrance, that's exactly what she does. A tiny pinch of Mugwort in a blend gives everything else a green backbone and a slight, witchy shadow. It keeps Roses from becoming too pretty, keeps Lavender from tipping into soap, pulls Ylang-Ylang and Jasmine back from the edge of headache-inducing. It adds a faint bitterness and a breath of wild air so things smell less like a duty-free counter and more like Flamingo at dusk. We tuck just a trace of her into blends when we want something to feel a bit witchier, a bit less well-behaved—as if the garden has been left to its own devices for a day, and the plants have decided to tell the truth instead of just being nice.

So Mugwort, for me, is both that old village woman and the plant in her hands: the first name on the healer's tongue, the belt worn to the bonfire, the dream herb under the pillow, the stubborn native lining the LA River. Some plants are pretty. Mugwort is something else entirely—a guardian at the edge of the garden, still willing, after eleven hundred years, to stand between us and whatever's lurking in the dark.

Nikolai Astrup's *Midsummer Eve Bonfire* (1915) captures the ancient, mystical atmosphere of St. John's Eve, a celebration deeply intertwined with the folklore of Mugwort. In European tradition, Mugwort was considered the most powerful of the "St. John's herbs" and was believed to reach its peak medicinal and magical potency on this night. It was common practice for celebrants to wear girdles or crowns made of Mugwort while dancing around the fires, as seen in this painting, to protect themselves from backaches and misfortune in the coming year. Before the night ended, these wreaths were often thrown into the flames to symbolically burn away any ill luck or disease, reinforcing the plant's ancient role as a "protector" that could purify both the body and the spirit.

Sioux Indian Medicine Man. Qu'Appelle, N. W. T., Canada

[GROUNDING] : A MAP OF PLEASURE FROM THE GARDEN

THE MEDICINE GARDEN

34°08' N / 118°12' W

LOS ANGELES, CALIFORNIA

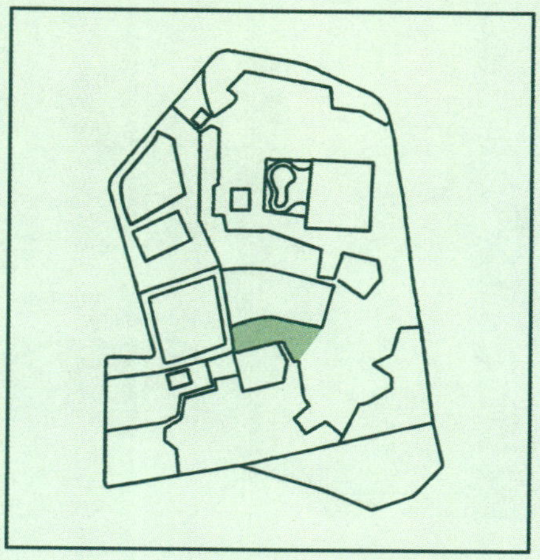

To the Navajo—or Diné, "the People"—health was never just about the body. It was a question of physics and philosophy. They believed that the universe operated in a delicate state of Hózhǫ́: a complex, vibrating equilibrium of balance, beauty, and order. Illness wasn't seen as a random glitch; it was a sign that the patient had fallen out of rhythm with the earth. The connection had been severed. To fix it, you didn't just need a remedy. You needed a realignment.

When a fever struck or a sickness wouldn't break, people didn't rely on a single village doctor. They activated a medical system as specialized and tiered as any modern hospital. The Hollywood trope of the solitary "medicine man" shaking a rattle is a lazy translation of a highly sophisticated network. In reality, if you were sick, you had access to four distinct types of practitioners, each with a specific clinical role.

←
Two mountaineers find Ötzi, Europe's oldest natural human mummy, in the Otztal Alps, September 1991.

[PAGE 128] A Sioux Medicine Man in Qu'Appelle, Canada, pictured in the early twentieth century. Though identified here as Sioux, he shares a profound cultural and linguistic lineage with the Navajo (Diné) of the American Southwest, who trace their ancestral origins back to the "Dene" peoples of the Canadian North. This image reflects a shared Indigenous medical philosophy that views the landscape as a living pharmacy.

First, you needed a diagnosis. You didn't go straight to the healer; you went to a diagnostician to find out why the harmony had broken. You might call for a Hand Trembler (Ndilniihii), who would enter a trance, his hand shaking involuntarily as it hovered over the patient's body like a seismograph, feeling for the source of trouble.

If the answer remained hidden, you might consult a Star Gazer, who read the refraction of light through a crystal or the patterns of the night sky to find the cause. Or you might seek out a Listener, who tuned into the subtle sounds of wind and earth, hearing the sickness that couldn't be seen.

Only once the diagnosis was confirmed were you referred to the fourth and most revered figure: the Singer (Hataałii). The Singer was the Keeper of the Cure. He was not a mystic guessing at solutions; he was an intellectual heavyweight who had committed to memory a library of hundreds of specific chants, complex sand paintings, and precise botanical protocols. A single ceremony, or Sing, could last nine nights and require the recitation of thousands of lines of poetry without a single error. He understood that to heal the body, he had to command the mind. The ceremony was a form of ancient psychoneuroimmunology—using ritual, rhythm, and awe to down regulate the nervous system and prime the immune system for recovery.

An illustration from a sixteenth-century edition of Dioscorides' *De Materia Medica*. Artist Gherardo Cibo depicts the labor-intensive harvest of Saffron, a vital "warm" remedy used by early modern doctors to treat liver blockages and respiratory issues, and to aid women in childbirth.

A fifteenth-century *Tacuinum Sanitatis* depicting the extraction of a Mandrake root. The dog reflects the folklore of the "fatal scream," as the plant itself was rumored to scream when plucked from the dirt. Once harvested, its juice was distilled into soporific sponges to induce deep anesthesia for surgery.

This instinct isn't unique to the American West. It's the oldest instinct we have.

In 1991, hikers in the Italian Alps found Ötzi, a mummy frozen in ice for 5,300 years. Tied to his belt was a leather thong holding two pieces of Birch Polypore fungus (*Fomitopsis betulina*). Scientists later discovered that Ötzi suffered from intestinal parasites; those fungi are toxic to the worms he carried. Five thousand years ago, freezing to death on a mountain, this man was carrying his own prescription.

Elsewhere, in Morocco's Taforalt Cave, a 15,000-year-old burial includes sprigs of Ephedra—a desert shrub still used today as a stimulant and decongestant—carefully laid beside the dead. In southern Africa, archaeologists found a 500-year-old antelope horn packed with plant extracts, the region's oldest "medicine bottle." In Arnhem Land, northern Australia, charred plant remains and grinding stones show Aboriginal people have been processing complex plant medicines for at least 65,000 years. And of course, we've all seen the herbal medicine shops in Asia: shelves lined with tightly packed jars, drawers full of roots and barks and dried things that once grew in the sun. My favorite is on Ko Shing Street in Sheung Wan, Hong Kong—still called "Medicine Street" because Chinese herbs are sold everywhere you look. Different continents, different languages, the same quiet conclusion: the garden has always been our first pharmacy.

The World Health Organization estimates that nearly 80–85 percent of the world's population still relies on traditional remedies as their primary healthcare—not as a TikTok trend, but because that's what is available and trusted. In many of those traditions, the boundary between "medicine" and "food" is thin: a root steeped in tea, an herb rubbed on the chest, a leaf burned as incense, a bark boiled into broth. Plants are not "alternative" medicine; they are where medicine started.

We like to think we've evolved past this "primitive" reliance on roots and leaves. We prefer our medicine in blister packs, white and sterile. But the truth is, we are still eating the earth. We just disguise it better.

Roughly 40 percent of modern prescription drugs are directly derived from plants or inspired by their chemical structures, and around half of our anti-cancer drugs trace back to natural products. Aspirin began life as salicin in Willow bark. Paclitaxel (Taxol), a cornerstone of chemotherapy, was discovered in the bark of the Pacific Yew. Digoxin came from Foxglove. Morphine from the Poppy. Metformin, the diabetes drug, came from a scruffy weed called Goat's Rue. We simply moved these plants from the garden to the lab, stripped them down to single molecules, and sent them out into the world in plastic bottles.

So when I walk into our Medicine Garden at Flamingo Estate, I don't see a quaint collection of greenery. I see a sunlit R&D lab.

←
A Chinese apothecary in San Francisco, 1882, captured by Isaiah West Taber. This shop served as a vital community hub where traditional Chinese medicine practitioners acted as both physicians and pharmacists. The shelves contained a vast collection of roots, barks, seeds, and dried flowers carefully selected to restore the Qi, or life energy of the patient. This nineteenth-century scene remains deeply relevant today, as plant medicine continues to be a cornerstone of Chinese culture. Unlike many Western remedies, Chinese medicine emphasizes a holistic, preventative approach, using complex botanical formulas to treat the root cause of illness rather than just the symptoms.

→
The Medicine Garden, painted by John Reagan, January 2026.

THE MEDICINE CABINET

ALOE VERA (*Aloe vera*) sits by the path like a dull, fleshy sword. Crack it open and the clear gel inside—99 percent water and 1 percent complex sugars, enzymes, and phytochemicals—is still one of the best things you can put on sunburn, kitchen burns, or irritated skin. Ancient Egyptians called it the "plant of immortality" and used it in embalming to keep skin elastic after death.

Nearby is MORMON TEA (*Ephedra virdis*). This native shrub looks like a bundle of green twigs stuck in the ground. Indigenous peoples brewed it to treat asthma and congestion. When Mormon settlers arrived in the West and were forbidden from drinking coffee or tea, they adopted it as a stimulant substitute. They were onto something: the plant contains ephedrine. Years later, science would synthesize related compounds into pseudoephedrine—the decongestant behind Sudafed and countless cold remedies. It was the original over-the-counter nose opener, growing wild in the desert.

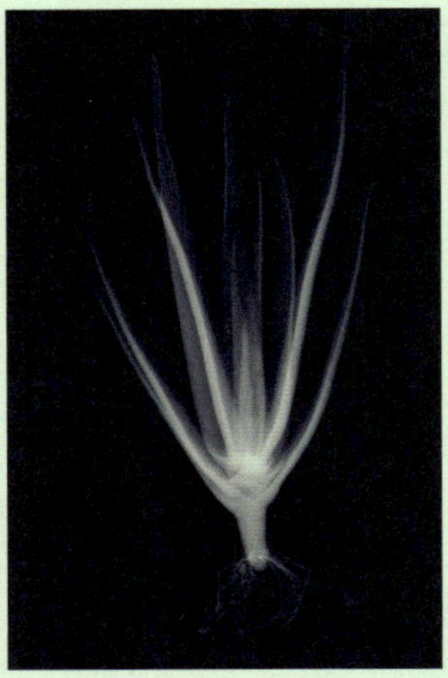

THE SEDATIVE BED

We grow GERMAN CHAMOMILE (*Matricaria recutita*), often dismissed as "sleepy tea" for children. The essential oil, when steam-distilled, turns an intense ocean blue because of chamazulene formed in the process. It looks beautiful, but it is also functional: apigenin in the flowers binds to some of the same GABA receptors targeted by anti-anxiety drugs.

Next to it is CATNIP (*Nepeta cataria*). We know it as the drug that sends cats into a euphoric frenzy (thanks to a compound called nepetalactone), but in humans it does the opposite. Catnip is a mild sedative. A tea of Catnip and Chamomile is a classic herbalist's trick for bringing down the nervous system of an anxious adult or an overtired child.

THE STRESS PLANTS

HOLY BASIL (*Ocimum sanctum*) anchors the corner. In India it is Tulsi, the "Queen of Herbs," considered so sacred it is the earthly manifestation of a goddess. In Vedic texts, Tulsi is described as one of the main pillars of herbal medicine. Inside the leaves live eugenol, rosmarinic acid, and other phenolics that researchers are now testing to help the body modulate cortisol, stress, and mood in people who are frayed by modern life.

Beside it sits ASHWAGANDHA (*Withania somnifera*). In Sanskrit, *ashwa* means "horse" and *gandha* means "smell." Crush the fresh root and you see why: it smells like sweat, musk, and wet animal fur. Ancient healers believed ingesting it gave you the stamina of a stallion. Today, multiple randomized trials and meta-analyses suggest its withanolides can nudge down anxiety, improve sleep, and support resilience to chronic stress.

THE GUT AND THE BLOOD

Perhaps the most complex character in the garden is **LIQUORICE** (*Glycyrrhiza glabra*). It is a vigorous shrub that originated in the Mediterranean, but its roots are the prize. They contain glycyrrhizin, a substance up to fifty times sweeter than sugar. In very small, occasional amounts it can soothe the throat and calm the gut; in larger amounts and over time, glycyrrhizin can seriously disrupt potassium and sodium balance, raising blood pressure and causing arrhythmias and other problems—especially in people with heart or kidney issues.

DANDELION (*Taraxacum officinale*), which most gardeners treat as an enemy, is a complete overachiever: leaves as a gentle diuretic and mineral tonic, roots for the liver, bitter compounds that wake up digestion. Naturopaths reach for it in every "spring cleanse," but the deeper truth is simpler: the human body likes a little bitter.

Winding through the shade of the Oaks is **YERBA BUENA** (*Clinopodium douglasii*). This is the true scent of California history. Before San Francisco was a city of tech and fog, it was a Spanish settlement named Yerba Buena ("good herb") because this creeping Mint grew so thick on the hillsides. It smells different from garden Mint—earthier, sweeter, like rain on dry soil. Indigenous Californians used it for ceremony, food, and daily medicine, especially for stomach aches and headaches.

THE WINTER ARSENAL

GARLIC (*Allium sativum*) is the winter wonder. In my grandmother's kitchen it was "as good as ten mothers" if you had a cold. Modern pharmacology calls its key compound allicin, and in the lab its extracts are convincingly antibacterial and antifungal. The evidence is not perfect, but it's strong enough that almost every culture on Earth has, at some point, told you to eat Garlic when you're sick.

ECHINACEA (*Echinacea purpurea*) stands there like a purple warning sign. Indigenous Plains tribes used its roots for coughs, sore throats, and even snakebite. Modern studies on colds are famously mixed—some show shorter or milder colds, some show no significant effect—but it is clearly doing something to the immune system: nudging white blood cells and cytokines, changing the way our bodies respond to viral insults.

ELDERBERRY (*Sambucus nigra*) is another winter ally. Black Elder flowers and berries have been used for centuries to fight colds and "inflammations of the chest." Syrups made from the berries have shown promising results in one small human trial, where people with influenza-like illness recovered a bit faster and had slightly less severe symptoms than those who didn't.

Then there is Honey—especially MANUKA HONEY. My father harvested it with friends on the top of a volcano in New Zealand, decanting this thick, medicinal nectar from hives battered by wind and salt. Manuka is made from the Manuka tree (*Leptospermum scoparium*) and is fiercely antimicrobial. Doctors now use Manuka-impregnated dressings on chronic wounds and burns because it can help fight off bacteria and support healing; after the Los Angeles fires, rescuers coated Manuka on the paws of burned animals to speed their recovery. In the kitchen, a spoonful in hot water with Lemon has been shown to be as good as, or better than, many over-the-counter cough syrups at calming a sore throat. Again, not a miracle cure, but a very elegant combination of sugar, acids, and antibacterial molecules doing quiet work.

GINGER (*Zingiber officinale*) is another old soldier. For generations people have used it to ease nausea, wind, and cold chills. The Latin *officinale* in its name means "pharmacy," marking it as a staple of the monastery medicine chest. Fresh Ginger smells bright and spicy, like Lemons and Pepper; dried, it warms and sweetens. Clinical evidence now supports what grandmothers knew: Ginger can help reduce nausea and vomiting in pregnancy, in motion sickness, and after surgery, and may support digestion in general. It warms the blood and settles the stomach with a reliability few modern drugs can match.

OREGANO (*Origanum vulgare*) and SAGEBRUSH (*Artemisia tridentata*) live on the sharper, more aggressive end of the spectrum—heavy in compounds like carvacrol, thymol, and cineole. In the lab they show strong antimicrobial activity against a grab-bag of bacteria and fungi. In the kitchen they show up as steams, teas, and gargles when someone first says, "I think my throat is sore." At Flamingo, a handful of Oregano and Sagebrush in hot water with Lemon and Honey is our version of a preemptive strike.

SMALL REVOLUTIONS, NOT MIRACLE CURES

There are others tucked into corners of the Medicine Garden: THYME (*Thymus vulgaris*) and PEPPERMINT (*Mentha piperita*) for steams, VALERIAN (*Valeriana officinalis*) for the kind of sleep that doesn't respond to podcasts, LEMON BALM (*Melissa officinalis*) for days when your worries feel louder than your appetite, TEA TREE and WITCH HAZEL for small skin rebellions, CALIFORNIA POPPY and HOPS and SKULLCAP for the nights when your thoughts won't lie down. Each one has its own tradition, its own science, its own caution label.

Put all of this together and the Medicine Garden stops looking like a quaint side project and starts to look like what it really is: a tiny, living annex to the pharmacy—and a tribute to all the plant knowledge that got us this far.

The herbs in these beds are not substitutes for antibiotics, chemotherapy, or vaccines. They do not replace doctors, nurses, or urgent care. I can't say that strongly enough. What they offer is something different: support, comfort, small corrections. A first circle of care.

If the last few years have taught us anything, it's that the system is delicate. Pharmacies run out. Insurance lines go dead. You spend two hours on hold to talk to someone about a rash. The Medicine Garden is there for the moments before that: when a handful of leaves or flowers can help you sleep, soothe your stomach, cool a burn, ease a sore throat, or take the sharp edge off a bad day.

The old medicine women and men may not have called it "evidence-based," but they knew something we're in danger of forgetting: that healing rarely happens in one grand gesture. It happens leaf by leaf, cup by cup, day by day, in a thousand small, attentive acts. That's the medicine I'm interested in now.

[IV]
APRIL

SPRING

DIRTYWORK

"Where flowers bloom, so does hope."

—LADY BIRD JOHNSON

GARDEN TASKS:

- [ ] Feed all fruit trees (Citrus, Figs, Pomegranates, stone fruits) with compost.
- [ ] Get summer crops in the ground: Tomatoes, Basil, Peppers, and Cucumbers.
- [ ] Harvest spring herbs (Parsley, Mint, Dill) and pinch back Basil and Mint to prevent flowering.
- [ ] Cut back overwintered Sage, Thyme, and Rosemary to encourage new growth.
- [ ] Sow quick crops like Arugula, Chard, Radish, and Lettuce in partial shade.
- [ ] Deadhead spring bulbs like Narcissus and Freesia; plant summer bulbs like Dahlias and Iris.
- [ ] Sow summer seeds: Zinnias, Cosmos, and Marigolds for color.
- [ ] Cut bouquets freely—Roses, Sweet Peas, Ranunculus, and Lavender.
- [ ] Prune non-spring blooming shrubs, ornamental grasses, and old perennial foliage.
- [ ] Top-dress beds with compost and mulch everything to retain moisture.
- [ ] Add crushed eggshells around Tomatoes and Peppers to prevent blossom end rot.
- [ ] Turn compost piles; they should feel like a wrung-out sponge.
- [ ] Release ladybirds to control aphids and check leaves for caterpillars.

TASK

MAKE A EUCALYPTUS VAPOR RUB

Pick a handful of clean, unsprayed Eucalyptus leaves. Bruise them between your palms to wake up the oils, then warm them gently in a small pot with Olive oil (or Jojoba) on the lowest heat until the oil smells like a spa. Don't let it simmer; you just want a slow, fragrant steep. Turn off the heat, cover, and let it sit as long as you can (even overnight), then strain. Melt a small spoonful of beeswax into the warm Eucalyptus oil, stir until it turns into a soft balm, and pour into a little jar to set. Rub a pea-sized amount over your chest and throat before bed (or lightly under your nose), breathe deeply, and let the whole house turn medicinal and calm.

TASK

RUB SOME MUSCLES

Arnica is the classic "I worked too hard in the garden" plant—best used topically for sore, tired muscles. Fill a clean jar halfway with dried Arnica flowers, cover completely with Olive oil (or Sunflower or Almond oil), seal, and let it infuse in a dark cupboard for 2–4 weeks (shake it when you remember), then strain. Warm the infused oil gently and stir in a little beeswax until it sets into a soft balm, then finish with a few drops of Rosemary and Peppermint essential oil for that cooling, wake-up feeling. Massage into shoulders, forearms, calves, and hands after gardening—like a thank-you note to your body.

QUICK SAFETY NOTE: *Do not ingest Arnica, don't use it on broken skin, and avoid if you're sensitive to the Daisy family (Ragweed allergies). If pregnant, nursing, or on blood thinners, ask your clinician first.*

TASK

TAKE A BHUTANESE BATH

In Bhutan, high in the Himalayas, we took one of the traditional "medicine baths": a very hot soak with big bundles of freshly cut herbs dropped straight into the water—no tea, no prep, just the whole garden going in at once. Gather armfuls of Mugwort, Calendula, Cannabis, Geranium, Artemisia leaves, Lemon balm, Chamomile, Lavender, Eucalyptus, Peppermint, Rosemary, Ginger, and Thyme. Bruise everything between your hands to wake up the oils, then toss the bundles directly into the tub as it fills, and soak until the steam turns the bathroom into a fragrant cloud.

TASK

Make Medicine for Your Plants

Your garden deserves something filthy, truly filthy, and compost tea is exactly the kind of microbial medicine that makes plants perk up and act grateful. Fill a bucket with water and let it sit for 24 hours to off-gas chlorine, then add 1–2 cups of finished compost or worm castings (and a small glug of unsulphured molasses if you want to feed the microbes). Stir once a day for 2–3 days until it smells earthy and alive, then strain, dilute about 1:4 with water, and pour it at the base of your plants. Use it fresh, and don't spray it directly on leafy greens you're about to eat.

TASK

GIVE MEDICINE TO GARDEN WITCHES

A spiritual guide once told me to do this in the garden—to reward the protective spirits that live there. Leave a thoughtful gift at the garden's edge: a few flowers, a bowl of water, a splash of wine, or a spoonful of Honey (the more intentional, the better). I like to wrap the flowers in a little basket made from Palm leaves, then add one extra detail—a single bloom, a shiny object—whisper a quiet thank-you, and walk away without looking back (very important).

TASK

STACK UP ON FENNEL

Cut a few tall Fennel stalks with their feathery fronds and seed heads, tie them into a tight bundle, and hang it over your front door (or tuck a pinch of Fennel seeds into a keyhole if you want to be extra).

In old folk tradition, Fennel is a guard plant—meant to keep out bad luck, bad spirits, and the kind of energy that ruins dinner. In Greek myth, Prometheus even smuggled fire to humanity hidden inside a hollow Fennel stalk, which feels like the ultimate Fennel résumé: protection, warmth, and a little rebellion. Leave it up until it dries and rattles, then replace it and compost the old bundle like you're renewing a contract.

TASK

BUILD AN ALUX HOUSE

In Maya folklore from the Yucatán, Aluxo'ob are small land guardians—part sprite, part spirit—who watch over fields, forests, and properties when they're treated with respect (and get mischievous when they're ignored). Build them a tiny home: a simple mini house or shrine made from local stone, brick, or wood, about knee-high, with a little doorway and a roof that can handle rain. Place it at the edge of the garden (where the wild starts), tuck it into greenery, and make a small offering the way farmers do—a gourd or bowl of water, a spoonful of Honey, a few kernels of Corn, maybe a sweet or a flower—then whisper a quiet thank-you and leave it there. The only "maintenance" is attention: refresh the offering now and then, keep the house tidy, and let the garden feel like it's being looked after from the inside.

RECIPE

MUGWORT AND TARO MARBLED SHORTBREAD

INGREDIENTS:

2 egg whites, gently whisked
1 cup toasted black and white Sesame seeds, set in a shallow sheet pan

MUGWORT DOUGH:

10 Tbsp unsalted butter, room temperature
1½ Tbsp dried green Mugwort powder
½ cup powdered sugar
½ tsp pure Vanilla extract
1½ cups all-purpose flour
½ tsp kosher Salt

TARO DOUGH:

10 Tbsp unsalted butter, room temperature
1½ Tbsp dried purple Taro powder
½ cup powdered sugar
½ tsp pure Vanilla extract
1½ cups all-purpose flour
½ tsp kosher Salt

METHOD:

DOUGH PREPARATION:

Place butter into the bowl of a stand mixer fitted with the paddle attachment. Mix on medium speed until fluffy and pale (about 3 minutes).
Turn the mixer down to low and add either mugwort or taro powder, powdered sugar, vanilla extract, flour, and salt. Mix until a dough forms.
Turn the dough out onto a lightly floured work surface and roll into a rectangle approximately 13 inches by 8 inches.

ASSEMBLE AND BAKE:

Preheat oven to 350°F.
Place the taro dough on top of the mugwort dough and roll together to form a log. Gently press down as you roll to create a thinner log. Cut the log into 2 pieces for easier handling.
Brush each log with whisked egg white and roll in the toasted black and white sesame seeds until fully coated.
Slice logs into ½-inch slices and place each cookie on a lined baking sheet, 1 inch apart.
Bake for 12–14 minutes, in batches if necessary, until crisp.
Allow cookies to cool completely before serving.

TASK

MAKE TULSI DRINKING CHOCOLATE

☐

This drinking chocolate doesn't just taste divine—the Holy Basil (Tulsi) in it is loved for calming the nervous system, smoothing stress, helping digestion, and bringing a little mental clarity back online. Brew a strong cup of Tulsi tea and set it aside. Warm 1 cup of milk (or your favorite alternative) in a saucepan until steaming. Whisk in 2–3 Tbsp of chopped dark chocolate or Cacao paste until melted and glossy. Stir in ½ cup of the brewed Tulsi tea, and sweeten with 1–2 tsp of Honey to taste (add a pinch of Cinnamon or Cardamom if you want it extra). Put on some jazz and sip slowly.

RECIPE

CONFIT GARLIC OREGANO OIL

This is one of the most fragrant things you can make in the kitchen. Garlic and Oregano are simmered slowly, allowing their aroma and flavor to gently infuse the Olive oil, resulting in a golden elixir that is simple and worthy of being drizzled on just about everything.

INGREDIENTS:

- 2 heads Garlic, peeled and trimmed
- 2 bunches fresh Oregano, stems included
- 5 cups Olive oil
- Pinch of Salt

METHOD:

[1] Preheat oven to 300°F.

[2] Place garlic, oregano, olive oil, and a pinch of salt into a shallow, heavy-bottomed ovenproof dish or pan.

[3] Cover with a piece of parchment paper cut to fit, pressing lightly so it touches the surface of the oil.

[4] Bake in the oven for 1 hour, until garlic is soft and aromatic.

[5] Remove from the oven. You can use the confit immediately over fresh bread or allow it to cool and transfer to an airtight bottle for storage.

MEDICINE GARDEN TACHIN

RECIPE

INGREDIENTS:

2 cups Basmati rice
Salt
2 Tbsp melted butter
2-3 Dandelion leaves
6-8 Sage leaves
6-8 Parsley leaves
5 Chamomile flowers
1 tsp Saffron threads
2 Tbsp warm water
1 cup plain Greek yogurt
3 egg yolks

METHOD:

Parboil Rice: Fill a pot with water and add salt generously. Set the pot over high heat and bring to a rolling boil. Add rice and cook for 4-7 minutes until parboiled—the rice should be al dente and slightly firm to the bite. Drain the rice well and spread it on a paper towel-lined sheet tray to dry. Set aside.

Assemble and Bake Tachin: Preheat oven to 390°F. Brush the bottom of a 9-inch glass pie dish or ovenproof dish with melted butter. Arrange dandelion, sage, parsley, and chamomile on the bottom of the dish in a decorative pattern. In a small bowl, steep saffron in warm water for 10 minutes. In a large bowl, mix together parboiled rice, Greek yogurt, egg yolks, and 1 tsp salt. Spoon the rice mixture over the prepared dish, pressing down gently and smoothing the top. Bake for 60-80 minutes, until the rice is golden and crispy on the bottom. Carefully invert the tachin onto a serving plate and serve immediately while hot and crispy.

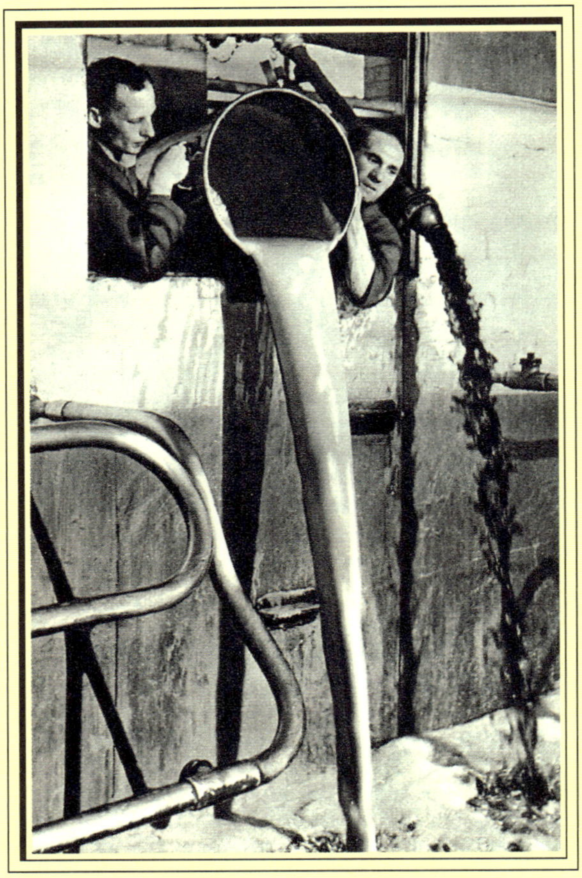

FERMENTATION

Before we made any perfumes, there was the smell of fermentation. Humans discovered that if you left Grape juice or crushed grain alone for a while, it changed: it kept, it nourished, it fizzed, and it made you feel different. Fermentation became one of our earliest collaborations with nature, shaping preservation, medicine, nutrition, and ritual.

Fermentation is the smell of life transforming. Yeasts and bacteria take simple sugars and break them down into new compounds: alcohols, acids, esters, and sulphur notes. These evaporate into the air as volatile molecules, and that is what we smell.

Bread is the most democratic miracle. As dough ferments, yeast produces carbon dioxide, alcohol, and a suite of aromatic molecules that leak out of the oven. Wine is bread's glamorous cousin. Yeast does the same work on Grape sugars, but the raw material changes the perfume: Muscat can smell of blossoms and Citrus, Syrah carries Black Pepper and smoke, Sauvignon Blanc hints at Passionfruit and cut grass, and a cool-climate Cabernet whispers green Bell Pepper. The nose reads the story long before the tongue does.

Lactic acid bacteria give us Cheese, Yogurt, Sauerkraut, and Kimchi. Their tangy, milky scent is bright and sour but never just one thing: fermented Capers smell cabbagey and floral; Yogurt is green and buttery with a lick of sea air; Kimchi is deeply sour with a buried vein of umami. Acetic acid bacteria take over when alcohol meets air, turning wine into vinegar and sweet tea into Kombucha, creating sharp, metallic fumes that make your eyes water.

I had to go to the bottom of the world to understand all of this. In Tasmania, I visited Adam James—the unofficial king of fermentation, arguably the most renowned fermenter in Australia (and one of the best in the world). He is the founder of Rough Rice, the fermentation project we now collaborate with at Flamingo.

[PAGE 146] Brewers pitching yeast, 1930s.

→

Our friend Adam James with his fermentation crocks in Tasmania. Photographed by Hugh Davison, spring 2025.

I found him barefoot in his garden, crocks lining the yard like small altars. He pried open an eleven-year-old "mothership" ferment and handed us spoons. It is crafted from sixteen varieties of fermented heirloom Chilies, Daikon, Hakurei, Tomato, Tomatillo, Eggplant, Cucumber, Radish, Fennel, Garlic Scapes, raw Apple vinegar, Sea Salt, and an herbaceous tangle of Shiso, Parsley, Tarragon, Lovage, Laksa leaf, Dill, and Chervil. What hit my nose was everything at once: heat, acid, Garlic, flowers, earth. The scent was primal and exciting.

For all its wildness, fermentation runs on balance. Too much heat or oxygen and the wrong microbes take control; the aroma tips into rot. That hairline between delicious and disgusting is what makes fermentation such a thrilling ride.

APR.

FERMENTATION MAY BE A GIFT OF THE MICROBES, BUT TURNING IT INTO ART— THAT'S OUR DIRTY WORK.

[1] Brewer Claude Arkwell testing the beer fermenter at the Donnington Brewery, 1963. [2] A man turning champagne bottles, circa 1950. This is a process known as riddling, used for settling sediment for later removal. [3] Inside the Fala factory in Strasbourg, 1935, showing the ethyl fermentation laboratory. [4] Capping beer bottles at a UK brewery circa 1930. [5] Tasmania, 2025. Photographed by Hugh Davison. [6] The fermentation of Grape juice after harvest in a French vineyard, 1949. [7] Sampling of Bass beer at the brewery, 1951. [8] A worker cleans the inside of a brewing kettle. [9] View of a worker using a shovel to help mix dried ground malt, or grist, with hot water in a mash tun to produce wort. This occurs during

GIFT OF THE MICROBES

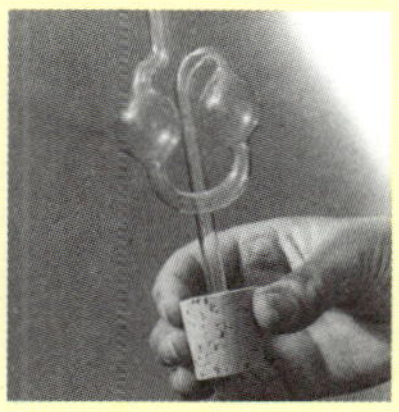

the fermentation stage at a Highland malt whisky distillery in Scotland, 1971. [10] Rough Rice fermentation jars, Tasmania, 2025. Photographed by Hugh Davison. [11] Yeast rising to the top of stainless steel vessels in the fermenting process, 1950. [12] Fermentation airlock. [13] Tasmania, 2025, by Hugh Davison. [14] Stainless steel wine Grape fermenters at Sequoia Grove Winery, Napa Valley, California, 1985. [15] Making mead, 1950s. [16] Two men working with metal wine fermentation vats, Frescobaldi Estate, Italy, 1988. [17] Pickling and fermenting at the Agrarian Kitchen, Tasmania, 2025. [18] A man guides a 10-ton stainless steel fermenting tun, constructed in Glasgow, onto a ship en route to the Guinness Brewery in Dublin, 1945.

May is about spectacle (or a preview of it). Above us, the Jacarandas explode into a violet haze, dropping their sticky, electric confetti onto the streets and sidewalks. It is a visual shout that demands we look up, even as the garden below demands we get to work. Lavender and Sage start humming in the heat, and the Roses—Damask, Tea, and wild—blow open in a show of color and scent. Backstage we're

MAY

racing to keep up: the summer heat is coming, so we mulch the trees deep to hold the moisture in and harvest the last cool herbs for the drying room. We stake the Tomatoes, pinch back the Dahlias, and sow the last of the heat-loving Beans and Melons. The Garden is moving fast now, shifting from the gentle green of spring into the full, riotous performance of summer. It's almost showtime.

When I open my bedroom curtains at sunrise, the Jacaranda is the first thing I see. Her strong, maternal arms stretch high above the garden, protecting the infant flowers from the menacing sun rising above. Her sudden splash of violet reminds me to chase and encourage spontaneity—a rare, seductive quality in a world marching to the predictable drumbeat of Google calendars, monthly revenue numbers, and endless Zoom calls. While our lives are meticulously planned—every minute accounted for, every outcome predicted by an algorithm—the Jacaranda operates on a different logic: she chases adventure.

Cities do too, sometimes. Buenos Aires is painted lavender in November when the Jacarandas bloom along Avenida del Libertador and around the Congress building—so much so that the Jacaranda has been declared the "emblematic tree" of the city. In recent years, the city even wrote this into law, naming *Jacaranda mimosifolia* its official tree in honor of the way it turns the streets violet each spring. Pretoria and Johannesburg are nicknamed the Jacaranda Cities; students call it "exam season" when the streets turn purple, and there's a superstition that if a flower falls on your head, you'll pass your finals.

In Australia, they call it "purple panic"—by the time the trees bloom around Brisbane and Sydney, assignments are due and exams are looming, and the sight of those flowers is a reminder that time is short. In Grafton, a small Australian town near where I grew up, whole streets planted in the 1880s now explode each spring in a violet canopy so famous they built a festival around it, complete with a Jacaranda Queen and a half-day public holiday. Across the world, entire towns wait for this tree to do its one big, unnecessary, spectacular thing each year: turn the streets into a dream for a few weeks, then quietly disappear again.

In Los Angeles, sometime between April and June, whole neighborhoods suddenly flip to Lavender. The *LA Times* publishes interactive "Jacaranda maps," based on city tree inventories, showing where to find the best blooms. One analysis of city data counted around 148,530 Jacaranda trees in Los Angeles alone—a kind of accidental perfume map, if you think about it—148,530 purple diffusers wired into the sidewalks. Instagram fills with pictures of Del Mar Boulevard in Pasadena and streets in Westwood and Koreatown, cars dusted in petals like frosted cakes. People complain about the sticky mess on their windscreens and secretly pray for a slightly longer bloom.

Each tree, like my own beautiful *Jacaranda mimosifolia*, has its own temperament. No two ever flower on the same schedule, even if they've endured the same winter storms and the same dry winds. With their own internal clocks and genetic predispositions, Jacarandas take their time, don't look sideways, and don't bow to peer pressure. For us spectators, the whole affair is a lesson in joyful unpredictability. One street in Los Angeles will go purple overnight, while the next block down is still all green. Glendale might be in full bloom while Burbank is barely thinking about it. Instagram fills with purple canopies, then just as suddenly the feed goes back to beige brunches. The Jacaranda never explains herself.

This devotion to inconsistency extends into the Jacaranda's aromatic life. In a single tree, there's a long, diverse scent story—ranging from flowers to seed pods to trunk. The Tupi-Guarani people, who lived with these trees long before any of us, are said to have given it the name Jacarandá—meaning "fragrant." They weren't thinking of fancy niche perfumes; they were thinking of the way the air around the tree changes through the season.

In the fresh flowers, you find a mild, sweet scent that some people describe as Grape soda, Honey, and powdery Lilac. It's faint—you have to get close—but it's there, sitting at the edge of perception. Once the flowers fall and begin to soften back into earth—cloaking cars, cement, and soil in a hypnotizing coat of violet—the fragrance of transformation begins. The first breath is warm, humid, and faintly sweet—like crushed petals and rain-damp grass. There's often a fruity, fermented edge—not unpleasant, but slightly winey, like overripe Pear or a forgotten glass of white wine. As the petals begin to brown, earthy, slightly musky notes emerge—wet bark, soil, fallen leaves. That smell is summer, if you grew up anywhere they grow: the scent of the year tipping over into heat and exams and long evenings.

↑
In an era before color photography, James Ackerman used a blend of machine-printed outlines and meticulous hand-painting to bring exotic species to life for an American public hungry for a glimpse of the world's natural wonders. This Jacaranda was painted in New York, 1847.

→
The Grafton Jacaranda Festival is an annual 10-day celebration of the blossoming trees held each November in Grafton, NSW, Australia. Jacaranda trees are not native to Australia but can be found around the country and are popular for their stunning purple blooms in spring.

The seed pods tell a different story. When fresh, they are green and vegetal, slightly resinous, with a sharp herbaceousness if you snap them. When they mature and harden, flattening into little brown castanets, there's a woody warmth, like sun-baked bark and smoke. Children in South America use them as rattles; in Paraguay, they're nicknamed "monkey applause" because they clap together in the wind. Then there's the trunk itself: standing firm and unpretentious, carrying a quiet scent of resin and earth and slight spice—only appearing after rains or on hot afternoons when sap is moving. Each part of the tree is like a different chapter of the same story.

In perfumery, there is no true Jacaranda oil; the flowers don't give up their fragrance under steam. When a perfume lists "Jacaranda" as a note, it's a fantasy mixture—a mix of Lilac, Violet, soft musks, a faint grapey sweetness, and something green, meant to feel like walking down a Jacaranda street at dusk. Perfumers borrow the memory, but like so many things in Los Angeles, the real thing on the sidewalk in late spring is stranger and better than anything in a bottle.

Like many of us in Los Angeles, the Jacaranda is far from her first home. She is native to the forests of northwestern Argentina, southern Bolivia, and parts of Brazil—places now heavily cleared for agriculture, particularly Soybeans and cattle. One theory says she might have arrived here during the Gold Rush on schooner ships out of Buenos Aires; another traces her to plant crates imported by adventurous nurserymen. Either way, she has no pristine homeland left to return to, so she has made herself a citizen of the world: Pretoria, Sydney, Buenos Aires, Grafton, Los Angeles—a commuter tree with multiple passports, dropping the same violet calling card wherever she lands.

In many places, the Jacaranda is classified as an invasive alien species. In South Africa, it's now illegal to plant new Jacarandas in certain public spaces without a permit; existing trees are loved, but no more may be added. In parts of Australia, councils grumble about the leaf litter. Yet she is adored by Los Angeles, so much so that we now have heat maps and articles dedicated to their whereabouts, and foresters defending them as ideal street trees: lacy leaves, open canopy, real shade, a moment of enchantment each spring. Almost like having 148,530 variations of our own perfume sprayed all across the city.

We have botanist Kate Sessions to thank for the Jacaranda's early California growth. Kate was also a masterclass in spontaneity and unpredictability. She was a brilliant, pioneering woman who single-handedly transformed the Southern California landscape. After getting her degree from Berkeley in 1881, she moved to San Diego in 1884 and started a nursery a year later. In 1892, she made a spontaneous contract with the City of San Diego to plant 100 trees per year for 10 years, and to provide 300 more for planting elsewhere. In exchange, the city gave her land in what is now Balboa Park to operate her commercial nursery full of exotic species from Europe, Mexico, and South America.

Among the plants she introduced or popularized: Bougainvillea, Birds of Paradise, Star Jasmine, Yellow Oleander, Poinsettia, Orchid tree, and our beloved Jacaranda. A wildly successful and tireless business owner, over her lifetime Kate operated nurseries in Coronado, Pacific Beach, Mission Hills, and other corners of greater San Diego. She worked 12-hour days, and when it grew too dark to garden, she would read botany books in her home office late into the night. She took only two vacations in 60 years.

The prolific Kate Sessions with a young sapling, circa 1935. A trailblazer in botany, she is credited with introducing the Jacaranda to California, forever changing the color of Los Angeles. Image from the San Diego Historical Society.

Long before the Jacaranda was the "official tree" of several LA neighborhoods, it was part of a strategic vision to beautify the city's new arteries. Here, the Home Garden group establishes a legacy on the Cahuenga Freeway in 1950—planting trees that now shade the city.

In 1925, Sessions told a journalist that an interest in growing things and a habit of gardening were the only recipe for health, joy, and longevity. "The garden was a tonic," she said. She had no children and never married, rejecting at least two proposals. In a letter to a friend, she said her flowers were her children—like the Jacarandas that brought her world to life. "If you want to do something for me, let's make a garden," she said after a long illness, when friends offered a celebration. She asked for a garden instead.

She died on Easter Sunday, 1940, following a lengthy hospital stay that resulted from falling and breaking her hip while watering plants in her garden. Among her final acts was to summon San Diego's city planner to her bedside so she could tell him what ought to be planted alongside a new stretch of the 5 Freeway. She is buried in Mount Hope Cemetery, where her grave lies along the road named after her—Kate Sessions Avenue—under a twisted Juniper tree, her favorite.

After her death, real estate developers of tract-house suburbs in Southern California in the 1950s fueled the expansion of Jacarandas. They were building communities with identical, uninteresting homes. To give them some exoticism, they would plant small, glorious purple specimens from "the jungle" to bring some excitement to the area. Jacarandas were an easy sell: drought-tolerant once established, fast-growing, spectacular for a few weeks a year. By the 1920s and '30s, they were already being planted extensively in Los Angeles and Santa Barbara; by the 1950s, they had become the default way to give a bland subdivision a bit of drama.

Thanks to them, numerous streets and neighborhoods today are lined with Jacarandas reaching 40 feet in height, spreading nearly as wide as they are tall, forming an oval canopy. They famously explode in big spontaneous patches around the city during spring and summer—lining the streets in an electric lavender haze, becoming Instagram stars for a brief moment in time.

But as a metaphor or warning for all those who come to LA—the flowers fade quickly after their annual brush with fame, and the showy celebrities become horticultural nobodies once more. The petals turn to mush; the city trucks come to sweep them away. Yet in their decay, the flowers that have fallen begin to transform, and the scent story continues. Spontaneity is a two-way street, and life is too short not to enjoy the summer and the winter of it all. The Jacaranda reminds me of this every morning: to enjoy the bloom and the bust equally. There is life-giving perfume in both.

One last note about the Jacaranda. Writer Alissa Walker has a compelling argument that they are LA's future. "Think Purple, not Palms," she says. The city has lost a shocking number of trees over the last decade, according to studies that use aerial imagery to track the degreening of LA. Our streets remain glaring and unsheltered, especially in less affluent neighborhoods. Shade is becoming a thing of the rich. Trees are now our best line of defense to protect the city from the reality of extreme heat and the public health risks of air pollution, and their presence alone can help promote pedestrian activity.

For the better part of a century, the Palm tree has been our city's most famous tree. But Palms—which are, technically, not trees at all—don't produce any shade. They don't possess meaningful air-purifying qualities. And there's a fungus that's slowly destroying them. Walker suggests we need a new tree to symbolize a cooler, cleaner, shadier LA. She votes for the Jacaranda: drought-tolerant, fast-growing, wildlife-friendly, shade-providing, and sidewalk-protecting. "Think Purple, not Palms" is more than an aesthetic suggestion; it's an urban survival strategy.

When I begin my day, I'm greeted by the wide arms of my Jacaranda. I think about her journey from the forests of northwestern Argentina to the garden at Flamingo Estate. I think about the Tupi-Guarani people who named her, and the students in Pretoria counting on a petal to fall on their head, and the Lisbon resident claiming the honor of seeing the first bloom. I think about the horticultural shepherd, Kate Sessions, who tended to her flock of trees, and the developers who planted them in rows to sell houses they didn't love. They all remind me to choose adventure and spontaneity every day—to be a little invasive in the best sense, to take root where you're not expected, and to throw a sudden, generous cloud of purple over whatever street you land on.

Jacarandas in full bloom, stretching their arms wide over the streets, 1960.

The Martha Stewart Rose, harvested from our garden and photographed by Hugh Davison in winter 2025.

[GROUNDING] : A MAP OF PLEASURE FROM THE GARDEN

THE ROSE GARDEN

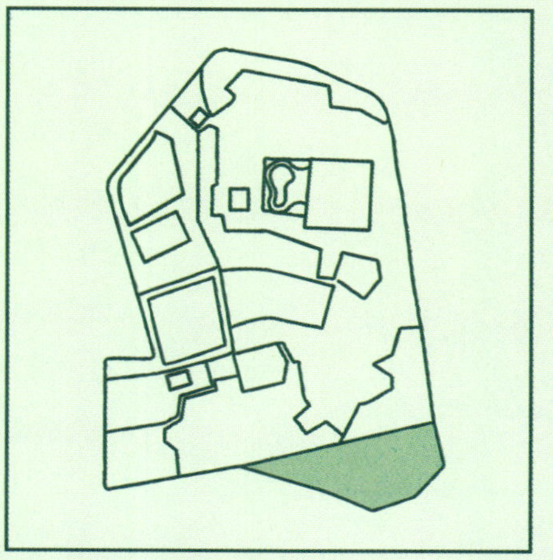

34°08' N / 118°12' W LOS ANGELES, CALIFORNIA

At first blush, the Rose feels a bit ubiquitous, almost boring. We all know, somewhat wearily, that it has become the world's most common cut flower—cut as buds, packed in refrigerators, flown around the globe. Many modern varieties have almost no scent at all, bred for stem length, vase life, and transport rather than perfume. Genetically coaxed into being "perfect" versions of an ideal that was never real. But what interests me is not this commodity Rose. It's the story of the flower that bites back.

My first introduction to Roses began at church. There was a white, chisel-bodied Jesus above our altar, wearing no more than a loincloth and a crown of Roses. The flower has been entwined with the Catholic imagination for centuries. Every time my mother and grandmother went to Mass and got on their knees to pray to the Virgin Mary, they held a strand of Rosary beads dedicated to the flower that symbolized her purity and their salvation. "Rosary" itself comes from *rosarium*—a garland of Roses. That looping strand of beads is literally a floral crown offered to Mary, while I stared up at Jesus.

An eighteenth-century "portrait" of the Prophet Muhammad. Islamic devotion avoids figural portraits, so the Rose becomes a stand-in for the Prophet's beauty, mercy, and perfume.

Aubrey Beardsley's *The Mysterious Rose Garden*, 1895. The piece is famously a parody of the Annunciation (where the Angel Gabriel visits the Virgin Mary). In traditional art, Gabriel often holds a Lily for purity. Here, the "messenger" whispers to a nude woman amid Roses, which historically symbolize Venus, passion, and carnal love. The Rose Garden is not a "closed garden" signifying virginity, but rather a space of sexual awakening.

Elsewhere, the beauty of the Rose was linked directly to the Prophet Muhammad. Devotional stories say that the first white Rose sprang from the Prophet's sweat on the night of his ascension, and that the scent of Roses echoes the scent of his body. Because of that, Rose water and Rose oil are still used to honor his memory—sprinkled at Mawlid (the Prophet's birthday), poured over shrines, handed to guests in mosques and homes as a gesture of respect and blessing.

Indeed, many religions are draped in Roses. But the thorns were often reserved for people shunned by them. The flower has quietly become the bloom we reach for whenever love is a bit dangerous, a bit complicated, or a bit "wrong" for its time. The drama and metaphor are built into the plant's sharp spikes below the bud.

For centuries, that duality has been written straight into proverbs. In Europe you get the old French and Italian sayings—*pas de rose sans épine, non c'è rosa senza spine*—"there is no Rose without thorns." In Persian: "He who wants a Rose must respect the thorn." The point is always the same: beauty and pain are a package deal. By the Middle Ages, the image is everywhere in Christian and Islamic thought—the Rose as divine love or Paradise, the thorns as the suffering that comes with it. In Rumi and other Sufi poets, the Rose is the soul reaching for God, the thorns the wounds of that longing. The flower was being asked to carry both ecstasy and suffering at once.

In Japan, "Rose"—*bara*—became a slur for gay men. Artists like Mishima Yukio and Eikō Hosoe reflected it back in their work, showing the male body wounded, draped in Roses and shadows. Jean Genet, writing about prison boys and criminal lovers in *Miracle of the Rose*, takes the pious Rose imagery he stole from the church and smears it over thieves and murderers. Critics talk about his work as "the contradiction of the Rose with thorns": the idea that when you finally dare to seize beauty with your hands, you're going to bleed, and you still

Simon Vouet, *The Virgin and Child with a Rose*, circa 1627. The central focus is a delicate Rose held between them—a poignant symbol of Mary's purity and a foreshadowing of Christ's future passion and the Crown of Thorns.

The "fist and rose" emblem, a symbol of the French Socialist Party, designed in 1969 by Marc Bonnet.

choose to hold on. That's queer love under criminalization in a nutshell. You can witness the same idea today in tattoos: the classic Rose-with-thorns, or Rose wrapped around a knife, inked on sailors, bikers, incarcerated men, trans girls, anyone whose love life or gender has never been straightforward.

The flower raises its fist elsewhere, too. Since the late nineteenth century, the red Rose has been one of the main symbols of the fight for change. In France it was picked up after the revolutions of 1848 and the Paris Commune, and by the 1880s it was widely understood as a flower for workers' struggle—beauty and a better life growing out of blood and hardship. In 1969, a French graphic artist drew the now-classic "fist and Rose" emblem: a clenched fist holding a red Rose. It was adopted by the French Socialist Party in the 1970s and quickly spread—you still see versions of it in the logos of socialist and labor parties around the world, including the British Labor Party's stylized red Rose.

Recently the red Rose emoji 🌹 has been quietly adopted by online democratic socialists—thrown into bios and tweets as a tiny, pretty way to say "I'm with the workers." That's the nineteenth-century red Rose resurfacing in an app. You also get the phrase "Bread and Roses" from the 1912 textile workers' strike in Lawrence, Massachusetts—an early women-led, immigrant-led labor uprising. It became a slogan for socialist feminism: we want bread, yes, but also Roses—not just survival, but joy and beauty.

On the other side of the left, there's the Black Rose. It doesn't really exist in nature, but it has become a kind of emblem for anarchist and libertarian socialist currents—especially ones that explicitly fold in feminism and anti-racism. The Black Rose is understood as the darker sister of the socialist red Rose—a flower that stands for love and solidarity, but also for mourning, resistance, and the refusal to be domesticated. It's the Rose that admits the revolution is going to be messy, and that a lot

薔薇族 7

of the people in the room are going to be queer, weird, poor, or otherwise thorny.

So, yes, a Rose is a celebration of our thorns. As a gay man, my own coming-out was uncomfortable and a bit painful. If you're lucky you get to be a Sunflower or a Camellia, all sunny and unchallenging. But for some of us, to blossom fully means you're going to get cut. You're going to be called names. You're going to be punched at school. You're going to lose people. You're going to bleed a little. Perhaps this is why I developed a late respect for the Rose, and wanted to plant a huge Rose Garden with rare varieties. But the other reason was Morocco.

In Jan Davidsz. de Heem's *Vanitas Still-Life with a Skull, a Book and Roses*, circa 1630, the Rose serves as a primary vehicle for a reminder of the inevitability of death. While the skull represents the permanence of death, the Rose represents the transience of life. In seventeenth-century Dutch art, flowers were chosen for their "ephemeral" nature; they are at their most beautiful right before they begin to rot.

In Vincent van Gogh's *Roses*, May 1890, the significance of the flower is rooted in a rare moment of optimism and recovery during the final months of his life at the asylum in Saint-Rémy. Unlike his earlier, darker works, these Roses represent a sense of hope and revitalization. He viewed the act of painting Roses as a "remedy" for his mental health, describing his work during this period as a way to calm his "shattered nerves."

After I bought Flamingo Estate, I visited Marrakesh and landed at the Beldi Country Club. It's a vast Rose garden outside the city, punctuated with swimming pools and sun lounges. The most clichéd flower in the world suddenly looked sexy, scattered between hot bodies and overflowing glasses of rosé. In another religious, semi-repressed corner of the world, hedonistic pleasure and the naked bodies that accompany it had found an abundant haven behind thousands of Roses. Botanists estimate something like thirty thousand cultivars now. Most wild species are simple—five-petalled, usually white or pink—but we have coaxed them into every shade of yellow and orange and red, and into petals so doubled they barely look like the original plant.

My own collection leans toward Old World varieties—Damasks, Bourbons, Teas—with abundant blooms and rich fragrance. These are Roses bred before the age of refrigeration and air freight, when scent still mattered more than stiffness. Fresh on the stem they smell of Citrus and Green Tea at the top, jammy Fruit and Honey in the middle, and a faint Clove or Pepper dry-down underneath. Of special note are the Roses I was given by Martha Stewart—a cultivar named in her honor. We have an entire bed of her pink blooms. And the Jane Goodall Rose, planted as a reminder of my friend, who first kick-started the idea of Flamingo years ago.

So the Rose Garden here is not just about prettiness. It's a living archive of everything the Rose has been asked to stand for: Mary and Muhammad, martyrs and mystics, unions and uprisings, drag queens and prison boys, hedonism in Marrakesh and quiet domestic courage in the suburbs. Underneath it all is a simple, furious wish: that everyone who walks through the Rose Garden will leave with a deeper appreciation of the thorns it also represents—for all the people whose lives and loves have never been smooth, but who decided to bloom anyway.

THE ROSES OF FLAMINGO ESTATE

THE CLASSIC SPECIES

Autumn Damask (*Rosa damascena semperflorens*)
Cabbage Rose (*Rosa centifolia*)
California Wild Rose (*Rosa californica*)
Damask Rose (*Rosa damascena*)
French Rose (*Rosa gallica*)
Musk Rose (*Rosa moschata*)
Rugosa Rose (*Rosa rugosa*)
Tea Rose (*Rosa odorata*)

CLIMBING ROSES

Bathsheba
Colette
Eden Climber
Quicksilver
Senateur LaFolette
Lady Banks' Rose (*Rosa banksiae*)

HYBRID TEA ROSES

Avant Garde
Barbra Streisand
Bewitched
Chrysler Imperial
Dr. Jane Goodall
Eau de Parfum Berry Bliss
Eleganza
Eleganza Fiji
Elle
Firefighter
Grande Dame
Heavenly Scented
Just Joey
Lasting Love
Martha Stewart
Mellow Yellow
Memorial Day
Midas Touch
Neptune
Oklahoma
Parfuma Bliss
Parfuma Earth Angel
Perfume Delight
Perfume Factory
Princess Charlene de Monaco
Princess Leia
Romantica Ball Gown
St. Patrick
Stainless Steel
Sweet Mademoiselle
Tropicana
Wedding Bells
Yves Piaget

LANDSCAPE, GROUNDCOVER & RUGOSA

Apricot Drift (Groundcover)
Bonica (Landscape)
Diamond Eyes (Miniature)
Hansa (Rugosa)
Kolorscape Kardinal (Landscape Floribunda)
Moje Hammarberg (Rugosa)
Peachy Knockout (Landscape)
Pink Double Knockout (Landscape)
Pink Knockout (Landscape)
Pink Ruby Meidiland (Landscape)

GRANDIFLORA ROSES

Fun in the Sun
Parade Day
State of Grace
Sunshine Daydream
Tiamo
Twilight Zone
Uptown Girl

ENGLISH SHRUB ROSES

Darcey Bussell
Desdemona
Evelyn
Gabriel Oak
Princess Alexandra of Kent
Scepter'd Isle
The Alnwick Rose
The Ancient Mariner
Tranquility
Winchester Cathedral

FLORIBUNDA ROSES

Candy Cane Cocktail
Celestial Night
Cherrytini
Earth Angel Perfume
Ebb Tide
French Lace
Hot Cocoa
Ketchup and Mustard
Oranges and Lemons
Our Lady of Guadalupe
Power Puff
Queen of Elegance
Scentimental
Silver Lining
Sweet Madame Blue
Winning Streak

[V] MAY SPRING	# DIRTY WORK	*"May, more than any other month of the year, wants us to feel most alive."* —FENNEL HUDSON

GARDEN TASKS:

Lavender and Sage begin flowering; harvest stems just before full bloom for the strongest scent.	☐	Mulch all trees before the summer heat—two to three inches thick, leaving space around trunks.	☐
Jasmine and Gardenia: prune lightly after flowering; feed with acid-loving plant food.	☐	Stake or cage the Tomatoes, pinch off suckers, and mulch. Feed every 10-14 days with compost tea.	☐
Stake and pinch back Dahlias to help encourage bushier growth.	☐	Peppers, Cucumbers, Zucchini, and Eggplants should be thriving—keep soil moist but not soggy.	☐
Harvest Basil, Parsley, Chervil, Mint, and Dill before they flower. Dry or freeze excess for later use.	☐	Zinnias, Cosmos, and Marigolds: direct sow or thin seedlings for space.	☐
Turn and aerate your compost. Decomposition accelerates in warmer weather.	☐	Sow second rounds of quick crops like Arugula, Radish, and Lettuce in partial shade.	☐
Apply compost tea or worm-casting extract to boost microbial life.	☐	Cut back flowering herbs (Thyme, Sage, Rosemary) after bloom to keep them compact and stimulate growth.	☐
Plant Beans, Corn, or Melons if the soil has fully warmed; May is the last good planting window before summer.	☐	Start saving seeds from early-blooming flowers or bolting greens.	☐

TASK

MAKE A ROSE WATER MIST

☐

Simmer a generous handful of Rose petals in water until the steam smells like a garden, then cool completely and strain. Bottle the Rose water and use it as a face toner, linen spray, or after-sun mist. For extra calm, blend in a little Aloe Vera gel or a splash of strong, cooled Chamomile tea.

Keep your Rose water mist refrigerated, and make sure to use it while it is fresh.

TASK

HOST A PARTY

☐

Every May, when the garden hits its peak flush, we host a Celebration of the Roses. It is a happy accident that this coincides with Harvey's birthday—my own Rose between the thorns—so we toast to both.

The menu is a love letter to color: vibrant, petal-strewn dishes that look like the garden on a plate. We ask our friends to arrive in their best pinks and florals, creating a living bouquet around the table. We dine immersed in the blooms, the air thick with perfume, while the staff pin fresh Rose corsages to their lapels. It is a night of total immersion—a moment to eat, drink, and dress like the flower that defines us.

TASK

Get Pickled

PAMELA ANDERSON'S ROSE PICKLES ARE BASED ON A RECIPE FROM HER AUNT VIE. WE MADE THEM IN THE SUMMER OF 2025, AND THEY SOLD OUT INSTANTLY. THE SIGNATURE FLAVOR COMES FROM ROSE, DILL, MUSTARD, AND GARLIC, WITH PINK PEPPERCORN, GUAJILLO, AND A LITTLE SMOKY SALT HEAT.

Ingredients:

CUCUMBERS:

2 lb	small Cucumbers (Kirby or Persian), whole or spears

THE BRINE:

2 cups	water
1 cup	distilled white vinegar
1 cup	Apple cider vinegar
2-2½ Tbsp	kosher Salt
1-2 Tbsp	sugar (optional)

PER QUART JAR (scale up as needed):

3-4	Garlic cloves, smashed
2-3 sprigs	fresh Dill
1 tsp	Mustard seeds
1 tsp	Pink Peppercorns
½-1	Guajillo Chile, torn
½	Fresno Chile, sliced
1-2 tsp	edible dried Rose petals

Method:

Pack cucumbers into clean jars with the garlic, dill, mustard seeds, peppercorns, chiles, and rose petals.
Warm the water and vinegars just enough to dissolve the salt (and sugar, if using). Do not boil—just heat and stir.

Pour brine over the cucumbers to fully cover. Tap the jar to release bubbles, then seal.
Cool, then refrigerate. They are good in 24 hours, best at 48-72 hours, and will keep (refrigerated) for about 3-4 weeks.

MAY ROSE ROCKY ROAD

INGREDIENTS

3 cups	white chocolate melting buttons
1 tsp	Rose water
$\frac{1}{4}$ cup	Pistachios
$\frac{1}{4}$ cup	dried Cherries
$\frac{1}{4}$ cup	dehydrated Strawberries
$\frac{1}{2}$ cup	Strawberry marshmallows, cut into halves
$\frac{1}{2}$ cup	Turkish delight, cut into cubes

METHOD

Line a 9" x 4" loaf pan with a sheet of parchment paper, cut large enough that it hangs over the sides. Set aside.

Place the white chocolate melting buttons in a heatproof bowl and set aside. In a large mixing bowl, combine all other ingredients and set aside.

Fill a 2-quart saucepan with 2 cups of water and bring to a boil. Once boiling, turn down to a simmer and then set the bowl of chocolate over the saucepan.

Use a rubber spatula to stir occasionally until all the chocolate has melted.

Pour the melted chocolate into the bowl with all other ingredients and mix gently with a rubber spatula.

Transfer the rocky road mixture to your prepared loaf pan and press down to remove any gaps. Leave in the refrigerator for the chocolate to set (up to 20 minutes).

Remove the rocky road and slice to serve or wrap for a sweet gift.

RECIPE

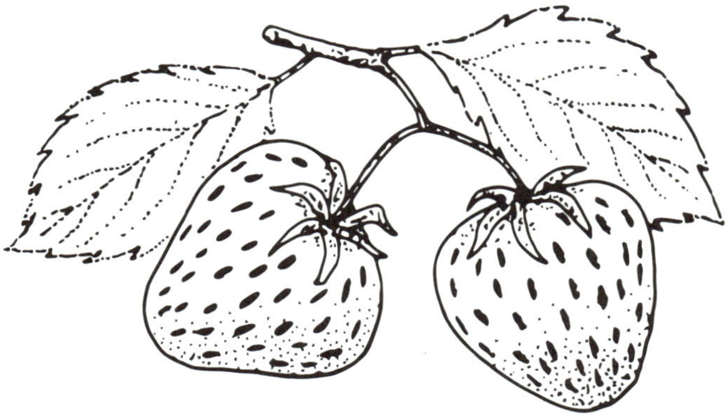

STRAWBERRY & ROSE CAKE WITH ROSE BUTTERCREAM

STRAWBERRY ROSE CAKE

1½ tsp	baking powder
1½ cups	all-purpose flour
1 cup	fine cane sugar
8 Tbsp	unsalted butter, softened
2 Tbsp	Olive oil
2 tsp	Rose water
½ tsp	fine Sea Salt
2	large eggs
½ cup	plain whole-milk yogurt
½ cup	Strawberry Rose compote

Preheat your oven to 350°F and line a 9” by 4” loaf pan with parchment paper. Sift together baking powder and flour into a small bowl and set aside. Add sugar, butter, oil, rose water, and salt to the bowl of a stand mixer with the paddle attachment and beat on medium-high speed until light and fluffy (about 5 minutes). Turn the mixer down to medium speed and add eggs one at a time. Add yogurt and prepared flour mixture and mix to combine. Scoop batter into the prepared loaf pan and drizzle with strawberry rose compote. Use a butter knife to create swirls of compote in the batter. Bake for 40 minutes, or until golden and a cake tester comes out clean. Remove from the oven and leave to cool on a wire rack. Cool completely before decorating with buttercream.

STRAWBERRY ROSE COMPOTE

1 cup	Strawberries, washed, trimmed, and quartered
1 Tbsp	Rose water
¼ cup	fine cane sugar

Add all ingredients to a saucepan and set over medium-low heat. Cook for 5–6 minutes, stirring occasionally to prevent the compote from catching on the bottom of the pan. Remove from heat and set aside to cool.

ROSE BUTTERCREAM

1 cup	unsalted butter, softened
2 cups	powdered sugar
1 Tbsp	Vanilla extract
2 tsp	Rose water

Place butter into the bowl of a stand mixer with the whisk attachment and begin to beat on medium-high until the butter is light and fluffy (about 5 minutes). Turn the mixer down to low speed, adding powdered sugar gradually until you have added all the sugar. Add vanilla and rose water. Turn the mixer up to high speed and beat for another 5 minutes until your buttercream is light in color and texture.

TASK

FACE THE ROSES

In a small bowl, mix 1 tablespoon Rose Clay (or any gentle clay) with 1-2 teaspoons Rose water (or cooled strong Rose tea) until it becomes a smooth paste. Add ½ teaspoon Honey for softness, and a few drops of Camellia oil (or Olive/Jojoba) if your skin runs dry. Spread a thin layer over clean skin, avoiding the eyes. Let it sit for 5-10 minutes. Do not let it crack completely—then rinse with warm water and finish with a simple oil or moisturizer. Patch test first if you are sensitive.

TASK

MAKE A ROSE STEAM

A Rose steam is a fast reset: the vapor softens skin and helps loosen congestion, while the aroma calms your nervous system and makes your whole bathroom feel like a spa.

Bring a pot of water to a boil, turn off the heat, and toss in a handful of Rose petals, plus any supportive herbs you love–Chamomile, Lavender, Rosemary, or a little Sage.

Lean over the pot with a towel draped over your head and let the steam bathe your face for a few minutes. Keep your eyes closed, stay comfortably back from the heat, and finish with a splash of cool water.

TASK

HAVE A ROSE NAMED AFTER

☐

Yes, it's real. Martha Stewart has a Hybrid Tea Rose named for her, and Dr. Jane Goodall has a Hybrid Tea Rose in her name, too. We have both at the Estate.

PICK A LANE

OFFICIAL & PUBLIC

THE MOST LEGIT OPTION.
THE REAL DEAL.

Find a nursery who offers commemorative naming, and pay a fee to name a new variety. You are essentially sponsoring the final stretch: testing, introducing, and naming. Expect it to cost real money and take time—because breeding a Rose is slow, picky work.

NAMING RIGHTS

A RARE PATH TO FIND,
MUCH LESS WORK.

Some nurseries will offer a limited number of Rose-naming opportunities each year, where they already have an unreleased Rose, and you get to name it. This is often the cleanest and simplest path forward if you want a Rose, but don't want to breed it yourself.

DIY

EXTREMELY HARDCORE.
NOT FOR THE FAINT OF HEART.

Breed your own Rose (yes, amateurs can do it, too), then register it properly and give it its official name. This is a long game, but it is the purest example of the precious things being "earned, not gifted."

WHAT YOU WILL ACTUALLY DO (PRACTICALLY)

Write your story in one sentence. Why this Rose should carry your name (or your project's name).

Choose your vibe. Color, fragrance, disease resistance, meaning—what do you want it to be famous for?

Find the right partner. Look specifically for "Rose-naming opportunity," "commemorative naming," or "name a Rose" programs from established Rose growers or breeders.

Make it official. The "real" name is a cultivar registration, and there are rules about uniqueness and what can be used as the official name; many Roses also have a separate marketing name.

Bring it into the world. The magic isn't just the naming—it's getting the Rose propagated, sold, planted, photographed, gifted, and grown. That is how a Rose becomes a legacy instead of a label.

JAN.

FEB.

MAR.

APR.

MAY.

JUN.

JUL.

AUG.

SEP.

OCT.

NOV.

DEC.

NOSE DIVE
[V]

THE GARDEN CENTER

When I was a little boy, my parents owned a garden center in Canberra, Australia. My brother and I spent entire days wandering through aisles of pots and seedlings, hiding between bags of soil, learning plant names, and making up stories about the flowers. I don't remember every detail of that place, but I remember the smell perfectly. It smelled like almost nothing else on Earth. Even now, when I walk into a big nursery or wholesale greenhouse and that warm, musty, green, slightly sweaty air hits me, something in my nervous system lights up. I feel so emotional, fast. It is, honestly, the most comforting smell I know. Damp, green, mossy—for me it smells like promise and family. There isn't a smell I love more.

MAY.

At the heart of it all is soil: damp, loamy, fertile. That smell is not poetry; it's chemistry. The main molecule is geosmin, produced by soil-dwelling bacteria and released when you disturb the earth. It's what you smell in the first seconds of rain on dry ground—that sharp, earthy, almost mushroomy hit. Geosmin and its cousins are rare in our indoor lives, so when they appear under a plastic roof, we notice. We are smelling the outside world, inside.

Layered over the soil are the fragrances of living plants. When they are watered, brushed against, or unpotted, they release "green leaf volatiles"—the spicy, cut-grass, crushed-leaf smell that signals growth, damage, and life all at once. Even faint traces of compost, fertilizer, and the plasticky odor of pots and trays fold into the mix.

And then there is the air itself. Walk through the automatic doors and the humidity wraps around you like a warm blanket. The greenhouse roof traps heat; sprinklers and misters soak the benches; the plants exhale water vapor. Runoff hits warm concrete and evaporates, releasing that unmistakable scent of rained-on pavement in a summer storm. It's subtle, but your skin and sinuses register it immediately: we're indoors, but the weather has followed us.

The concentrated scent cloud of a garden center presses every nostalgia button at once. Scroll through Reddit and you'll find thread after thread of people trying to describe it: "the smell of my childhood," "Sundays with my dad," "the smell of possibilities." For me it is exactly that—the smell of standing in an aisle, begging for one small plant to take home, already imagining the life it might have, and feeling the whole future of a garden in a plastic pot in your hands.

Bodnant Garden Nursery, Wales, 1992.

June is about surprise. It begins with the ocean rolling over the hills—the famous “June Gloom” that is really a delivery system for Sea Salt, coating the garden in a cool, mineral breath at daybreak. By noon, the sun burns it off and everything wakes up at once: Citrus tighten their tiny green fruit, Figs begin to blush, Olives and Pomegranates quietly knit their jewels. While the mornings are gray, the evenings are full of secrets from faraway lands. The Cactus Garden wakes

JUNE

up after hours, unfolding satin petals and releasing a seduction that doesn't belong to the day. The air turns thick with the scent of Lavender, Rosemary, and Sage, shocking the Estate into a Mediterranean disguise. It is a time when the garden feels most like a traveler, transporting us to the Amalfi Coast or the deserts of Mexico without ever leaving home. The discipline of spring is over; now, the pleasure begins.

On some late June nights in Los Angeles, the city exhales. The summer heat loosens its grip and the orchestra of Flamingo Estate begins to play: sprinklers tick, cicadas click, and crickets keep a steady percussion. Pollinator moths fly silent, but you'll hear the faint tap at the glass and the soft flutter around bulbs. Long-horned grasshoppers keep time like a metronome, and a great horned owl adds its deep, classic "hoo-hoo." Occasionally we hear the goats bleat, and coyotes in the distance add yips, barks, and high, cascading howls. Above it all, the sky competes with helicopters and late planes.

This is an after-hours concert: the Jasmine has already gone to bed. Citrus has folded its fans. The California Poppies have buttoned their silk cups shut. But during the encore, a leafless green stem the size of a palm begins to change. The flower untucks itself from its tight scroll, petals begin to unravel, and a perfume rises that doesn't belong to the day. From a Cactus comes a fragrance so rich it feels like a seduction. The night moths quickly arrive like ghosts with a job to do.

This is the Queen of the Night—like Whitney Houston in that scene in *The Bodyguard*, where she appears at the club for a quick song, then dashes away, leaving only rumors behind. She is a Cactus that learned to climb, an epiphyte (a plant that grows on other plants) who prefers the company of trees to the ground—living in their crooks, drinking moonlight and humidity. Most of what the world calls "Queen of the Night" in gardens is *Epiphyllum oxypetalum*, sometimes nicknamed the Orchid Cactus. Her origins are the warm, shaded forests of southern Mexico through Central America—Chiapas to Guatemala, Belize, Honduras, Nicaragua, and Costa Rica—where she opens for moths (and sometimes bats) that navigate by scent and star.

There's also her Caribbean cousin, *Selenicereus grandiflorus*, another rightful "Queen," born across the Greater Antilles and the Yucatán. And the third Queen—*Peniocereus greggii*—who rules over the Sonoran Desert, located in the southwestern United States (Arizona and California) and northwestern Mexico (Baja California and Sonora). Three monarchs wearing similar crowns, all blooming in the late night.

Cacti are a New World plant family, born on the long spine of the Americas—starting in Canada's dry flats and running all the way down to Patagonia's cold shoulders. Not all are the desert cacti we know from Western movies. A surprising number are forest creatures—epiphytes that perch high in tropical canopies, using tree bark as scaffolding, catching filtered light and warm night air.

Although there are some exceptions, the majority of these blooms are white-ish. It's the most visible color in low light or darkness, and wide petals create an easy landing pad. Cacti know that the darkness can be an amplifier. The flowers also offer up a contradiction: a hard, spiky, sharp, tough family of plants that produce tender perfumes. They are the very definition of soft power. Perhaps that is why these scents and plants feel so at home at Flamingo. We love to play it tough, but at the end of the day we're sweet as can be.

Here are some of the fragrant Cacti from the Flamingo Garden that make up our favorite fragrance notes. Each one of them has a very special story to tell, and I am very grateful to have them in the Cactus Garden.

NIGHT-BLOOMING CEREUS
[*Peniocereus greggii*]

For eleven months it pretends to be nothing—just a fist of gray pencils hiding inside Creosote and Mesquite—while the real plant sleeps underground as a starchy, human-heart-sized tuber. Then the desert changes the schedule: a run of breathless heat, a shift in pressure, the first signs of a monsoon (dozens of plants keep this same appointment). At full dark, a satin trumpet unrolls with a scent you can follow across roads: cool Honey, rind of Lime, a faint Coconut cream. Hawk moths arrive like small aircraft, guided by that perfume; they thread the scrub at chest height, dust themselves in pollen, and leave you blinking at the speed of it.

Farther south it's called *reina de la noche*, a name said with the same respect you'd give a visiting aunt who only comes once a year. Old stories swear you can feel the flower open as a small coolness on the skin. By dawn, the trumpet is a crumpled handkerchief, and a few days later an egg-shaped red fruit ripens, juicy and sweet enough for thrashers, foxes, and anyone lucky enough to find it before they do. If you grow it in a pot you must offer it no winter water, because a single deep drink can tip a plant into bloom; in cool weather, leave it bone dry. When it finally spends its energy on flowers, it spends lavishly—one perfect night financed by an entire year of thrift.

PERUVIAN APPLE
[*Cereus repandus*]

Night Trumpets, a tall cactus with candelabra-like stems, produce long white flowers at night (sometimes bronze-tinted) and fruit by day. The fragrance is restrained—cool nectar, green Apple skin, a whisper of Clover—enough to compass moths in the dark. By late summer, smooth orb fruits arrive: pale, crisp, quiet sweetness. Born to the Caribbean rim and northern South America, this Cactus has a long practical history.

Along coastal towns it's trained into living fences—post a cutting, and it will root and rise—while the fruit, named Pitaya, "Peruvian Apple," or cadushi on the ABC islands (Aruba, Bonaire, and Curaçao—just off the Venezuelan coast) gets eaten out of hand, chilled, or pressed for a soft, clear juice. In some places, old columns become an ingredient in homestyle soups after careful de-spining; in others, the summer crop is a children's rite of passage: climb, pick, pass down, laugh at the inevitable seed on the shirt. It's a plant that turns heat into height, darkness into flowers, and patience into fruit.

SAGUARO
[*Carnegiea gigantea*]

The scent of the Saguaro flower is generous and direct—sweet nectar with a faint warm, bready note. Up close it smells like sugar water and pollen with a hint of rising dough. As the night moves the fragrance shifts slightly: just after opening, it turns bright, sugary, clearly floral. Around midnight it gets a warm, yeasty edge. And before sunrise it gets a bit fresher and greener. Touching the anthers leaves a light malty smell on your fingers.

Saguaro fruits form from the fertilized flowers. The red, split-open fruits then ripen a few weeks later—typically June into July. The Tohono O'odham (the Indigenous nation of the Sonoran Desert, living in what is now southern Arizona and northern Sonora, Mexico) mark the fruiting with songs and a Saguaro fruit wine made from the first red harvest—not Grapes (we have the recipe later in this book).

Ecologically the Saguaro Cactus is a vertical village. Desert woodpeckers chisel nest cavities (the Cactus walls them off into smooth, watertight "boots"), and when birds move on, elf owls, kestrels, and other tenants take the lease. White-winged doves track blooming and fruiting across the desert like a moving food truck; coyotes and foxes scatter the seeds farther still. Each column is a water tower, a pantry, a bar, and an apartment block disguised as a plant.

THE DUTCHMAN'S PIPE CACTUS
[*Epiphyllum oxypetalum*]

A flat, jointed Cactus with no theatrics by daylight, it keeps its secret in a long, tapered bud. After dusk, everything happens quickly: sepals unlatch, the corolla opens like a pale sea creature, and a silky fragrance—white-floral with a cool, almost Cucumber lift and a breath of sweet cream. Native to Mesoamerica's warm forests, it traveled early to Asia and took root in Chinese courtyards as *tanhua* (昙花). Here the bloom became a community event. Families stayed up late with tea, neighbors were called, groups gathered. Fortune was read in the hour the flower chose to bloom—earlier for luck in business, later for longevity. So the saying *tanhua yixian* (昙花一现) entered the language to mean a brilliance too brief to keep. In scholar gardens from Suzhou to Guangzhou, the tanhua became a small rite of culture—poems improvised on fans, a quick charcoal sketch before the petals loosened.

The plant gathered other names as it roamed East Asia: in Japan it's *Gekka Bijin* (月下美人, "Beauty Under the Moon"), and in Vietnam Hoa Quỳnh, where families likewise keep vigil for a midnight bloom. In modern Chinese cities, apartment balconies become miniature stages—friends text "开了！" ("it's opening!"), and everyone hurries out with a phone and a cup of tea, repeating an old courtyard ritual with new props. Everyone waiting for the lacquer-smooth fragrance of white petals to float around. We too wait patiently for it every year at Flamingo.

ORGAN PIPE
[*Stenocereus thurberi*]

The garden's night choir has multiple arms that rise from a single base, each one lifting creamy flowers that open at night and linger into morning. The aroma is nectar-rich and slightly resinous—think warm Agave and cut Melon—originally for lesser long-nosed and Mexican long-tongued bats that commute along the Ajo valleys in southwestern Arizona. Faces dusted gold, they do the heavy pollinating before dawn; bees and orioles take the day shift. By high summer the Pitaya dulce swells: dark-skinned, crimson-pulped fruit packed with glossy seeds, eaten fresh from the chill or cooked down to syrups and leathers—food for people long before borders, and fuel for birds and foxes when the desert runs lean.

At Organ Pipe Cactus National Monument in southern Arizona, you can read the landscape by these plants: where the cold drains away, where stone holds the day's heat, where bat corridors pass like invisible rivers. In Los Angeles it wants the same logic—maximum sun, radiant stone, ruthless drainage, and a little shelter from winter rain while young—and then it plays on its own schedule, a magnificent organ that opens when the air is hot enough to carry the sweetness all around the garden.

MOONLIGHT CACTUS
[*Selenicereus*]

This is a Cactus that behaves like a vine: three-ribbed jointed stems climb posts and trees, then drape from the top like a chandelier. On hot evenings the long, furred buds tip upward and open into porcelain flowers. The scent is clean and precise—cool nectar with a light Vanilla note and a bit of green Melon. Weeks later come the famous scaled fruits: skins blushing Rose, magenta, or yellow; flesh from snow-white to electric fuchsia (the yellow species is the sweetest). The flavor is gentle and refreshing, a Flamingo favorite (we have a recipe later in this book).

Most of our night-blooming Cacti are desert columnars (Saguaro, Organ Pipe, Cardón): upright water towers tuned to arid heat, heavy ribs, and thick skin. Dragon Fruit is tropical and epiphytic—born in the warm, humid forests of Mesoamerica, it climbs rather than stands, often rooting into bark and trellis instead of anchoring deep in desert soil. It flowers and fruits in multiple flushes through the warm season (not a single brief window), and many varieties are self-sterile, asking for a second clone—or a midnight paintbrush—to set heavy crops. In short: the same family (*Cactaceae*), but completely different lifestyle choices. Sound familiar?

[GROUNDING] : A MAP OF PLEASURE FROM THE GARDEN

THE MEDITERRANEAN GARDEN

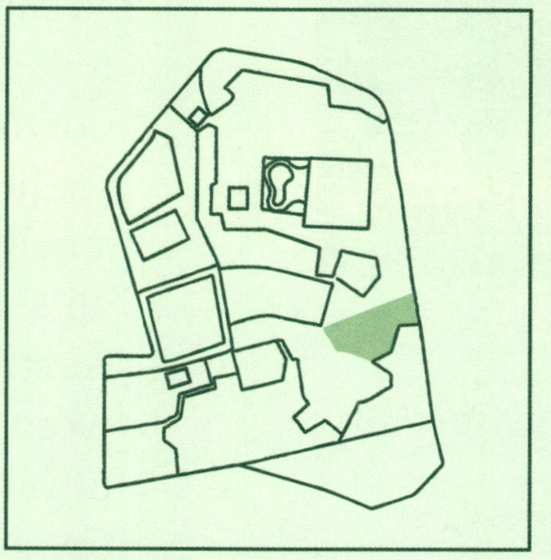

34°08' N / 118°12' W LOS ANGELES, CALIFORNIA

Children live in a more delicious world than we do. They're born with thousands of taste buds not just on the tongue, but scattered across the cheeks and the roof of the mouth, and they're exquisitely sensitive—especially to bitterness and sourness, which is part of why kids often hate Broccoli, Radicchio, and strong Cheese. As we grow up, many of those extra taste buds simply die off. The ones outside the tongue disappear first; the tongue's taste buds slowly thin out and become less responsive. As adults, our "taste" has been turned down, and food and wine have to shout a little louder to get our attention.

Sometimes I think the opposite was true of me. I moved to Italy when I was in my twenties, to work at Benetton. Here, in the sleepy town of Treviso outside Venice, my taste buds woke wide awake. The first thing you notice is the Treviso Radicchio–

The giant eagle urn, overlooking the Olive grove in the Mediterranean Garden. Photographed by Hugh Davison, 2025.

Flamingo Estate Capers in the kitchen, 2025.

"Veneto's red gold," a bitter, curled Chicory that only really makes sense once you've eaten it there. We'd often wash it down with Fragolino, the "forbidden" wine of Veneto, made traditionally from the Isabella or Fragola Grape, a variety that smells and tastes like wild Strawberries. And then there were all the other things I never really tasted growing up in rural Australia: balsamic vinegar and Figs. My happiest memories were eating Olive arancini in a bar on the main square; a slice of blistering hot pizza with Rosemary on top, eaten standing up; an espresso "corrected" with a splash of grappa. Treviso also quietly claims tiramisu as its own. One version of the story says it was invented at Le Beccherie in the 1970s by Alba Campeol, who wanted a "pick-me-up" dessert for new mothers and the elderly.

It was here that I first drank Prosecco, which in Treviso isn't a brunch cliché but a daily vitamin. The hills of Conegliano and Valdobbiadene are just up the road, and their wine flows into every osteria glass. You drink it standing at the counter with a plate of cicchetti—little Venetian bar snacks that hop the lagoon and land here too: crostini topped with baccalà mantecato, Tomato jam, and anchovy, handed over on a napkin. It's all very unceremonious and completely perfect: bubbles and salt and fried things and the feeling that time has briefly left the room. Italy taught me to TASTE life.

I'd spend many sun-kissed summers on the island of Pantelleria, staying at the home of my friend Andreina Longhi. Pantelleria is a small, wild, volcanic island sitting alone in the middle of the sea between Sicily and Tunisia—closer to Africa than to mainland Italy. It's all black lava terraces, wind, and low stone dammusi houses with white domes, flanked by Caper bushes. There are no sandy beaches, just dark cliffs dropping into deep, electric-blue water, hot springs steaming out of rocks, and a feeling that you're standing on the skin of the Earth itself. The island is difficult to reach, and unwelcoming of most tourists, with a couple of hotels and the rumor of a taxi.

On Pantelleria, the Caper is not a garnish; it's a religion. For decades it was one of the island's only real crops alongside zibibbo Grapes. Families still tend a patch of Caper bushes the way others tend vines or Olives. There's a Protected Geographical Indication label—Cappero di Pantelleria IGP—to protect the plant, but the real proof of how precious it is is in how people talk about it: they call it "green gold," they argue over the best size, they rinse each bud like a jewel before it goes into a pan. When you open a jar there, you're not just seasoning your food—you're uncapping a whole island's stubbornness and pride.

Caper picking on the small, wild, volcanic island of Pantelleria, Italy, circa 1980. Here the mineral-rich soil makes Capers like nowhere else on Earth. It's one of my favorite places and favorite flavors.

Freeway in the Lavender Garden at Flamingo Estate,
with a bronze sculpture by Klaas Gubbels.

Unlike most fruit, the Fig is technically a *syconium*—a fleshy, hollow shell that contains hundreds of tiny flowers blooming internally. This nineteenth-century diagram illustrates the internal structures of the fruit and reproductive organs. The dense cluster of internal flowers require specialized wasps for pollination.

A botanical illustration of Rosemary (*Rosmarinus officinalis*) by William Clark in 1833. Today a sea of Rosemary covers the Flamingo Olive grove and floor of the Mediterranean Garden. When it flowers it's a feast for our nearby bees who wait patiently for the blooms.

They're special partly because of where they grow. Pantelleria is volcanic and brutal: almost no rain, fierce winds, and mineral-rich soils. Capers hate comfort; they love hardship. On those stone terraces the bushes stay low and stressed by the wind, which means the buds are smaller, denser, and more intensely aromatic than most Capers from elsewhere. They're picked by hand at dawn, all summer long, when the buds are still tight, then packed in layers of local Sea Salt and turned again and again until they shrivel and concentrate. I became obsessed with Pantelleria Capers on my first visit (try making ice cream with them!).

Since then, I've spent my whole life trying to perfect Italian hospitality, with the flavors and scents of Italy. When we finally made a home of our own, I realized I wanted Italy not just on the plate and in the glass, but growing in the soil outside the back door. So I began to plant a Mediterranean Garden: Rosemary and Thyme along the paths so that every step brushes perfume into the air. We planted a grove of Olive trees, Fig trees for their generous shade, and a Pomegranate that splits open like a ruby in late summer. There are Citrus trees whose blossoms can make the whole garden smell like an Amalfi morning, and in the hottest, stoniest corner, Caper bushes that cling to the rocks as stubbornly as their cousins on the islands.

Recently, we visited my friend Rozemarijn de Witte in the Balearic Islands. Here the Lavender grows almost like a weed, spilling over paths and stone walls, thriving in the same dry, stony soil that Capers and Olives love. Lavender is another Mediterranean stoic: it likes sun, neglect, and wind. Crush it between your fingers and the scent rises up—clean and herbal, with a soft sweetness underneath, like Honey and warm linen. There's something both calming and sharp about it, as if it clears your head and slows your breathing at the same time. That scent has become

Bundles of Lavender from the Flamingo Estate garden.

part of our everyday rituals at home; we use Lavender in our body wash and hand soap so that even a quick shower or a run of the tap smells faintly of those sunburnt hillsides and island afternoons.

Rozemarijn is a Dutch entrepreneur and former magazine publisher who cofounded the iconic hotel, restaurant, and store Los Enamorados with her husband, Pierre. In her garden above the hotel stood a towering bronze sculpture by Klaas Gubbels, a Dutch painter and sculptor who, even at ninety-something, can't be tamed. "This sculpture is a tribute to the Mediterranean sun and sea here," she told me. "He has another one. Would you be interested in it for your garden?"

We said yes, of course. Back home, we converted what was once an unused corridor at the bottom of the garden into a Lavender walk, planting it thickly along both sides so everyone can run their fingers through the foliage as they pass. The oils release on your skin, and for the rest of your stroll your hands smell like the Balearics. At the end of the path you come to a small, hidden landing, and there is Klaas Gubbels's sculpture—tall and quietly joyful—catching the light and watching over the sea of purple.

Now our garden has become a little theater for the senses: bitter Radicchio on the table, Pantelleria Capers in the kitchen, Prosecco in the glass, Lavender in the air, and a bronze sculpture at the end of a fragrant path reminding us to live a more Mediterranean life—to slow down, to use our hands, to smell and taste everything like a child again.

La dolce vita, indeed.

Prickly Pear from the Opuntia Cactus, a classic California summer jewel
from our garden, photographed by Hugh Davison, 2024.

ROSEMARY
[*Salvia rosmarinus*]

Cascading down the terrace with its azure-blue flowers and parade of honeybees trailing behind, Rosemary does what it's always known to do: provide pleasure. Compulsively growing along seashores in its native Mediterranean (and now world over), its Latin name writes the story of its fragrance—with *rosmarinus* meaning "dew of the sea." Smelling it mirrors this act: submerging us in a cool bath of menthol and salt, mixing in the breeze of warm, camphorous hillsides.

An emblem of clarity, Rosemary's fragrance emits a sharp sense of vitality said to enhance memory and light up creative dreaming. Making it one of the oldest raw materials known to perfumery, and leading to its use as the primary ingredient in the first alcohol-based perfume, formulated in the fourteenth century, called Hungary Water.

ROCK ROSE
[*Cistus ladanifer*]

Though an emblem of Andalusian heritage, the Rock Rose extends its aromatic mysticism to the world—providing perfumes with the first-ever leather note derived from the plant kingdom. The aromatic story begins in the scorching hills of southern Spain, where delicately wrinkled white flowers are splattered everywhere in early April, only lasting for two days. If one were to smell these ephemeral snowflakes, one would be met with clean air. For the scent does not house itself in the flower, but rather in the branches. As soon as the blossom appears, the plant secretes a resin that protects the branches from the sun, producing an ambery smell that pervades the whole area.

This indispensable raw material is known by the name of Labdanum Gum, carrying an intensity full of animalic warmth, where wood, grass, and resin come together to entrance. Known as Christ's Tears in Spanish, the white flowers carry deep crimson spots in each of its five petals—venturing into the sacred with a scent that carries the religion, the scorching heat, and the resilience of the Mediterranean. Lucky for us, they feel right at home in the blazing heat of Los Angeles.

POMEGRANATE
[*Punica granatum*]

In Greek mythology, the Pomegranate was associated with Persephone, who, as a result of eating it, was forced by Hades to return to the underworld for a third of each year. Upon her return to Earth, spring would begin.

In most cultures, from Persia to Egypt, the Pomegranate is a symbol of beginnings—with its dozens of seeds winking toward fertility and prosperity. When piercing through its pillowy rind, one is met with a green and lightly tannic scent—something like Green Apple and Rose. Cracking it open reveals rows of ruby seeds, lightly glinting through red translucent flesh. Popping them releases a cool, watery freshness at first. Then, hints of Cranberry, Cherry, and Red Grape. Juicy, sweet, godlike.

Rosemary.

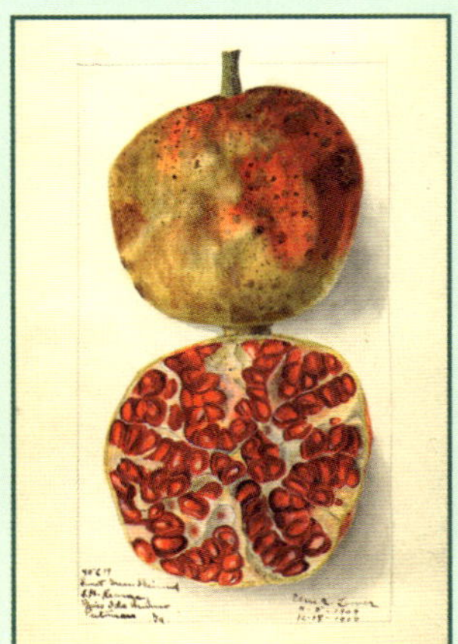

CAPERS
[*Capparis spinosa*]

Clinging to the sun-bleached stones of the Mediterranean, the Caper bush endures where little else grows. As its roots thread through limestone, its unopened buds hold the promise of a flower never meant to bloom. Immature and unripened, fresh Caper buds are bitter and inedible on their own. Yet when brined or salt-cured, an enzymatic reaction occurs that gives it a volatile whisper of Mustard and sea air. Its sharp, floral brine—layered with sulfurous warmth and citric lift—stirs the appetite as it has for millennia.

Ancient Greeks scattered them across fish and Barley, the Romans prescribed them for digestion, the Italians made them holy in pasta puttanesca. Yet their story doesn't just end in the unopened bud. If left to bloom, these buds form delicately scented white flowers, eventually turning into plump Caper Berries. Tumbling elegantly out of the unassuming nooks and crannies of ancient ruins, they're perhaps the toughest Mediterranean survivor. Thus its nickname, "flower of the stones."

FENNEL
[*Foeniculum vulgare*]

Once fed to gladiators, Fennel is marathon spirit made incarnate. In Greek, *Marathon* means "a place with Fennel." It's a real town near Athens that still exists where the famous run began. The plain was filled with it, and its powerful aroma was fuel. Just a drop of its essential oil is enough to cast its sweet, herbal sparkle. When I first tasted it infused in Olive oil in the town of Sant'Agata di Militello, I was set on recreating it.

We wild-harvest it here in California by hand, while the blooms are fresh. Infusing it slowly in our extra virgin Olive oil, filling it with its warm and sweet perfume. The result is a delicately peppery, floral flavor and scent reminiscent of Anise. It will bring you to tears.

OLIVE TREE
[*Olea europaea*]

The Olive tree releases its quiet alchemy with a perfume that smells like Pine and Citrus over stone and dust. When pressed, its fruit gives off the sharp green bite of E-2-hexenal and hexanal, the same living molecules that rise in cut grass—redolent of sharp Artichoke and Peppers. Yet in its blossom, one finds something much softer, sweeter, honeyed. It's why professional Olive oil tasters don't just rely on taste—they "nose" the oil first.

A fragrant, fresh aroma signals high polyphenols. A musty smell, on the other hand, indicates fermentation and poor storage. To the ancient Greeks, the Olive tree was perhaps the most venerated of them all. A symbol of wisdom, purity, and endurance, they anointed athletes and kings with its oil, and trusted its clean, vegetal scent to bridge the mortal to the divine.

[VI] JUNE SUMMER	# DIRTY WORK	*"If a June night could talk, it would probably boast it invented romance."* —BERNARD WILLIAMS

GARDEN TASKS:

- [ ] LAVENDER: Harvest stems for drying when buds open; hang in small bundles in a cool, airy place.
- [ ] CITRUS: Reduce watering slightly to strengthen skins and deepen flavor.
- [ ] BEANS & OKRA: Begin to sow late crops now that all of the soil is fully warm.
- [ ] ROSES: Deadhead spent blooms and cut hard after the first flush to encourage a second show.
- [ ] PEPPERS & EGGPLANTS: Feed with potassium-rich fertilizer as they begin to flower.
- [ ] CUCUMBERS & ZUCCHINI: Harvest them daily before they become too oversized.
- [ ] TOMATOES: Stake, prune, and feed with potassium-rich fertilizer. Water once or twice a week.
- [ ] HERBS: Harvest Basil, Mint, Dill, and Parsley. Pinch stems preflowering for the best fragrance.
- [ ] WISTERIA & JASMINE: Prune and train new vines before they become hard and woody.
- [ ] HYDRANGEAS & GARDENIAS: Feed lightly with acid fertilizer while in full bloom.
- [ ] GREENS: Succession plant quick crops like Arugula, Chard, and Lettuce in partial shade.
- [ ] FRUIT TREES: Feed again before midsummer with compost, seaweed, or worm tea.
- [ ] POMEGRANATES: Buds are opening; feed with compost and keep soil evenly moist.
- [ ] OLIVES: As flowering ends and fruit forms, prune lightly for shape and airflow.

TASK

WARD OFF THE VAMPIRES

Peel a few cloves of Garlic, then smash them to wake up the stink. Rub a little on your door frames, windowsills, and the back of your neck like invisible armor. We also tie Garlic to the front gate to ward off anyone who sucks the energy out of your day. Hang a braided Garlic string by the door for extra theater, then cook something outrageously garlicky for dinner—because if anything supernatural shows up tonight, it's not getting past the front porch.

TASK

SMOKED SEA SALT

Smoke a tray of flaky Sea Salt over low, indirect heat until it smells like a beautiful bonfire, let it cool completely, then stir in crushed Rosemary and a small pinch of Lavender so the whole thing tastes like an herb garden near Formentera.

To get that ink-black "midnight" look, finish with a tiny pinch of food-grade activated charcoal, mix well, and jar it up. Use it on roast vegetables, grilled fish, eggs, buttered bread—or a cocktail rim when you want dinner to feel a little dangerous.

TASK

BAKED GRAPES ☐

Heat the oven to 300°F, spread fresh Grapes on a baking sheet, drizzle lightly with Olive oil (or a little Honey if you want), and roast for 20–30 minutes until they're soft, slightly shriveled, and caramelized.

Spoon them over your favorite yogurt, ricotta, ice cream, toast, or (our favorite) pop them straight into your mouth like candy.

TASK SPICE THINGS UP ☐

Start with a handful of dried Guajillo Chiles (4-6 for a glow, 8-10 for real trouble). Wipe them clean, snip off the stems, shake out most of the seeds, and tear the flesh into big confetti pieces.

Toss them into a dry pan over low heat and toast for 30-60 seconds a side, just until they smell like sun-warmed leather, dried fruit, and smoke. (If they blacken, you've gone too far.)

Tip the warm Chiles into a heatproof jar with a pinch of Salt and, if you like a sharper bite, one or two dried Árbol or Cayenne Chiles. Gently heat good extra virgin Olive oil until it's hot to the touch but nowhere near smoking—about 150-175°F.

Pour the warm oil over the Chiles so they're fully submerged, stir, and let it cool to room temperature. Cover and leave to infuse in a cool, dark place for 24-72 hours, tasting each day until the heat and flavor feel right.

Then strain through a fine sieve or cheesecloth to remove all the solids, and bottle the clear, ruby oil. Store in a cool cupboard (or the fridge if you're cautious) and use on fried eggs, veggies, and anything else within a month or two.

TASK *LAVENDER DREAMS* ☐

Put a generous handful of fresh or dried Lavender in a pot and add distilled water, just enough to cover. Place a small heatproof bowl on an upside-down ramekin in the center of the pot (so it sits above the waterline), then cover with the lid upside down and pile ice on top. Simmer on the lowest heat so the Lavender steam hits the cold lid and drips into the bowl as fragrant hydrosol, replacing the ice as it melts. Cool completely, pour into a clean spray bottle, and mist over pillows, sheets, and the air to calm a racing mind. Store in the fridge and use within 1–2 weeks (or add a small splash of vodka/Witch Hazel to help it keep a little longer).

JAN.

FEB.

MAR.

APR.

MAY.

JUN.

JUL.

AUG.

SEP.

OCT.

NOV.

DEC.

NOSE DIVE
[VI]

SALT

JUN.

Ed Ruscha, *Salt*, 1967,
Graphite on paper, 14 1/2 × 23 in. © Ed Ruscha.

When early June arrives in Los Angeles, we wait for a special morning visitor. A thick marine layer rolls in from the Pacific and begins its 20-mile journey inland—sliding through canyons, draping freeways, slipping over Downtown, and finally spilling over the hills of the Estate.

June Gloom is really the ocean, delivered by air. Gray and omnipresent, it cools the heat and gives us all a sip of moisture. It also brings a very specific message to the nose: the smell of Sea Salt. We are obsessed with Sea Salt because in it lives the ocean itself—once Earth's crust, then a tumbling wave.

The smell we call "sea air" is a complex blend of ocean-born molecules. Fresh, cold, mineral, faintly sulfurous, and metallic. The key player is dimethyl sulfide (DMS), a gas released mostly when phytoplankton break down. In the crest of a breaking wave, spray and foam fling DMS into the air, where it smells faintly of cooked Cabbage, raw clams, freshly shucked oysters. Those molecules hitch a ride on fog and wind and find their way to our noses, miles from the shoreline.

Pure salt (sodium chloride) itself is odorless. What we smell is life. In seawater, only about 3–3.5 percent is dissolved salts; the rest is water. Yet we've all felt the presence of those minerals: tasting the air on the coast, feeling the crystals dry on our skin after a swim, catching that crisp, clean ache in the lungs that says "ocean" long before we see it.

Our Sea Salt comes from the pristine waters of Big Sur, California—a stretch of coast with no phone service and more poetry than roads. Driving north on Highway 1, you know you've arrived when the air turns electric. Ocean and forest collide in resin, fog, and salt spray. Waves rumble and detonate against cliffs; the deep blue smell of the Pacific tangles with Sage, Redwood duff, and wet stone. It is Mother Nature at her loudest.

Our friend Carlo Overhulser at Big Sur Salts gathers this water, and lets it evaporate. What's left is a complex mix of minerals, trace elements, and organic matter—a salt that's defiantly alive, carrying whispers of phytoplankton and bacteria from that season. We fold these crystals into our soaps and scatter them over everything in our kitchen. The only rock we eat, salt is flavor and energy and the great equalizer. It is grand and granular at once: proof that the ocean moves through us every time we breathe, that tears are just another way salt and water make us human.

July is about stamina. The days are long and the air the hottest, and the garden stops being an idea and starts being exercise: water at dawn, mulch deep, shade what's tender, cut what's finished so it blooms again. Pomegranates swell into small green globes; Olives set their fruit and test our consistency. The pollinator beds go into overdrive—Zinnias, Cosmos, Marigolds, Dahlias, Yarrow, Buckwheat, and California Fuchsia throw open their runways, and the bees work

JULY

them with ferocity—back and forth, back and forth, dusted in pollen, never late. And it's not just the bees enduring. It's the team—so many hands tending, cutting, cooking, carrying, cleaning—catching ball after ball the heat throws at us, and turning it into something generous, from garden to hive to kitchen. Every day, we do it again. Stamina is the month's only real religion.

Vanilla planifolia by Sri Lankan artist and scientific illustrator George De Alwis, found in his book *Mon Jardin à Ceylan*, released in 1896.

My friend Gonzalo Samaranch Granados built a Noah's Ark in the middle of Mexico's Yucatán Peninsula. Two by two they come, but they are not saving animals from the flood. They are saving plants for the world. Gonzalo and his wife purchased 6,500 acres of the thickest jungle I have ever seen, and created a project to cradle the most rare and endangered—extinct heirloom seeds, wild Vanilla vines, rare bees, and the old Mayan ways of farming—turning that dense green tangle into a huge living project, named Mestiza de Indias.

Here, in the low forests of Gonzalo's jungle, there is a vine that does not know it is famous. It climbs in slow spirals up the trunks of Sapodilla (*Manilkara zapota*) and Chicozapote trees, pressing its flat green leaves against the bark. The jungle here is a study in green—Lichen, Moss, Bromeliads, Ferns—and in the middle of all that, the Vanilla vine looks almost shy. No grand buttress roots, no showy crown. Just a slender body, inching upward. Most days, it disappears into the understory and you could walk right past it. But once a year, and only for a day, it remembers that it is an Orchid.

The bud unfurls with a kind of soft urgency. A pale waxy flower opens, and for a few daylight hours the vine becomes a chandelier. The petals are the color of cream just before it boils, the throat washed with yellow like pollen dusted by hand. The scent is like Almond milk, crushed Jasmine, and green Banana peel; a faint, buttery sweetness. There is a green, almost Cucumber-cool edge at the top and a soft, powdery floral note underneath (like talc on sweaty skin). It's Vanilla stripped of its costume—no sugar, no cream, just this vegetal whisper of what it will one day become. By nightfall, if nothing has happened, the petals fold in on themselves and the chance is gone.

Somewhere in that window, a rare bee (once thought extinct) becomes the perfumer of the jungle. It is small and green, with a metallic sheen like oxidized copper—an Orchid bee. The male Orchid bee spends his days traveling from blossom to blossom, from fungi to rotting wood, composing a fragrance. He scrapes resins from bark, steals scent from rare Orchids, collects invisible molecules from places we would never think to smell, and stores them in tiny pockets on each hind leg like miniature perfume bottles.

Over weeks, he blends and edits this collection until it becomes his perfume—a species-specific cocktail with his own slight signature. Then he chooses a perch: a bare patch of trunk, a favorite branch. He fans his wings, rocking back and forth, and releases the fragrance into the air. To us it would be a faint, strange cloud—green, resinous, smoky, floral—but to a female Orchid bee, it is everything. She chooses her mate by the quality of this perfume: its complexity, its composition, the exact balance of molecules that tells her, without a doubt, who he is.

Researchers like Philipp Brand and Santiago Ramirez at UC Davis have shown that these perfumes are so specific they can actually help create new species. Two Orchid bee species can look almost identical, but differ in the chemistry of their scent bouquets and in a single smell-receptor gene that tunes what the males collect and what the females prefer. Change the perfume, and you change who talks to whom. So when a male Orchid bee visits a Vanilla flower, he isn't just running errands for the plant. He is also shopping for ingredients for his own love life.

He lands at the lip, nudges past the pale curtain of tissue that hides the pollen—that little hinged flap that defeated Europe for three hundred years—and, in the simple hunger of his own life, joins two pieces of the plant that cannot reach each other. When he flies off, dusted and satisfied and perhaps a little richer in scent, he carries the future of Vanilla on his back.

Around him, another bee hums through the understory: the *Melipona*, the stingless bee the Maya call Xunáan Kab—princess bee. For a long time, everyone said that she was the one who pollinated Vanilla, and in the old stories she still is. The truth is more complicated, as it usually is in forests. Orchid bees, *Melipona* bees, tiny wasps, and unexpected visitors—the work is shared between many small bodies and a great deal of luck. What matters to the Orchid is that someone arrives, during that brief, tender opening, and knows what to do.

When the Spaniards arrived in Mexico, they took Vanilla beans of this forest flavor and carried them across the ocean, tucking them into ships' holds alongside Cacao and Cochineal and sugar. Vanilla arrived in Europe as a celebrity. Apothecaries wrote about it as a medicine. Perfume houses obsessed over it. Noble kitchens used it to flavor desserts. The world fell in love with Vanilla.

But the plant itself refused to cooperate.

For three centuries, outside of Mexico and Central America, Vanilla vines twined politely up glasshouse trellises and refused to bear fruit. They opened their elegant waxy flowers and then let them wither, over and over again, without a single pod to show for it. The Spanish could move the vine, but they could not move the invisible choreography between flower and pollinator. The Mexican bees were too far away.

So Vanilla became a kind of horticultural riddle. Gardeners tried to brush pollen around with feathers and knives. Botanists dissected the blossoms, writing about the mysterious flap that separated male from female inside each flower, like two shy strangers at opposite ends of a room. No one quite knew how to introduce them.

It wasn't until the nineteenth century that it happened, in a colonial plantation on Réunion Island, a small French island in the Indian Ocean (east of Madagascar and southwest of Mauritius). Here, an enslaved twelve-year-old boy named Edmond Albius found the trick: lift the flap with a sliver of wood, press pollen and stigma together with a thumb, and in one quick gesture replace an entire missing insect. Suddenly, Vanilla flowers all over the tropics began to set fruit. Réunion and later Madagascar built huge Vanilla industries on his technique.

Many people on Réunion tried to secure an official stipend or public recompense for him "in recognition of his discovery," but the request stalled in colonial bureaucracy and never materialized. After the island was emancipated from slavery, he worked as a servant, was later imprisoned for a theft, and eventually had part of his sentence commuted because of his contribution to Vanilla—a grim sort of acknowledgment, but not a real reward. He died in poverty in 1880.

This is a wild inequity to sit with. Today, even if you look only at natural Vanilla beans, extracts, and flavors, you're already in big numbers with US$3–4 billion a year generated from Edmond Albius's hand-pollination method in 1841. The figures overlap a bit, but if you count Vanilla as an ingredient, it's an additional US$5 billion per year.

So even if you only counted the last 70–80 years of industrial Vanilla, and even if you assume totals from earlier decades were much smaller, you're easily into the hundreds of billions of dollars of accumulated value from natural Vanilla and extract alone. Spread that over 120–150 years since Vanilla really took off globally, and that already lands you in the ballpark of US$250–400+ billion of direct Vanilla value tied to Albius's method.

And that is still under-counting. Albius didn't just create beans. He created a flavor infrastructure. Once you can grow Vanilla at scale, you get:

(1) Ice cream: Vanilla is the #1 ice cream flavor. Vanilla accounts for roughly a quarter to a third of ice cream sales in some big markets—around US$80–120 billion a year.

(2) Bakery and confectionery: Vanilla is the invisible base note in cakes, biscuits, custards, chocolates. If even 10 percent of that market depends on Vanilla as its signature "blank canvas," that's almost US$50 billion a year of baked goods and sweets leaning on Vanilla.

(3) Fragrance: The global fragrance market is around US$50–60 billion a year, headed toward US$70–90 billion by 2030. Vanilla is one of the most widely used base notes in perfumery. If only 5–10 percent of that value involves Vanilla accords, that's another US$3–6 billion a year linked to the smell Albius made scalable.

You can argue about exact percentages, but even with painfully conservative assumptions, you're quickly in a world where Vanilla generates something like US$25–60 billion each year in goods where Vanilla is the central flavor or scent. And that's before you touch synthetics. In the US, about 90 percent of "Vanilla" used is actually synthetic vanillin, which only became a mass obsession because the world already knew and craved the real thing.

No one can give a precise number, but it's completely fair to say that the technique a twelve-year-old enslaved boy invented has created over a trillion dollars of economic value over the past 150 years. And he died penniless and almost forgotten.

Back in the wild forests of southeastern Mexico, *Vanilla planifolia*—the mother of nearly every bottle labeled "pure Vanilla extract"—still relies on rare encounters with bees and other small, anonymous couriers. Natural pollination is so unusual that botanists are still arguing about who exactly does what, and how often. The *Melipona* bee keeps her place in Maya stories and in the Honey boxes under the trees. Orchid bees glide through the air like living jewels, their perfumes shaping who they are allowed to love. Somewhere between them and the other quiet workers of the canopy, the wild pods appear.

What has become perfectly clear is how precarious all of this is.

Wild *Vanilla planifolia* in southeastern Mexico is now considered threatened. The forests where it once looped itself effortlessly from branch to branch have been thinned by cattle and Soy, roads and resorts. Climate change nudges the seasons off-key; flowers open a little earlier, or a little later, than their pollinators are ready for. On cleared land, farmers plant rows of cloned vines descended from a single genetic line, brought in from far away. They are productive, efficient, and almost identical—a green army of vines marching up posts and trellises, their flowers waiting for the toothpick method from Edmond Albius, instead of the bee.

Those tangled, half-hidden vines in Gonzalo's Yucatán jungle project are more than just plants. They are the genetic memory of Vanilla before it was industrialized—all the subtle variations in flavor, resilience, and timing that the forest bred over thousands of seasons. Lose them, and we are left with a flavor that technically still exists, but has forgotten half of what it knew.

Gonzalo and his team treat the Vanilla vines almost like elders. They leave the native forest standing, because the Vanilla needs the shade of older trees and the architecture of a real canopy. They keep pesticides far away, because the pollinators don't recognize a sprayed forest as home. They harvest sparingly, taking pods from vines that have already given some of their future back to the understory. In a world that now knows how to make Vanilla behave in a straight line, this is a decision to let it remain a little wild.

The scent that comes off those pods is not the soft, anonymous Vanilla of supermarket ice cream. Split one open with your thumb and the scent is intoxicating: First comes the familiar blanket: warm, creamy, sweet. Then the layers unfold. Dark caramel that borders on burnt sugar. A thread of pipe Tobacco and old leather, the smell of a secondhand bookshop in the rain. Dried Figs, Raisins, and Prunes soaking in rum. A hint of smoke, as if someone has just blown out a candle in the next room. There is a green brightness too, almost like

Vanilla plants growing up the tree trunks in the rainforest at Mestiza de Indias.

Martha Elena Chan Tuz harvesting heirloom Tomatoes.

Our friend Gonzalo Samaranch Granados at Mestiza de Indias, harvesting *Melipona* Honey—an arduous process that must be done with a needle and great patience. It cannot be exposed to the sun or other properties, as it ferments easily and the boxes can explode. In Mayan, the *Melipona* is called Xunáan Kab, meaning "Princess Bee." She really is a princess. Together, we've embarked on a project to help save the endangered *Melipona* bee by building a sanctuary. Photographed by Hugh Davison, winter 2025.

A detail of the *Melipona* hive.

Gonzalo's Vanilla vines growing up trees inside his bee sanctuary.

Gonzalo in front of the bee sanctuary we're helping support, built in the middle of the dense and pristine Mexican jungle with traditional materials found in the jungle.

crushed Bay leaves or the skin of an underripe Mango (*Mangifera indica*), a reminder that this started life as a green, breathing thing.

If you lean in closer, there are smaller notes, the ones you only notice if you have the time: the waxy cream of the original Orchid flower, a ghost of Lily and Almond; the sour-sweet breath of fermenting fruit; the tiniest suggestion of Cacao husk, as if the pods remember the centuries they spent married to chocolate in the same cup. It is Vanilla, yes, but it carries with it an entire ecosystem: bark and blossom, soil and sunlight, bees and humans and all the accidents that connect them.

To grow Vanilla this way, in its own home, is less like farming and more like listening. You leave the jungle standing. You let the vines choose their hosts, wrapping themselves around trunks in slow embraces. You stand back from the flowers and wait for a bee. Flamingo Estate has become quietly entangled in that listening. For the past few years we have been funding the Melipona Bee Project in Gonzalo's jungle to build habitats for these endangered bees and increase their population. It is because of these bees that every kitchen drawer in the world rattles with a bottle labeled "Vanilla."

Isn't it strange we also call something "Vanilla" when we classify it as ordinary. But there is nothing ordinary about a plant that blooms for a single day, relies on a handful of endangered insects, and then spends nine slow months turning light and rain and jungle into a black, wrinkled pod that smells like paradise. There is nothing normal about a twelve-year-old boy, enslaved on a small island, who created a way to make the world's most famous fragrance and make other people billions of dollars.

There's absolutely nothing "Vanilla" about Vanilla.

A walk through Mestiza de Indias, a 600-acre living laboratory in the middle of the Yucatán, looking for Vanilla vines growing up the trees.

Vanilla Orchid, painted by John Reagan, winter 2025.

[GROUNDING] : A MAP OF PLEASURE FROM THE GARDEN

THE POLLINATOR GARDEN

34°08' N / 118°12' W LOS ANGELES, CALIFORNIA

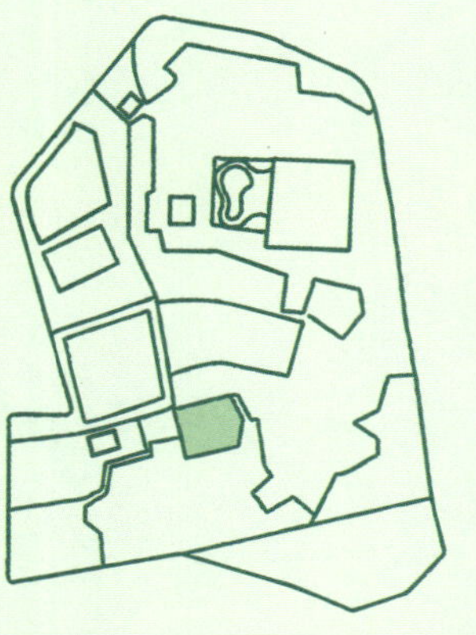

On certain afternoons, if you stand very still by the vegetable beds, you can hear a faint papery sound—the soft clap of monarch wings moving through the valley. She drifts up from the hillside, skirts the Macadamia trees, pauses over the Olives, and then beelines for the Narrowleaf Milkweed. No passport, no border control. Just a tiny body following an ancient map.

A few hundred miles from here, we've drawn hard lines across that same map. During the Trump Administration, steel bollards rose across the desert—30 feet high, 4 inches apart. They are meant to stop people, but they also stop almost everything else—the Sonoran pronghorn who travels to find water, the jaguar who needs vast, unbroken territory to find a mate, the bighorn sheep and mule deer who look for food and shade. Their corridors have been closed shut. The only ones who move freely through this fortified border are the smallest travelers: insects, birds, bats, and butterflies. Creatures light enough to slip between the bars, or high enough to fly over them. Freedom, for now, has become an airborne privilege.

The monarchs that visit Flamingo Estate belong to the Western population—cousins to the famous migrants who glide from Canada to the high forests of Central Mexico. Ours make a different pilgrimage. Each year a "super generation" is born: butterflies with longer wings, stronger bodies, wired with a mysterious inner compass. They travel astonishing distances on a tank the size of a fingernail. They have never seen the groves where they will spend the winter, yet they find them anyway, reading the position of the sun and something older—the whisper of Earth's magnetic field.

By the time they appear above our garden, they are hungry. The world they are flying through is harsher than it used to be. We've sprayed away Milkweed, traded hedgerows for highways, poured herbicides over the very plants monarch caterpillars need to live. So here, on a hillside in

Los Angeles, we decided to do something that felt both radical and embarrassingly simple: we planted flowers.

We began with the nonnegotiables. Narrowleaf Milkweed (*Asclepias fascicularis*)—the true native, not Tropical Milkweed (*Asclepias curassavica*), which refuses to rest and can throw monarchs out of rhythm. Our Milkweed knows how to disappear in winter, collapsing back into the soil so the butterflies can fall into their own seasonal sleep. In late spring it rises again, stems tipped with soft white and blush-pink flowers—a nursery and dining table in one. The monarch lays her eggs there, trusting this plant to raise her children when she is gone.

Around the Milkweed, we built a kind of pollinator airport. Not the Newark kind—the good, welcoming kind. A small, efficient terminal with great restaurants. The sort of place that stays open late because someone always arrives hungry after their flight.

California Aster (*Symphyotrichum chilense*) comes online in late summer and fall, when everything else is tired—a final gate call of purple petals before migration. California Buckwheat (*Eriogonum fasciculatum*) throws out its tiny cream pom-poms that age into rust-colored seedheads, hosting dozens of native bees who arrive in a blur, legs dusted in pollen like they've been rolling around in gold. Cleveland Sage (*Salvia clevelandii*) and Hummingbird Sage (*Salvia spathacea*) perfume the air with a wild sweetness, while Anna's hummingbirds and Allen's hummingbirds sword fight around the blossoms like tiny fencers.

Milkweed by Canadian watercolorist Robert Holmes, depicting monarch butterflies and a caterpillar on their host plant. Created for the 1916 book *Rambles of a Canadian Naturalist*.

In the hottest, driest months—when the hillsides outside the gate go beige—California Fuchsia (*Epilobium canum*) keeps burning. Little red trumpets that seem to glow from within, feeding the hummingbirds when they need it most. Coyote Brush (*Baccharis pilularis*) stands at the edges like

→
Flowers photographed by Craig P. Burrows using a technique called ultraviolet-induced visible fluorescence (UVIVF) to reveal the hidden "glow" of the natural world that is often invisible to the human eye. The chlorophyll-bearing bracts fluoresce a vivid red, contrasting sharply with the teal fluorescence of the flowers themselves, creating the striking, glowing appearance seen in the images.

a waiting room, then suddenly bursts into cream-colored flowers as autumn arrives—late-season fuel and refuge for butterflies and beetles and all the small lives that don't make it into nature documentaries.

Underfoot, California Poppies (*Eschscholzia californica*) and Tidy Tips (*Layia platyglossa*) appear in spring like spilled confetti—orange cups and yellow-and-white Daisies—feeding the first daring bees who venture out on cool mornings. Matilija Poppy (*Romneya coulteri*) throws those enormous white crepe-paper flowers like a diva in full voice. Yarrow (*Achillea*). Marigolds (*Tagetes*). Sunflowers (*Helianthus*). Rosemary (*Salvia rosmarinus*) and Lavender (*Lavandula*) edging the walkways, always busy, always giving.

Very quickly, the traffic increased. Our patch of nectar began welcoming a whole neighborhood of travelers: northern mockingbirds, lesser goldfinches, swallowtails in lemon-striped gowns. Painted ladies stop to tank up on Aster before continuing their own mysterious journeys. At dusk, bats zigzag overhead near the Bathhouse, vacuuming up the moths who spent the day hidden in the Buckwheat. Sometimes a skunk shuffles through the leaf litter, snuffling for dropped fruit and fallen seeds, becoming an accidental gardener as he goes.

The bees are the only full-time residents at our pollinator airport. And for them, the landing lights look different.

Bees do not see the world as we do. Where our spectrum runs red-orange-yellow-green-blue-indigo-violet, the bee's rainbow is shifted: ultraviolet-blue-green. They lose red almost entirely (many reds read as dark or black), but gain something we can barely imagine—the ability to see ultraviolet patterns on flowers that are invisible to the human eye.

Flowers, in turn, have learned to speak "bee" fluently.

A white Daisy or a Yarrow head that looks subtly uniform to us can be blazing with a bull's-eye to them: a distinct ultraviolet target at the center, surrounded by bright UV-reflective petals. California Poppies, Marigolds, Sunflowers—many carry fine UV stripes pointing inward like runway lights. Rosemary and Lavender often have tiny nectar guides acting as arrows, telling a bee exactly where to land and where to sip.

The bee is built to read all this. Her big compound eyes don't give her a pretty postcard—they give hard edges and contrast so she can separate flower from leaf at top speed. Above her head sit three tiny simple eyes—the ocelli—which don't form images at all. They measure light. They help her keep track of the sky. They are, in a way, the instruments on her dashboard.

And she isn't just passively looking. Watch closely and you'll see it: the bee approaches a bloom with a kind of deliberate choreography—repeated paths, small adjustments, a tilt of the body, a pause in just the right place—simplifying what she needs to solve. Her vision runs in fast-forward. Moving petals. Shifting shadows. A breeze turning the whole scene into a kaleidoscope. She still threads through it cleanly, like she has done it a thousand times. Which she has.

This is the secret choreography of a pollinator garden: flowers broadcasting instructions, bees decoding them in flight, then carrying the message onward as pollen. It is humbling to think about. We build fences and walls and think we control the map. Meanwhile, the garden is lit up with codes we can't read, and the bees are out there translating. So suddenly the monarch makes even more sense.

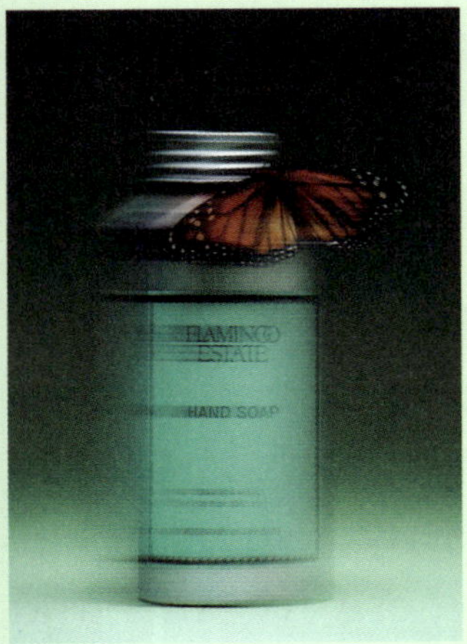

Our products are made with natural oils, like Olive and Babassu, and thickened with natural Sea Salt. They are Palm-free and fully biodegradable, made with regeneratively grown ingredients that benefit water, soil, and pollinators alike. Photographed by Hugh Davison.

The monarch is not just following Milkweed. She's following a broadcast too—a landscape that still knows how to say welcome. She arrives on empty. She needs a landing strip. She needs nectar timed to the exact weeks she passes through. She needs places to lay eggs that won't be poisoned, paved, mowed down, or sprayed away because they aren't "tidy."

When you plant for butterflies, you are building the long-haul route: host plants, nectar, seasonal continuity. When you plant for bees, you are building the neighborhood: density, variety, nutrition, and the tiny, daily transactions that keep a place alive. One is movement across distance. The other is language up close. Together, they turn a garden into infrastructure.

That's why a pollinator garden is never just a pretty border. It's a duty of care. It's also an act of civil disobedience against concrete and convenience. Each Milkweed and Buckwheat and Fuchsia becomes a refusal to believe our only job is to consume, scroll, and stay inside. When you put a plant in the ground for a bee, you are voting—quietly, with your hands—for a future that includes her. For an international airport—arrivals and departures at all hours, no visas needed.

The Pollinator Garden, painted by John Reagan, 2025.

THE FLOWERS OF FLAMINGO ESTATE

[1] Pig's Ear (*Cotyledon orbiculata*) [2] Dancing Lady Orchid (*Oncidium*) [3] Palo Verde (*Parkinsonia aculeata*) [4] Round Headed Garlic (*Allium sphaerocephalon*) [5] Fire Star Orchid (*Epidendrum radicans*) [6] Rattlesnake Plant (*Calathea crotalifera*) [7] Pincushion Protea (*Leucospermum*) [8] Sweet Coneflower (*Rudbeckia subtomentosa*) [9] Calendula (*Calendula officianalis*) [10] Stiff Sunflower (*Helianthus pauciflorus*) [11] Mexican Marigold (*Tagetes lemmonii*) [12] Wild Radish (*Raphanus raphanistrum*) [13] New Zealand Rock Lily

(*Arthropodium cirratum*) [14] California Buckwheat (*Eriogonum fasciculatum*) [15] Fennel (*Foeniculum vulgare*) [16] Mexican Tree Daisy (*Montanoa bipinnatifida*) [17] Matilija Poppies (*Romneya coulteri*) [18] Protea (*Protea*) [19] Plains Coreopsis (*Coreopsis tinctoria*) [20] Angel's Trumpet (*Brugmansia*) [21] Green Amaranth (*Amaranthus viridis*) [22] Beaked Yucca (*Yucca rostrata*) [23] Tomatillo (*Physalis philadelphica*)

[24]

[25]

[26]

[27]

[28]

[29]

[30]

[31]

[32]

[33]

[34]

[35]

[36]

[37]

[38]

[39]

[40]

[41]

[24] Red Hot Poker (*Kniphofia linearifolia*) [25] Epidendrum cinnabarinum (*Epidendrum cinnabarinum*) [26] Cymbidium devonianum (*Cymbidium devonianum*) [27] Crimson Bottlebrush (*Melaleuca citrina*) [28] Snapdragon (*Iris xiphiuelatum*) [29] Dahlia (*Dahlia*) [30] Scarlet Banksia (*Banksia coccinea*) [31] China Aster (*Callistephus chinensis*) [32] Lily (*Lilium*) [33] Redflower Gum (*Corymbia ficifolia*) [34] Garden Cosmos (*Cosmos bipinnatus*) [35] Red Calla Lily (*Zantedeschia aethiopica*) [38] Tulip (*Tulipa*) [39] Peruvian Lily (*Alstroemeria*) [40] Zinnia (*Zinnia elegans*) [41] Damask Rose (*Rosa damascena*) [42] Cabbage (*Brassica oleracea*) [43] Carnation (*Dianthus caryophyllus*)

[44] Spanish Iris (*Iris xiphium*) [45] Lacy Phacelia (*Phacelia tanacetifolia*) [46] Common Poppy (*Papaver rhoeas*) [47] Coyote Mint (*Monardella villosa*) [48] Grand Crinum Lily (*Crinum asiaticum*) [49] Canary Island Sage (*Salvia canariensis*) [50] Artichoke (*Cynara cardunculus*) [51] Fragrant Sage (*Salvia clevelandii*) [52] Passionfruit (*Passiflora edulis*) [53] Rosemary (*Salvia rosmarinus*) [54] Pride of Madeira (*Echium candicans*) [55] Candle Larkspur (*Delphinium elatum*) [56] Delphinium (*Delphinium*)

BUTTERFLIES AT THE ESTATE

CHECKERED WHITE BUTTERFLY

CABBAGE WHITE BUTTERFLY

BECKER'S WHITE BUTTERFLY

CALIFORNIA DOGFACE BUTTERFLY

CALIFORNIA HAIRSTREAK BUTTERFLY

BROWN ELFIN BUTTERFLY

JUNIPER HAIRSTREAK BUTTERFLY

GREAT PURP HAIRSTREAK BUTTERFLY

ANISE SWALLOWTAIL BUTTERFLY

GIANT SWALLOWTAIL BUTTERFLY

PALE SWALLOWTAIL BUTTERFLY

PIPEVINE SWALLOWTAIL BUTTERFLY

WESTERN TIGER SWALLOWTAIL BUTTERFLY

MOURNING CLOAK BUTTERFLY

BAY CHECKERSPOT BUTTERFLY

GULF FRITILLARY BUTTERFLY

ORANGE SULPHUR BUTTERFLY

CLOUDLESS SULPHUR BUTTERFLY

QUEEN BUTTERFLY

ECHO AZURE BUTTERFLY

ACMON BLUE BUTTERFLY

MELISSA BLUE BUTTERFLY

CERAUNUS BLUE BUTTERFLY

PACIFIC DOTTED-BLU BUTTERFLY

HARFORD'S SULPHUR BUTTERFLY

THICKET HAIRSTREAK BUTTERFLY

MOSS'S ELFIN BUTTERFLY

BLUE COPPER BUTTERFLY

PURPLISH COPPER BUTTERFLY

GOLDEN HAIRSTREAK BUTTERFLY

BEHR'S HAIRSTREAK BUTTERFLY

SYLVAN HAIRSTREAK BUTTERFLY

NORTHERN CLOUDYWING BUTTERFLY

FUNEREAL DUSKYWING BUTTERFLY

GREAT BASIN WOOD-NYMPH BUTTERFLY

WEST COAST LADY BUTTERFLY

PAINTED LADY BUTTERFLY

RED ADMIRAL BUTTERFLY

LARGE ORANGE SULPHUR BUTTERFLY

TWO-TAILED SWALLOWTAI BUTTERFLY

ARROWHEAD BLUE BUTTERFLY

GREENISH BLUE BUTTERFLY

CORONIS FRITILLARY BUTTERFLY

UNSILVERED FRITILLARY BUTTERFLY

FIELD CRESCENT BUTTERFLY

YUCCA GIANT-SKIPPER BUTTERFLY

COMMON RINGLET BUTTERFLY

GREAT BASI WOOD NYMPH BUTTERFLY

THE GARDENS AT FLAMINGO ESTATE HOST A WIDE
VARIETY OF RESIDENT AND TRAVELING SPECIES.

34°08' N / 118°12' W

BLE STREAK ERFLY	SQUARE-DOTTED BLUE BUTTERFLY	WESTERN PYGMY-BLUE BUTTERFLY	MARINE BLUE BUTTERFLY	GRAY HAIRSTREAK BUTTERFLY	HERMES COPPER BUTTERFLY	SOUTHERN DOGFACE BUTTERFLY	DAINTY SULPHUR BUTTERFLY

RCH ERFLY	PALMER'S METALMARK BUTTERFLY	FATAL METALMARK BUTTERFLY	MORMON METALMARK BUTTERFLY	COMMON SOOTYWING BUTTERFLY	SMALL CHECKERED-SKIPPER	AFRANIUS DUSKYWING BUTTERFLY	PACUVIUS DUSKYWING BUTTERFLY

RDINO D-BLUE ERFLY	COMMON CHECKERED-SKIPPER	MOURNFUL DUSKYWING BUTTERFLY	GORGON COPPER BUTTERFLY	GREAT COPPER BUTTERFLY	SPRING WHITE BUTTERFLY	CALIFORNIA MARBLE BUTTERFLY	MEXICAN YELLOW BUTTERFLY

HUNTER'S STREAK ERFLY	MOUNTAIN MAHOGANY HAIRSTREAK	HEDGEROW HAIRSTREAK BUTTERFLY	NELSON'S HAIRSTREAK BUTTERFLY	WESTERN PINE ELFIN BUTTERFLY	MALLOW SCRUB-HAIRSTREAK BUTTERFLY	WESTERN TAILED-BLUE BUTTERFLY	REAKIRT'S BLUE BUTTERFLY

ORLD LOWTAIL RFLY	AMERICAN SNOUT BUTTERFLY	CALLIPPE FRITILLARY BUTTERFLY	MILBERT'S TORTOISESHELL BUTTERFLY	CALIFORNIA TORTOISESHELL BUTTERFLY	SATYR COMMA BUTTERFLY	MYLITTA CRESCENT BUTTERFLY	NORTHERN WHITE-SKIPPER BUTTERFLY

R-SPOTTED ER RFLY	MOJAVE SOOTYWING BUTTERFLY	SALTBUSH SOOTYWING BUTTERFLY	WOODLAND SKIPPER BUTTERFLY	SACHEM BUTTERFLY	WESTERN BRANDED SKIPPER BUTTERFLY	EUFALA SKIPPER BUTTERFLY	ORANGE SKIPPERLING BUTTERFLY

[VII] JULY SUMMER	# DIRTY WORK	*"July is a blind date with Summer."* —HAL BORLAND

GARDEN TASKS:

- [ ] The first harvest arrives.
- [ ] Pomegranates: Small green globes appear; keep watered, but reduce feeding to harden growth.
- [ ] Olives: Fruit is setting—maintain consistent irrigation to avoid fruit drop.
- [ ] Mulch deeply to keep roots cool and conserve moisture (straw or leaf litter in veg beds).
- [ ] Harvest daily: Tomatoes, Zucchini, Cucumbers, Peppers, and herbs thrive with constant picking.
- [ ] Pinch Basil flowers as they form (flowers are edible); pinching encourages bushy growth.
- [ ] Cut back Mint, Dill, and Parsley—they'll regrow fresh after the heat breaks.
- [ ] Feed Tomatoes every two weeks with compost tea or worm castings.
- [ ] Water early morning to minimize evaporation and avoid fungal growth.
- [ ] In late July, start seeds of Kale, Broccoli, and Chard in trays for transplanting in late August.
- [ ] Deadhead constantly: Roses, Cosmos, Dahlias, and Marigolds bloom more with regular cutting.
- [ ] Cut Lavender, Sage, and Yarrow for drying; hang in bundles in a cool, dry place.
- [ ] Prune Wisteria and Jasmine after flowering to keep them contained.
- [ ] Feed Roses after pruning with diluted seaweed or fish emulsion.
- [ ] Feed ornamentals with compost only; stop fertilizing for the season.
- [ ] Collect seeds from Calendula, Poppies, and Nasturtiums to save for autumn sowing.
- [ ] Shade tender plants and new Cycad growth with cloth or branches during heat waves.
- [ ] Leave shallow dishes of water for birds, bees, and other thirsty visitors.

TASK ☐

GROW AN IMPRISONED PEAR

For years, we dreamed of making Imprisoned Pears the French way. The Poire Prisonnière is a Pear that grows inside its own bottle—ripening in glass before being cradled in brandy—a quiet act of suspended nature.

First practiced by artisans in Olivet, one of France's most storied fruit-growing regions, and later shown at Paris's 1889 Exposition Universelle, it became a symbol of craft and quiet elegance.

We've resurrected that delight at the Estate, and we make them for Christmas. In late spring, right after fruit set, choose one tiny Pear (marble-sized) with a long, healthy stem and slide a clean, dry glass bottle up over it so the baby Pear sits inside while the stem stays outside; tie the bottle securely to the branch and angle it slightly downward so rain or condensation can't pool inside.

Let the Pear grow all season until it fills the bottle, then harvest by cutting the stem from the tree and leaving the Pear trapped inside.

Add Vanilla bean (split) and one thin strip of Lemon zest (no pith), pour in a good brandy, seal, and stash it in a cool, dark place until it turns golden and fragrant—patience, bottled, with a perfect little treasure inside.

TASK ☐

START A SUMMER SEED COLLECTION

In summer, gather seeds from Calendula, Poppies, Nasturtiums, Sunflowers, and Zinnias—and add Cosmos, Marigolds, Sweet Peas, Nigella, Larkspur, Hollyhocks, Bachelor's Buttons, and Morning Glory if you've got them. The best hint they're ready for their next life is simple: the flower heads or pods look papery and dry, the seeds rattle when you shake them.

Snip the heads into a bowl or paper bag, let them dry a few more days, then rub them gently to release the seeds. Store everything cool and dry, in paper envelopes or little jars, and label each one with the name and date—as you will likely not remember in the future.

Come autumn, sow them back into the soil like you're planting your own time capsule.

TASK

MAKE AN ARRANGEMENT

☐

Harvey and I took an ikebana class in Tokyo and came to appreciate its meaning. Take one simple ikebana lesson, online or in person, and learn the basic idea: it's not "arranging flowers," it's composing a moment with line, space, and restraint. Ikebana comes out of Japanese tradition and treats stems like architecture; the empty space is part of the design, and every cut is intentional.

Practice Ikebana

Start with just three elements: one tall, one medium, and one short. Place them in a shallow bowl with water, and practice making the arrangement feel calm from every angle. The lesson isn't perfection—it's attention: fewer flowers, more meaning.

TASK

PLANT MILKWEED

☐

The single best thing you can do for butterflies is to plant Milkweed (*Asclepias*).

Choose the right regional Milkweed, give it full sun (at least 6 hours), loosen the soil, scatter the seeds shallowly, and water once deeply, then lightly as they germinate. Once it sprouts, you can mostly ignore it. Skip pesticides, and welcome the chewed leaves—that's how you know you did it right.

TASK

GIVE HUMMINGBIRDS NECTAR

☐

Give the birds something to eat by dissolving 1 part plain white sugar into 4 parts water.

SUGAR | WATER | WATER | WATER | WATER

Heat the water until it's just about to boil, stir until there are no crystals, then cool completely before filling your feeder. Refrigerate any extra for 3-4 days in a clean sealed container. Skip Honey, brown sugar, Agave, and anything "natural" (they can ferment or cause problems), and never add red dye—let the feeder be red if you want the color.

Clean the feeder often—every 3-4 days in cool weather, every 1-2 days in hot—rinsing thoroughly. If you ever need a short-term energy boost in colder weather, some people briefly use a 1:3 ratio, but 1:4 is the everyday gold standard.

TASK ☐

INFUSE VANILLA OLIVE OIL

We first made this for our Mexican Box in early 2025, and it was a hit. The sweetness of Vanilla is so unexpected with the grassiness of Olive oil.

Split 1 or 2 Vanilla beans lengthwise (use 2 if you want it bold), scrape in the seeds, then chop the pods into a few pieces and drop everything into a clean bottle.

Cover with good Olive oil, seal, and let it sit for 2–4 weeks in a cool, dark cupboard, shaking it whenever you remember, until the oil smells softly of Vanilla.

Strain if you want it perfectly clear, and use it on roasted Carrots and Squash, grilled seafood, salads, or ice cream.

TASK ☐

CREATE A POLLINATOR BATH

Birds, bees, and butterflies all need a different kind of garden bath. Small pollinators need a very shallow edge so they don't get stuck, and birds need a stronger perch to land and sit—most birdbaths are too deep for bees and butterflies, which is why they drown. So we made pollinator baths with different water levels with the design team at Kohler.

You can do the same at home with a shallow dish or tray filled with water, then layered with stones, pebbles, or broken terra-cotta so there are lots of tiny "landing pads" where bees, butterflies, and moths can sit, drink, and rest without falling in, while birds can perch on the larger stones and take their turn too.

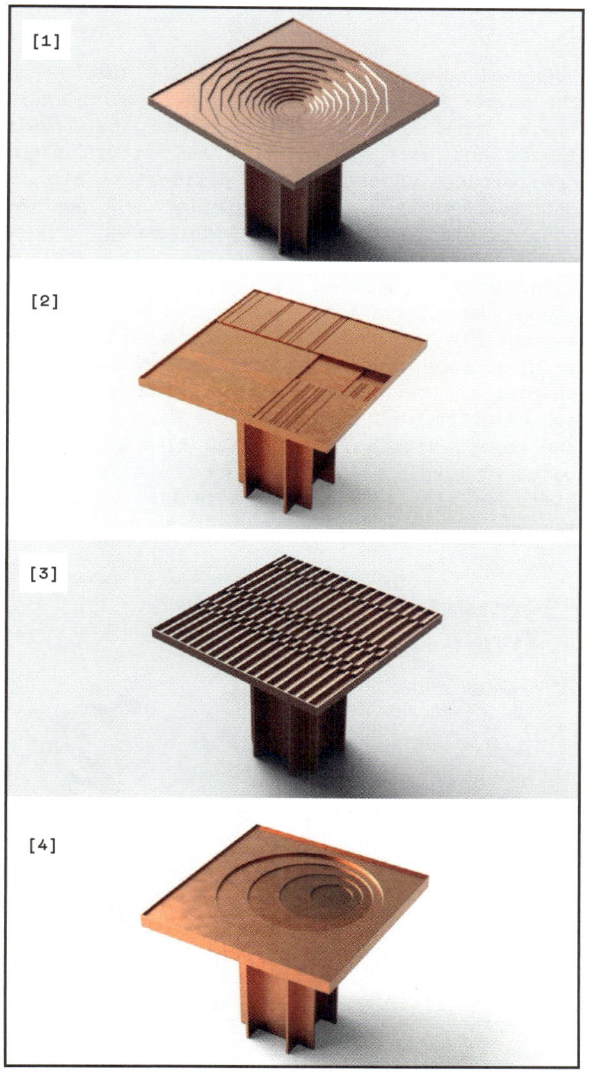

POLLINATOR BATHS MADE IN COLLABORATION WITH KOHLER FOR OUR PRESENTATION AT SALONE DEL MOBILE IN MILAN, 2026.

TASK

BECOME A BEEKEEPER

Backyard beekeeping is surprisingly doable—and the payoff is enormous: better pollination, more fruit, more flowers, and a garden that feels louder and more alive. It also matters right now, because bees and other pollinators are under real pressure. Start simple: one healthy hive is plenty. Check your local rules, choose a sunny spot with afternoon shade, add a shallow water source (pebbles in a dish so they don't drown), and get a basic setup plus a "nuc" from a reputable local keeper. Then it's mostly small, regular attention—short inspections in season, keeping the hive calm and clean, and staying on top of mites. And then comes the best part: your own Honey, bottled and labeled like a vintage—personal garden Honey is one of the most perfect gifts on Earth because it tastes like a place, a season, and your hard work.

Honey Trails

COLOR THE PATH TO CONNECT EACH BEE TO ITS FLOWER!

TASK

CRAFT Beeswax Candles

Gather your supplies: beeswax pellets, Cotton or Hemp wicks, a small pot (or double boiler), and a skewer or chopstick.

[STEP 1]
Melt the wax on low, stirring gently so it doesn't scorch.

[STEP 2]
Tie the wick to the stick, dip it into the wax to coat, let it cool until firm, and then dip again.

[STEP 3]
Keep repeating—dip, cool, dip—until the candle is the thickness you want.

[STEP 4]
If it gets a little lumpy, gently roll it between your palms to smooth it, then trim the wick and let the candle cool completely before lighting.

RECIPE

BLACK SESAME AND VANILLA JAM

INGREDIENTS:

½ cup	Japanese black Sesame paste
½	Vanilla bean, scraped
½ cup	kokuto (Okinawa dark brown sugar), cubes or granules
1 pinch	Sea Salt
1-2 Tbsp	untoasted Sesame oil

METHOD:

To a food processor, add the black sesame paste.
Cut 1 vanilla bean in half and, with a spoon, scrape the vanilla seeds from the pod and add them to the food processor.
If using kokuto cubes, simmer them in a small saucepan with 1 tablespoon of water over low heat until fully dissolved into a thick syrup. If using granules, you can add them directly to the blender.
Add the kokuto syrup (or granules), salt, and 1 tablespoon of sesame oil to the food processor. Process for 1-2 minutes until the mixture is uniform and reaches your desired "jam" thickness. Add an additional tablespoon of sesame oil if you desire a looser consistency.
In an airtight container, the jam will keep for a month in the fridge. We love to serve it with vanilla shortbread cookies.

RECIPE

FETA PHYLLO PARCEL WITH HONEY

INGREDIENTS:

1 large block	feta, drained and patted dry
1 package	phyllo pastry
¾ cup	unsalted butter, melted
1 bunch	fresh whole Chives
1 bunch	herbs and edible flowers of your liking: Lavender, Fennel blossoms, Parsley, Dill
1 drizzle	Honey, to serve

METHOD:

Preheat the oven to 415°F.
Cut feta into 4 even blocks and set aside.
Place a sheet of phyllo dough onto a clean, dry work surface. Paint a layer of butter to cover and top with another sheet of dough. Repeat until you reach 4 sheets.
Place 1 block of feta in the center and wrap to form a parcel, trimming any excess dough. Using the whole chive leaves, tie together the feta parcel and dress with a mini bouquet of herbs and flowers. Repeat with remaining pieces of feta.
Bake for 20-30 minutes, or until golden and crispy.
Serve with a drizzle of honey.

Stuffed Squash Blossom

INGREDIENTS

BEE POLLEN HONEY

1 Tbsp	local bee pollen
3 Tbsp	Wildflower Honey
¼ tsp	Salt
¼ tsp	Pepper

SQUASH BLOSSOM

1 cup	fresh whole milk ricotta
1	large egg yolk
1 Tbsp	chopped Parsley and Thyme
¼ cup	grated Parmigiano-Reggiano
12	Zucchini Squash blossoms

TEMPURA BATTER

3 cups	vegetable oil for frying
2 cups	white Rice flour
1 cup	cornstarch
1 tsp	Salt
½ tsp	baking soda
2 cups	cold club soda

METHOD

[STEP 01 : BEE POLLEN HONEY]

- In a small bowl, mix together the bee pollen, honey, salt, and pepper. Set aside.

[STEP 02 : SQUASH BLOSSOM]

- In a small bowl, mix together the ricotta, egg yolk, chopped parsley and thyme, and Parmigiano-Reggiano. Scoop mixture into a piping bag.
- Pipe ricotta mixture into each blossom and slightly twist the ends to enclose.

[STEP 03 : TEMPURA BATTER]

- Heat oil in a heavy-bottomed pan to 350°F.
- Mix remaining ingredients in a medium mixing bowl until a batter is formed.

[STEP 04 : ASSEMBLE & FRY]

- Dip each stuffed blossom into the batter and drop into the preheated oil.
- Cook for 2 minutes, or until crispy and golden, using a slotted spoon to carefully turn them as they cook.
- Drain on paper towels and finish with flaky salt. Repeat with remaining blossoms.

(NOTE: Make sure to give the batter a mix between dipping each blossom, as the rice and cornstarch can settle to the bottom over time.)

JAN.

FEB.

MAR.

APR.

MAY.

JUN.

JUL.

AUG.

SEP.

OCT.

NOV.

DEC.

NOSE DIVE
[VII]

BEE SMOKE

A beekeeper producing smoke with his smoker to calm down the bees, Germany, 1930s.

JUL.

Of all the scents at the Estate, this is perhaps my favorite. When we open the hives to harvest Honey, we pack the smoker with dried Lavender and a few Pine needles. Long after the work is done, I find myself lifting my hands to my face, inhaling the scent that clings to my fingers and clothes for the rest of the day. It is a deeply calming, woody fragrance—addictively smoky and grounding.

To understand this scent, you have to understand how a bee "sees." A hive is a dark environment; bees navigate it almost entirely through chemistry. When a guard bee senses a threat, she releases a volatile alarm pheromone, primarily isopentyl acetate, which smells sharply of overripe Bananas. It is a chemical siren that triggers a defensive cascade. Smoke works because it acts as an olfactory jammer. The heavy particulate molecules of smoke physically bind to the bees' antenna receptors, momentarily scrambling their ability to detect the alarm. It disconnects the network.

But the smoke itself is a study in transformation. When we burn dried Lavender, we are altering its molecular profile. The bright, camphorous top notes of fresh flowers (dominated by linalool) flash off quickly in the heat. What remains is the scent of the stalk and the oil undergoing pyrolysis—a process that creates phenols like guaiacol. These are the molecules responsible

Our Lavender Bee Smoke Candle. A limited-edition, 100 percent vegetable wax candle inspired by the scent of burning Lavender used to calm bees during harvesting. Featuring notes of Lavender, Piñon, Cedarwood, and smoke. Photographed by Hugh Davison, 2025.

for that deep, roasted, spicy-sweet smell we associate with incense. It is Lavender stripped of its floral vanity, reduced to its woody, herbal skeleton.

When this herbal smoke is pumped into the hive, it collides with the ambient scent of the colony: beeswax and propolis. Propolis is essentially a glue made from tree resins, rich in balsamic acids and vanillin. As the warm smoke hits the wax and resin, it heats them up, releasing a heavy, animalic musk.

The resulting fragrance is a distinct, fleeting masterpiece: the charred, sacred smell of burning Lavender and Pine; the warm, fatty scent of melting beeswax; and the sweet, caramelized note of heated Honey. It is an ancient smell that feels medicinal in the truest sense.

We became so obsessed with this specific, fleeting accord that we tried to capture it in our Bee Smoke candle and soap. We blended Lavender, Piñon, Cedarwood, Vetiver, Cypress, and Tobacco with smoked Sea Salt and charcoal to mimic that layered, resinous depth. It is a scent that relaxes me just as much as it relaxes the bees.

Photographed by Sean Hazen, 2024.

Harvesting the first spring Honey. Photographed by Pia Riverola, 2021.

August is about lust. The garden has lost all restraint. It is a month of heavy-hanging fruit—Tomatoes splitting their skins, Figs dripping with sugar, and Frangipani scenting the air like a drug. The heat is relentless, turning the orchard into a pressure cooker of smell: warm oil, crisping Lavender, and the green, feral scent of Nightshade. It is a season of absolute gluttony. We harvest faster than we

AUGUST

can eat, bottling the sun into jars, roasting the excess, and giving it away with frantic generosity. There is no modesty left; everything is ripe, sticky, and begging to be touched. The bees are drunk on Rosemary, the air smells of sweat and Basil, and the days stretch out like a long, hot exhale. We are sun-drenched and overwhelmed, surrendering to the sheer, exhausted pleasure of the peak.

Sunday by Ken Done, 1982. Currently in the collection of the Art Gallery of New South Wales, Sydney, Australia.

My earliest memories are all in the 1980s. The era of *Dynasty*, MTV, and early computer graphics—jagged fonts, grids, neon gradients. The visual language was loud and unapologetic. From Benetton to Esprit there was a kind of joyful aggression: fluorescent pink, electric blue, lime green, everything shouting over everything else. Minimalism was out; excess was in.

The Memphis Group appeared right on cue—an Italian design collective making furniture that looked like children's toys and sculptures all at once. Plastic laminate, zigzags, polka dots, impossible colors. Emotion and story were more important than function. Gaetano Pesce was one of the unruly uncles of that era, and I dreamed of meeting him. Years later, he would design the Flamingo Estate Olive Oil bottle, his last project before he died—a small piece of Memphis art sitting on our kitchen counter.

Australia, where I grew up, was busy inventing its own color language. Architects like Harry Seidler, Philip Cox, and Glenn Murcutt were building houses that belonged to the Australian landscape instead of copying Europe. Ken Done was painting Sydney Harbor, coral reefs, and the outback in brushstrokes of pure joy—hot pinks, acid yellows, unapologetic blues—and then printing them on everything from bedsheets to beach towels. He was our Hockney, but with more sunscreen.

We lived on a farm at the end of a dirt road. The closest thing I had to this world of glamour was the mailbox: an old milk barrel, turned on its side, where the postman dropped my mother's magazines each month. *Vogue Living* arrived like a visitation. I read it cover to cover, dreaming about a future house full of color and art, with a garden full of plants I had never seen in person. One of the houses that appeared again and again on my bedroom wall was Ken Done's own home on Sydney Harbor. Glenn Murcutt designed it—all white walls and clean lines—wrapped around a pool and a single magnificent Frangipani tree.

A Frangipani tree blooms over the pool at Australian artist Ken Done's home on Sydney Harbor, designed by the acclaimed architect Glenn Murcutt.

The Frangipani was the star. Its crooked branches and luminous flowers were framed perfectly by Murcutt's walls and Done's paintings. It turned up in his canvases like a recurring character: *Frangipani, 1984*; *Sunday, 1982*; and many others. As a little boy, all I wanted was to grow up and have a Frangipani tree leaning over my own pool, like Ken.

Seated along the bustling streets of Honolulu in the early twentieth century, these Native Hawaiian lei vendors showcase the thriving floral trade of the late Kingdom era. This hand-colored lantern slide by Christian J. Hedemann captures the transition of the lei from a sacred cultural symbol to a commercial emblem of Hawaiian hospitality. Among the blossoms are the then-recently introduced Frangipani, which would soon become the world's most recognizable symbol of the Aloha spirit.

The flowers felt made for the '80s. The most common variety in Australia was white with a fluorescent yellow center that looked almost airbrushed on—like an MTV logo drawn by nature. The natural palette runs from bright white and lemon through apricot, mango, hot pink, and bruised orange all the way to deep plum. They are Memphis in plant form: strong outline, high contrast, too much and just right at the same time.

It's a common misconception that the Frangipani is native to Hawaii, because it appears in almost every lei. In truth, the plant—Plumeria—is native to Mexico, Central America, and the Caribbean, spreading down into Brazil. It only arrived in Hawaii in the mid-nineteenth century with a German botanist, Dr. William Hillebrand, who planted it in Honolulu. From there, it slipped into every corner of island life. Hawaiians called it pua melia and folded it into the story of aloha—welcome, farewell, affection, and the promise of return. To be given a lei of Frangipani is to be told, without words, "you are wanted here."

Frangipani is also a plant of resurrection. In cooler months the tree drops all its leaves and sits there like a bundle of gray bones, absolutely lifeless. People who don't know it assume it's dead and dig it out. But when the warmth returns, the bare branches suddenly push out new leaves and spray the air with flowers that smell like nothing else on Earth. It is a masterclass in not judging a body by the state of its surface. This is part of why, in so many cultures, Frangipani stands for rebirth, immortality, and the soul's return: a plant that looks finished and then quietly decides not to be.

Which brings us to the fragrance.

The perfume of the Frangipani is color turned into air. The first inhale is bright and fizzy: Citrus sparkle and Green Apple, a bite of Peach. Then, as the waxy petals warm, a soft, creamy sweetness appears—custard, whipped cream, and a hint of Honey. In the base there is often a faint Coconut roundness, a touch of musk, sometimes even an Almond–Vanilla shadow, like the memory of a dessert. It is heady, tropical, and strangely refined: a scent that feels like standing on wet tiles by a pool at dusk, still in your swimsuit, sunscreen and salt clinging to your skin.

Curiously, the name "Frangipani" doesn't come from the flower at all. In the 1600s an Italian nobleman, Marquis Muzio Frangipani, created a scent for perfumed gloves—leather being one of the great luxuries of the time. His perfume, used to scent fine gloves in Europe, mixed Orris Root, spices, civet, and musk. It was creamy, exotic, Almondy, Vanilla-like, and became famous simply as "Frangipani."

About a century later, a French colonist encountered *Plumeria alba* in the West Indies. When its blossoms opened, he smelled something eerily like the Frangipani glove perfume from home. The name stuck to the plant. So you have this rare reversal: a flower named after a fragrance, instead of the other way round. Half the world calls it Frangipani, the other half Plumeria, but either way the plant is permanently tied to the idea of perfume.

Perfumers who want to work with it face a problem. The flowers are delicate and the yield of natural oil is tiny. True Frangipani absolute exists, but it is extremely rare and expensive, produced in only a few places by solvent extraction. Most "Frangipani" in modern perfumery is a fantasy accord—built from Jasmine, Ylang-Ylang, Orange blossom, lactonic notes, Coconut, Vanilla, and musk. This accord shows up in scents like Hermès Un Jardin sur le Nil and Tom Ford's Soleil Blanc—fragrances that are creamy, solar, and a little lazy, like the hour after lunch when the pool is warm and the air smells of lotion and fruit.

This 1903 postcard reflects the cultural revival spearheaded by King Kalākaua, who returned hula to public view after decades of missionary suppression. However, as a commercial product of the post-annexation era, the image utilizes "Orientalist" tropes, staging the dancers to appear "exotic" for a Western audience. The prominent use of Frangipani blossoms highlights the flower's rise as Hawaii's premier commercial emblem. While not used in the sacred hula rituals of Hawaii's past, the flower's hardy nature and intense fragrance made it ideal for a romanticized icon of the Pacific.

What I love most is that, for all this sunshine, the flower does its real work at night. Frangipani produces no nectar; instead, it evolved exquisite fragrance to trick its pollinators. In many places a sphinx moth is the main visitor: a night-flying, long-tongued moth that follows scent rather than color. The tree pumps out fragrance after dark, broadcasting an irresistible promise of food it doesn't actually offer. The moth, fooled, pushes deep into the flower, finds nothing, and flies to the next one to try again—carrying pollen on its body the whole time. It is a very beautiful scam.

Long before Europeans started pinning it to their moodboards, Frangipani was already heavy with meaning. In parts of Mesoamerica it was a flower of nobility and status: grown in palace gardens, worn by rulers, used in offerings and medicine. To have Frangipani in your courtyard was to announce that your life was doing better than most. In Aztec and Maya cosmology, flowers were a way to talk about the "flower world"—a heavenly place of music, perfume, and joy—and Frangipani was one of the plants that belonged to that realm.

When I was in my thirties, I walked into a Frangipani grove in India: dozens of trees planted around a courtyard, all blooming at

My Frangipani tree by the pool, painted by John Reagan, 2025.
Dreams do come true.

once. The air was thick with scent. In India, Frangipani is often linked to immortality and the soul's endurance, because the plant can continue to flower even from cut branches and stumps. You see it planted near temples, in ashrams, in graveyards: a quiet statement that life is not a straight line, and endings aren't always the end. When I finally moved into my own temple—Flamingo Estate—I went hunting for Frangipani trees to plant next to the pool. I had been dreaming of that picture since I was a boy staring at Ken Done's house in *Vogue Living*: white walls, blue water, and a Frangipani leaning in like a gossip. They are fragile and slow-growing, so large specimens are rarely available. After an exhausting search, I found some on Craigslist for around $30 each. A woman nearby needed to remove her trees to build a garage. I bought them immediately, closed the street, and craned them over the house into their new home.

Now they stand by the pool, just where I imagined them, throwing their crooked shadows across the water in summer and their bare bones across the tiles in winter. I look at them every morning with my coffee, breathe in that luminous scent when they flower, and thank them for being proof that some fantasies are worth holding on to. Inside, facing the pool, hang some of my Ken Done paintings, collected slowly in my thirties and forties. One of them is covered in what I imagine to be the most deliciously scented Frangipanis—the flower that gave my imagination wings. It is my most cherished possession, because it reminds me that a boy at the end of a dirt road in Australia can grow up to plant his own 1980s dream tree above a Californian pool and call it home.

The Lei Day Queen, along with her attendants, descending a flight of stairs in Honolulu adorned in traditional Frangipani leis. Honolulu, 1935.

[GROUNDING] : A MAP OF PLEASURE FROM THE GARDEN

THE TOMATO GARDEN

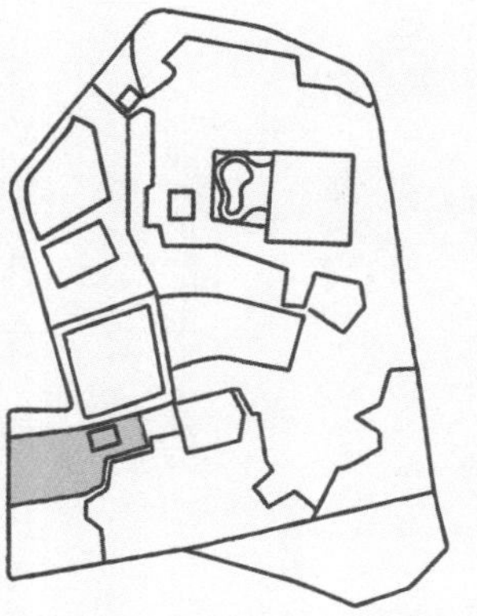

34°08' N / 118°12' W LOS ANGELES, CALIFORNIA

They were once small, wild things in the Andes and Mesoamerica, more like hard red Currants than the glossy supermarket cricket balls we know now. They came in colors we've almost forgotten: yellow, orange, brick red, black; some striped or marbled; some shaped like little Peppers, some like ox hearts, some like ribbed Pumpkins. The flavors were varied but powerful—spicy, sweet, sometimes tannic and very herbaceous. The Aztecs called them *Xitomatl* and stirred them into Chili, ground seeds, and Chocolate long before anyone in Italy thought to pair them with pasta.

When Tomatoes finally staggered into European gardens in the sixteenth century, they arrived as a handful of strange, shimmering fruits: often yellow ("golden apples"), often deeply ribbed, often bitter, always slightly suspect because of their Nightshade family. For a long time they were grown as curiosities in monastery gardens and villa courtyards, more conversation piece than dinner. It took two or three centuries for them to creep into peasant pots and then onto middle-class plates.

A huge harvest of Roma Heirloom Tomatoes washed in the garden fountain. Photographed by Leslie Kirchhoff, summer 2022.

A 1956 magazine ad for Hunt's Tomato ketchup. By using high-fashion aesthetics and the "Hunt . . . for the Best" campaign, the brand elevated this pantry staple to become a formidable national competitor, challenging the industry's long-standing leaders.

By the time the nineteenth century rolled around, the plant that had once been feared as poison had a whole cast list of local names and shapes: *Costoluto* from Genoa, *Cuore di Bue* from Piedmont, *Principe Borghese* from Lazio, *Stupice* from Czechoslovakia. In Mexico you might harvest small red-and-black Tomatoes with spicy, almost smoky juice; in Campania you'd be simmering long, thin San Marzanos into ragù and pizza sauce; on the slopes of Vesuvius people were braiding little Piennolo Tomatoes and hanging them from kitchen ceilings like red chandeliers, to be plucked all winter.

We have this idea that Tomatoes have always been one thing—the red circle on a burger—but they used to be wonderfully inconsistent. Every valley had its own favorite. Every Nonna, every Tío, every backyard madman saved seeds from their plant and called it by the family name. You could tell where you were in the world by what your Tomato tasted like.

Then we invented supermarkets.

As soon as we learned how to ship fresh produce at scale—on trains, then trucks, then planes—soft-skinned fruit quietly became a liability. It bruised. It leaked. It offended the spreadsheets. So breeders, especially in the mid-twentieth century in Florida, California, and southern Europe, began selecting Tomatoes that could be picked green, ripened later with ethylene gas, stacked six deep in a crate, and shipped halfway across the world.

They engineered varieties for hard skin, firm flesh, uniform color, and synchronized ripening. One famous gene, the "uniform ripening" mutation, gives that perfect, even red you see in the shop, but at the cost of sweetness—it switches off some of the leaf's ability to make sugars. Another set of mutations keeps Tomatoes firmer for weeks, but also keeps them tasting like damp cardboard. None of this was a conspiracy;

Farm trucks in Camden, New Jersey, packed to the brim with bushel baskets of ripe Tomatoes, ready for markets, 1930s.

Philadelphia seedsman Robert Buist was a pioneer in horticultural marketing, using vibrant lithography to turn functional crops into fine art. In the early- to mid-1800s, many people still viewed Tomatoes with suspicion (or even as poisonous). Pioneers like Buist helped change public perception by making them look irresistible and "solid" in these illustrations.

An illustrated crate label for 'Campy' tomatoes, one of many brands created by distributor J.V. Campisi to market Florida-grown produce nationwide, circa 1930–1950.

↓ Ads for Heinz Tomato soup, often featuring children in vibrant illustrations to promote health and well-being.

it was simple: shippability and profit came first. The same fate waited for countless other fruits and vegetables.

In the process, hundreds of varieties of Tomatoes fell out of circulation. Thin-skinned hearts that bruise if you sigh on them. Fluted Italian salad Tomatoes that collapse into sauce on the walk home. "Black" Tomatoes from Eastern Europe that look spoiled before they are ripe. Yellow Cherries that explode as soon as you pick them. All the fruit that only wanted to travel from the field to the kitchen vanished from the catalogs to make room for fruit that could survive a flight across the ocean. Now you can eat a Tomato in Honolulu that tastes almost exactly like a Tomato in Houston, and neither has much to say.

But the wild names are still out there if you go looking:

Brandywine—an Amish beefsteak from the 1800s that tastes like red wine and sunshine and has more lobes than is sensible. Cherokee Purple—dusky, smoky, sweet, said to come from seeds shared by a family in Tennessee who got them from the Cherokee. Green Zebra—neon green with yellow stripes, bred as a small rebellion against red sameness; tangy and sharp, like biting into a Lime. Black Krim, Paul Robeson, Carbon—so dark they look bruised, with a slightly salty, iron-rich flavor.

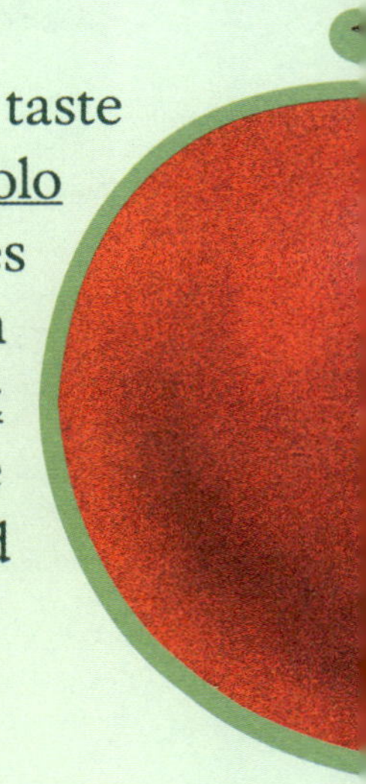

Jaune Flamme—small orange lanterns that taste like Tangerines and late afternoon. Piennolo del Vesuvio—tiny, pointed Tomatoes grown in volcanic soil and hung in clusters to sweeten over months. Aunt Ruby's German Green—big, chartreuse fruit that tastes of sweet white wine and Green Apple.

Tigerella—red-and-orange striped, like someone painted flames on a Tomato. Mortgage Lifter—huge, pink beefsteaks bred by a mechanic in West Virginia in the 1930s to pay off his debts; he sold seedlings until his mortgage was gone.

Down in Mexico, my friend Gonzalo Samaranch at Mestiza de Indias is hunting down endangered Tomatoes, begging for seeds from elders, swapping packets, smuggling in unusual varieties. His Tomato rows are full of fruit from another time—some striped, some half black and half red, some that taste like spice, some like sweet wine (you can read more about Gonzalo in the July chapter).

At places like Seed Savers Exchange in Iowa, thousands of Tomato varieties like these are being kept alive in jars and envelopes—each one with a story attached. "Sent in by an 82-year-old man whose father brought this variety from Italy in 1912." "Saved from a garden in Alabama, 1950s." "Grown by a Black farmer in Ohio who named it after his wife." Seed Savers Exchange now stewards tens of thousands of heritage crops; Tomatoes are one of their largest and loudest collections. But Seed Savers is just one ark. There are others.

In Missouri, Baker Creek Heirloom Seeds prints a catalog so thick it feels like a phone book from Mother Nature. Page after page of Tomatoes with names that sound like gossip or folk songs: Black from Tula, Barry's Crazy Cherry, Blue Beauty, Nepal, Purple Bumble Bee.

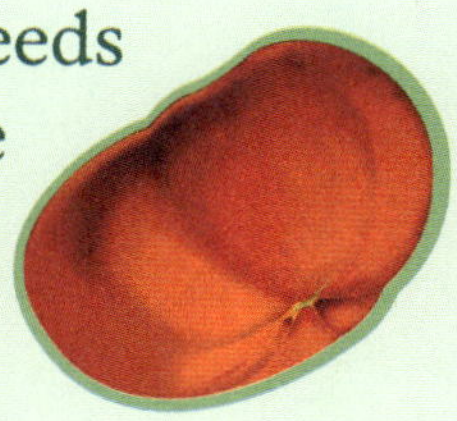

My favorite is Wild Boar Farms, which breeds the most unusual-looking varieties. Founder Brad Gates has given us things like Atomic Fusion, Apollo's Chariot, Berkeley Tie-Dye, Chestnut Chocolate, Cherokee Rose, Kryptonite, Justin's Fire Opal, and Solar Vortex—all of which are growing now in the Flamingo Tomato Garden.

↑

Giving our freshly plucked Tomatoes a quick rinse, which would inspire an entire line of Flamingo Estate Tomato products for the kitchen featuring Dish Soap, Hand Soap, and Surface Spray. Photographed by Pia Riverola, summer 2025.

→

The harvest! Photographed by Pia Riverola for us in Mexico City, 2021.

So if you're reading this and wondering where to begin, the answer is: with one packet of seeds from people like these. Growing Tomatoes is a powerful way to resist the industrial food system. Supermarkets have optimized Tomatoes to fit boxes and forgotten they were supposed to fit mouths. We've devoted a whole section of the garden at Flamingo to Tomatoes that would fail every supermarket test: too soft, too weird, too striped, too ugly, too alive. We save seeds. We trade envelopes with friends. We get possessive about a flavor and then share it anyway. This is how you fix a tiny piece of the world: you plant something that cannot survive a truck, and you eat it right where it grew.

Our Roma Heirloom Tomato Candle is the first Candle we ever made, and to this day our #1. It's the scent of Flamingo Estate—inspired by the green, peppery scent that's released on balmy summer nights when we've just watered the garden. Photographed by Hugh Davison.

No Tomato talk would be complete unless we also talk about the smell. Most people's first memory of a Tomato plant isn't the taste at all. It's that green, feral smell on your fingers after you've touched a vine.

Our Tomato candle was the first real hit we ever had, and it's still our most-loved product. People tell us they light it and suddenly they're eight years old again in their grandmother's garden, or in some rented house in Puglia, or standing barefoot in the Flamingo beds in August. It doesn't smell like pasta sauce or sun-dried Tomatoes. To me, Tomato leaf smells like trouble in the best possible way. Sharp, green, a little bitter. There's cut grass in it, and Nettles, and that strange metallic note you get when you snap a Bean in half. It's not polite. It rushes up your nose and wakes you up. It smells like chlorophyll and sap, like something that grew under a hot sun and isn't entirely sure it wants to be picked.

When we made the Flamingo Estate Heirloom Tomato Candle, I was very clear about one thing: it had to smell like the plant, not the pantry. I wanted that first noseful you get when you push open the gate to the Vegetable Garden in late afternoon. It's built around crushed Tomato leaves and stems, wild-harvested Tarragon, and Black Pepper Essential Oil from

Tomatoes hanging from our Terrace, drying in the sun. Photographed by Drew Escrivá.

Warhol's delicious masterpiece.

Andy Warhol,
Campbell's Soup I: Tomato,
1968.
Screenprint on white paper
35 × 23 inches

flowering vines in the forests of Madagascar. I am still amazed that so many people love our Tomato candle (and that so many brands have copied it). It was not a predictable scent, and not an easy idea.

In a way, the Tomato candle is the domestic version of everything I'm trying to say in this chapter. In a world where Tomatoes have been flattened into "product," insisting on the perfume of a real, misbehaving Tomato leaf is its own small act of rebellion against the synthetic Vanilla candles we see everywhere. So yes, plant the rare seeds, fight for the soft skins and the strange shapes. But also pay attention to the smell on your hands when you stake a vine or tie it up with string. Save that scent. Share your seeds. And celebrate everyone—and everything—with thin skin.

A slice of the impossible: Two women pose with "giant" Tomatoes in this 1911 tall-tale postcard by A. L. Johnson. Before digital editing, photographers used multiple exposures and careful cutouts to create these horticultural illusions.

Love Apples with Red Fruit by artist Basilius Besler, 1613.

[VIII] AUGUST SUMMER	# DIRTY WORK	*"August creates as she slumbers, replete and satisfied."* —JOSEPH WOOD KRUTCH

GARDEN TASKS:

- [ ] Harvest Figs daily when soft and fragrant—birds and wasps are waiting.
- [ ] Keep Citrus watered deeply but pause feeding for slow, steady development.
- [ ] Mulch trees deeply with compost to cool roots and retain moisture.
- [ ] Harvest Zucchini, Cucumbers, and Peppers often to keep plants fruiting.
- [ ] Cut Mint, Oregano, Thyme, and Rosemary for drying.
- [ ] Sow cool-season crops in shade: Kale, Chard, Carrots, Lettuce, and Beets.
- [ ] Feed tired soil with compost or diluted Seaweed extract.
- [ ] Prune Roses lightly and feed for a late-summer flush.
- [ ] Cut back Sage and Lavender by one-third after flowering.
- [ ] Plant heat-tolerant greens like Malabar Spinach, Amaranth, or Purslane.
- [ ] Turn compost piles weekly and keep lightly damp.
- [ ] Water trees deeply every 10–14 days to reach roots below the dry layer.
- [ ] Freeze Mint, Basil, and Tomato water in ice trays for drinks.
- [ ] Soak Tomato leaves in water overnight to make a natural aphid repellent.
- [ ] Shade tender plants and new Cycad growth with cloth or branches during heat waves.
- [ ] Blend Garlic and water with a drop of soap for a general pest spray.

TASK

MAKE BBQ SAUCE ☐

This is our twist on the classic, and an August favorite at the Flamingo table.

INGREDIENTS:

1½ lb	ripe Strawberries, hulled
1 cup	chopped ripe Tomatoes
¼ cup	Wildflower Honey
¼ cup	balsamic vinegar
2 Tbsp	Lime juice, optional: a little zest
1-2 tsp	Urfa Chili, start small, add more if you want heat
1 tsp	smoked Paprika
½ tsp	purple Peppercorns
½ tsp	smoked Sea Salt
2 Tbsp	Olive oil, stirred in at the end

OUR TWIST ON A CLASSIC

HOW TO MAKE IT:

Cook it down:
Add strawberries, tomatoes, honey, balsamic, and lime juice to a saucepan. Simmer gently 15-25 minutes, stirring, until everything collapses and turns glossy.

Blend:
Blend until smooth (immersion blender or countertop).

Season and thicken:
Return to low heat and stir in Urfa chili, smoked paprika, crushed peppercorns, and smoked sea salt. Simmer 5-10 minutes more, until it coats the back of a spoon.

Finish:
Turn off the heat and whisk in the olive oil for shine and depth. Taste and adjust—more Balsamic for tang, more honey for sweetness, more smoked salt for BBQ attitude, more Urfa for fire.

HOW TO USE IT:

Store + Use: Cool, jar, and refrigerate up to 2 weeks. Brush on grilled chicken or pork, spoon over roasted vegetables, or use as a sticky glaze for anything that hits a hot pan.

TASK

SCRUB WITH A TOMATO

This skin mask is for dull, tired skin. Your skin will be brighter, softer, more hydrated in 10 minutes. Tomato's natural acids help lift dullness and refine texture. Honey acts as a humectant, so skin feels plumper and less tight. Yogurt contributes gentle lactic acid and a cooling softness. Turmeric lends a warm, even-looking glow. A few drops of Lemon can brighten—but it's powerful, so treat it like seasoning, not a main ingredient.

INGREDIENTS:

½	sun-warmed Tomato
1 tsp	Wildflower Honey
1 Tbsp	plain yogurt
1 pinch	Turmeric
2 drops	Lemon

HOW TO MAKE IT:

Crush the tomato with your fingers until it becomes a fragrant, ruby pulp. Stir in the honey. Fold in yogurt, turmeric, or lemon—whatever your skin is asking for today. This is intuition, not instruction.

HOW TO USE IT:

With clean hands, smooth over your face. Leave on for 5–10 minutes, then rinse with warm water. Pat dry. Admire the radiance only plants can pull forward.

TASK

BITE THE BEST TOMATO SANDWICH

Slice 1 or 2 peak-season Tomatoes thick, salt them, and let them drip for 5–10 minutes.

Mayo two slices of soft white bread, add Dijon if you want backbone, then pile the Tomatoes high with zero regard for structural integrity.

Finish with flaky Salt and cracked Pepper. A proper Tomato sandwich should be a beautiful mess.

If it's tidy, try again.

TASK ☐

Drink the Bloody Mary

A Bloody Mary is basically a farmers market with a liquor license, and ours sticks to Pete Petiot's classic 1920s formula from Harry's New York Bar in Paris:

Shake 1.5 oz vodka, 3 oz Tomato juice, 0.5 oz Lemon juice, 2-3 dashes Worcestershire, 2 dashes Tabasco, plus pinches of Celery salt, black Pepper, and optional smoked Paprika or Horseradish.

Pour over ice and garnish with a Celery stalk, Lemon wedge, and Olives and/or a Pickle spear.

RECIPE

STEAMED EGG WITH CONFIT TOMATO

INGREDIENTS:

3 cups	Cherry Tomatoes, preferably on the vine
3 cloves	Garlic, crushed with a knife
1 tsp	Lemon zest
1 tsp	Salt
1 tsp	Peppercorns
2 cups	Olive oil
Optional	aromatics like Basil, Thyme, and Rosemary to the confit for added flavor

STEAMED EGG:

4	eggs
½ tsp	Salt
½ tsp	tamari
1 Tbsp	neutral oil
2 cups	warm water (95-113°F)

METHOD:

CONFIT TOMATOES:

Preheat oven to 300°F.
Place all ingredients into a heavy-bottom, oven-safe dish.
Top with a piece of parchment paper cut to fit the top of the dish and pressed down so it touches the top of the oil.
Bake to confit the tomatoes for 1 hour.

STEAMED EGG:
Prepare a deep-set pot with a metal steamer insert over medium-high heat and cover with a lid.
Whisk eggs, salt, tamari, and oil in a bowl, streaming in the water as you whisk.
Pour the egg mixture into small heatproof ramekins and turn the heat up on your pot to boil the water and create steam. Remove the steamer pot lid and gently place ramekins into the steamer basket.

Close the steamer lid, turn the heat down to low, and cook for 8 minutes. The egg custard should be jiggly and silky to the touch when done.
Carefully remove the ramekins using an oven mitt or tea towel.

ASSEMBLY:

Serve the steamed egg with a sprinkling of flaky salt, a generous amount of confit tomatoes, and topped with a drizzle of the confit oil and Flamingo Estate Balsamic Vinegar.

RECIPE

PICKLED MACKEREL & GREEN TOMATOES

INGREDIENTS:

1 cup	white wine vinegar
1½ cups	water
2 Tbsp	sugar
2 tsp	Salt, plus more for the mackerel
1 tsp	black Peppercorns
3	small green Tomatoes, cut into wedges
2	Shallots, peeled and thinly sliced
3	cloves Garlic, thinly sliced
2	mackerel fillets, pin-boned

METHOD:

Add vinegar, water, sugar, salt, and peppercorns to a saucepan over low heat, dissolving the sugar and salt to make a brine. While the pickle brine is still hot, add green tomatoes, shallots, and garlic, and set aside to cool completely.

To prepare the mackerel fillets, generously cover with salt and leave unwrapped in the refrigerator for up to 1 hour. Rinse the fillets well and pat dry.

Add the mackerel to the pickle brine and leave to pickle in the refrigerator for up to 4 hours.

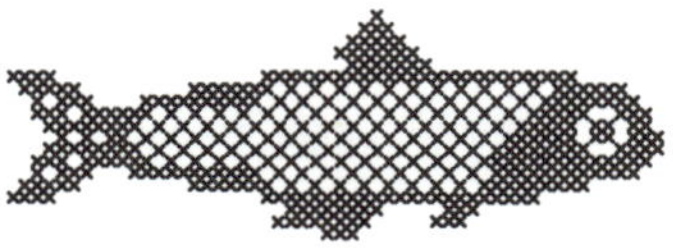

Enjoy slices of mackerel and pickled green tomatoes over a piece of toast with mayo, freshly cracked pepper, and olive oil.

GRAPE FRANGIPANE *Tart*

INGREDIENTS

ROASTED GRAPES

2 bunches	red Grapes
3 Tbsp	Olive oil
1 tsp	flaky Salt

ALMOND CREAM FILLING (FRANGIPANE)

½ cup	unsalted butter, room temperature
½ cup	granulated sugar
2	large eggs, room temperature
¾ cup	ground Almonds
5 Tbsp	all-purpose flour
½ tsp	fine Salt

TART SHELL DOUGH

2½ cups	all-purpose flour
½ tsp	Salt
1 cup	butter, chilled and cut into cubes
1	large egg
¼ cup	water, chilled
½ cup	cream, chilled

METHOD

[STEP 1 : ROASTED GRAPES]

- Preheat oven to 400°F.
- Prepare a sheet tray lined with parchment paper.
- Place the grapes on the prepared tray and generously drizzle with olive oil, and sprinkle with flaky salt.
- Roast the grapes for 30–40 minutes, until juices run and the skins have lightly crisped and charred.

[STEP 2 : FRANGIPANE]

- Using a whisk, cream the butter and sugar together in a bowl until light and fluffy.
- Add the eggs one at a time, whisking to fully incorporate each egg before adding the next.
- Switch to a spatula and mix in ground almonds, flour, and salt.
- Scoop mixture into a piping bag and set aside.

[STEP 3 : TART SHELL DOUGH]

- Gently whisk together flour and salt in a large bowl.
- Toss in butter cubes and, using your thumbs and index fingers, work in the butter by pressing the cubes into the flour to form flattened pieces. Keep the bowl in the fridge while you wash your hands and move on to the next step.

- In a small bowl, whisk together the egg, water, and cream. Remove the bowl of butter from the fridge and pour the egg mixture over the flour. Use a spatula to mix and gather into a dough ball. Turn out the dough and wrap tightly in plastic wrap. Leave to rest in the fridge for 30 minutes.
- Lightly flour a clean working surface.
- Unwrap dough onto a lightly floured working surface and roll out until you reach 2-inch thickness. Turn the dough as you roll and dust with flour as needed to prevent it from sticking to your work surface.
- Cut the sheet of dough to fit your 9-inch tart tin and trim the edges. Chill again for 5 minutes, or until ready to use.

[STEP 4 : ASSEMBLY]

- Preheat oven to 375°F.
- Pipe the frangipane filling on the bottom of the tart shell, filling halfway up.
- Place the whole roasted grapes and press down into the frangipane filling.
- Bake the tart on the middle rack of your oven for 40 minutes, or until golden brown and puffed.
- Serve with a generous wedge of blue cheese and honey.

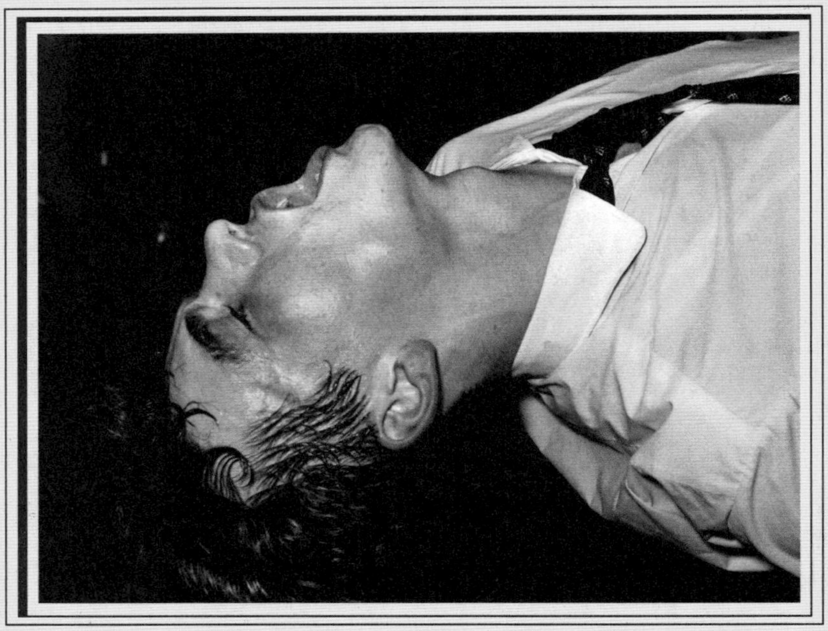

NOSE DIVE
[VIII]

SWEAT

Desire. What does it smell like? Perfume commercials have capitalized on the question of desire, but the truth is, it has nothing to do with what we spray on our bodies. It is about who we are when stripped bare. With nothing but skin and sweat, we remember the animals that we are. Sweaty and aroused, we inhale and know to be pulled toward the flesh of another. When it comes to sex, our primal, intuitive "YES" always begins with smell.

Sweat itself is mostly water and electrolytes. The smell arrives when it meets the skin's ecosystem: oils, minerals, and a bustling microbiome that breaks those secretions down into volatile molecules—musky, metallic, sometimes sweet. There are different kinds of sweat, too. Eccrine sweat (the watery kind) cools you down. Apocrine sweat (released around the underarms and groin) is richer in fats and proteins, and becomes much more aromatic once bacteria get involved. Emotional sweat often leans more apocrine-heavy—richer, stickier, quicker to develop a scent.

AUG.

We like to call these invisible cues "pheromones," but in humans it's more accurate to say "chemosignals": tiny chemical hints that can carry information about familiarity and desire. Skin is the canvas. It absorbs, warms, and transforms scent. That's why no perfume smells the same on two people, and why your lover's T-shirt can feel like a spell. In August, when someone comes in from the garden—sun-flushed, dirty at the edges, threaded with sweat—the smell is complex and alive: salty and warm, slightly ripe, intensely human. Get closer and it turns creamy and sweet, a little musky, like Sandalwood and Honey melted into cotton drying in the sun.

In the garden, this sexual chemistry is a life force. Courtship is clear and uncomplicated: bees swoon over Jasmine and moths court Brugmansia unabashedly. But nature can also be vulgar. The Bradford Pear—infamously known as the "cum tree"—releases a heavy, semen-like scent when it blooms. The

Sugar Ray Robinson, sweating in the dressing room after a win against Charley Fusari, in what would become an iconic photograph titled *Post Match Sugar Ray Robinson*, Atlantic City, 1950.

The sweaty taste of summer. Photographed at Flamingo Estate by Pia Riverola, summer 2022.

volatiles released by its white flowers are molecularly similar to ammonia, which is also found in human semen. It is a scent that is strong, metallic, and explicit in its purpose.

We, too, are meant to get tangled in these smells. The perfume industry often tries to scrub us clean, but sex is nothing without our own scent. The point isn't to eliminate our odor, but to listen to it. Sweat, hair, and real blood pumping in the folds—that is the true smell of desire.

AUG.

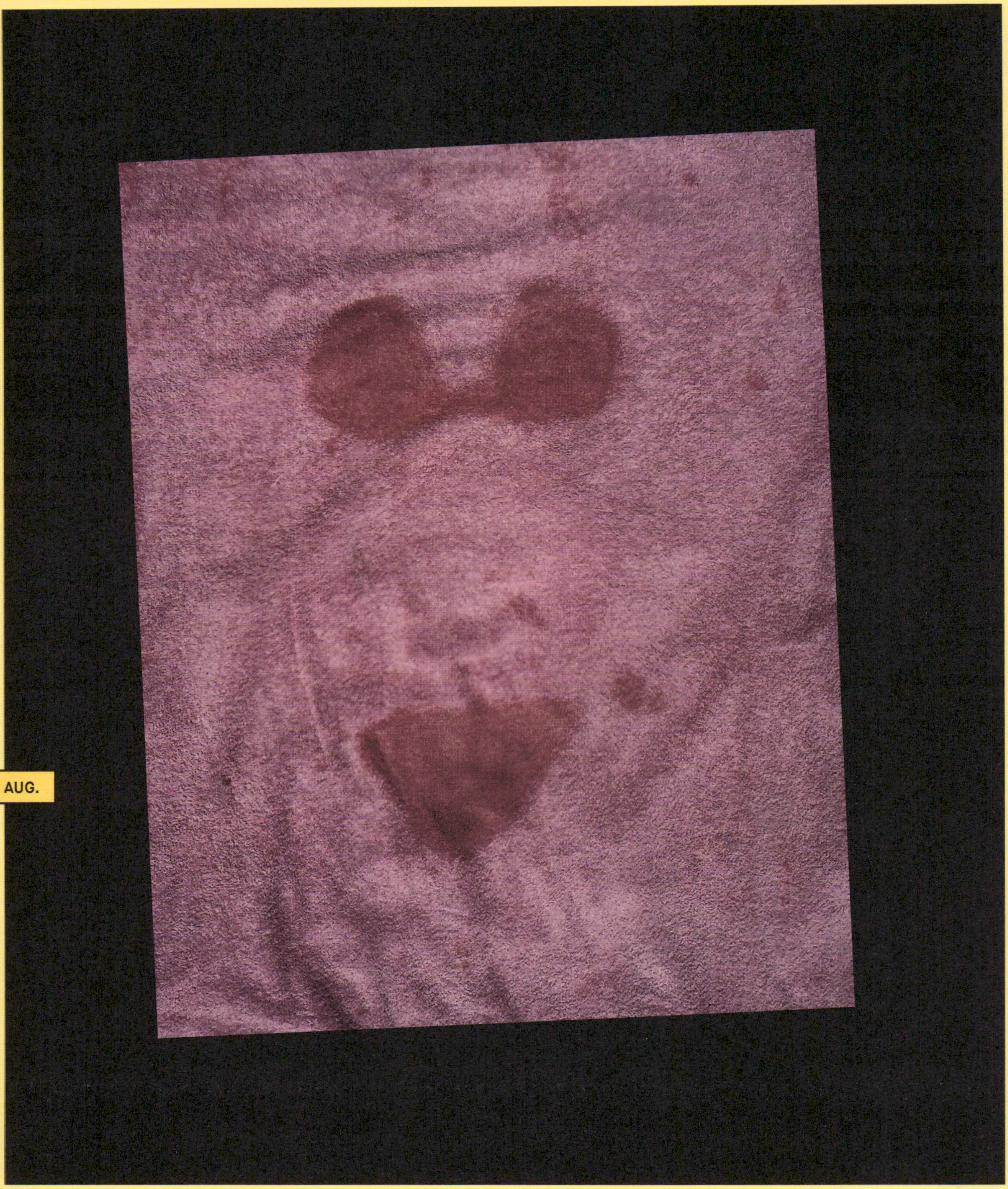

Sea taken in 2005 by Patrizia Laporta.

Ajigaura Ibaraki, 1977, by Suda Issei.

September is the ultimate after-party. If August was the riot, this is the vegetable garden refusing to go home. August heat keeps the dance floor warm, even as the nights cool. You can still eat outside without a sweater, but you can feel the season turning at the edges. The beds are still giving—Peppers, Eggplants, Cucumbers, Zucchini, Basil flowers—while we start the clean-up in the same breath: pull tired vines, cut back what's spent, turn yesterday into compost. This is the

SEPTEMBER

month of overlap: one hand holding summer, the other reaching for fall. Seedlings wait in trays like the next act backstage. We sow Arugula, Lettuces, Kale, Mustard, and Chard, and tuck Carrots and Beets into soil that's willing again. We top-dress, mulch, and water early and deep, like discipline. Bees keep working the Marigolds, frantic in the last bright hours. The garden throws ball after ball; the team keeps catching them—harvesting, washing, cooking, planting—until the music slows.

Computer scientist Alan Perlis once said, "A year spent in artificial intelligence is enough to make one believe in God." If you're actually looking for enlightenment, I'd suggest you start somewhere far less digital.

At Flamingo, the first thing you see is a Passionflower (*Passiflora*). We planted it above the entry gate so it twists overhead when you arrive and when you leave—a small reminder that this place belongs to another kind of thinking. Here, "natural intelligence" is the thing that saves us.

When sixteenth-century Spanish missionaries first saw the Passionflower in South America around 1553, they didn't reach for technology either; they reached for God. They read the flower like a vision: five petals and five sepals for the ten faithful apostles (subtracting Judas and Peter), three stigmas for the nails of the Crucifixion, the tendrils as whips, the wild halo of filaments as the crown of thorns. The blossom became a tiny theater of suffering and redemption, and they gave it the name we still use—*Passionflower*, from the "Passion of Christ." For them, this was proof. A plant had spelled out the entire Gospel in petals. Case closed.

I like to imagine the moment didn't truly land until they got close enough to smell it. You can't just look at a Passionflower from a distance; it pulls you in. Up close, the scent arrives as something quietly holy. *Passiflora* smells like a jungle trying to become a cloud—humid, green, thick with Jasmine (*Jasminum*), Honey, and ripe fruit. It's subtle but unmistakable, a little tropical ghost hanging in the air. Nobody mentioned that in the naming story, but it was right there, same as it is today, lifting a veil and deepening the spell.

Charles Darwin didn't believe in the missionaries' God, but he absolutely took the Passionflower seriously. He was obsessed with climbing plants—he couldn't look away from anything that reached, grabbed, held on—and in 1865 he published *On the Movements and Habits of Climbing Plants*. What captivated him was how busy they are. A tendril doesn't sit there like decoration. It behaves like a blind arm, like a hand in a dark room, feeling for the edge of something solid.

He described what he called revolving movement—slow, looping sweeps through the air, as if the vine is scanning the world in spirals. If you watch it long enough, you start to see the pattern: the tendril makes a wide circle, then a tighter one, then wide again, like it's changing its mind, like it's testing different radiuses. And then—this is the part that always feels like a little miracle—the instant it touches something that could hold it, the whole mood changes. The tendril commits. It begins to coil, sometimes within minutes, tightening itself into a living knot through touch-triggered growth responses we now call thigmotropism. There's nothing passive about it. It is a plant making a decision with its body.

Darwin didn't have calcium sensors or gene expression charts. He didn't have the science we have now. But the basic idea he was circling is still true: plants constantly sample their environment and translate information into action. And the more we learn, the more the "searching hand" metaphor stops being just poetry.

When a plant is wounded—by insects, scissors, weather, whatever—its tissues respond fast, sending internal signals and releasing volatile chemicals into the air. Those volatiles include the sharp, green notes we recognize as "freshly cut grass" smell: a biochemical broadcast that other plants can detect. Exposed to those cues, some plants prime their own defenses, getting their chemistry ready the way your body tightens when it hears a door slam at night.

Plants also register vibration. In controlled experiments, exposure to the specific tremor pattern of caterpillar chewing can change a plant's defensive response—almost as if the leaf can tell the difference between a gust of wind and a mouth. It's not "hearing" the way we hear, but it's sensing mechanical information through tissue, and then converting it into hormones, compounds, action.

And then there's the newest layer, which feels like science fiction even when you keep it sober: stressed plants can emit faint ultrasonic clicks that can be recorded and classified. The leading explanation is beautifully physical—cavitation events in the xylem, tiny changes in pressure and air bubbles as water transport strains under drought or damage. Not a scream, not a sob, not an emotion the way we mean it. But it is a measurable signal leaving the body. And some researchers have begun asking whether certain insects might be listening for those cues when they make decisions—like where to land, what to visit, where to lay eggs.

This is why I've always had a soft spot for the most infamous modern attempt to prove plants have inner lives. In February 1966, a prominent polygraph examiner named Cleve Backster hooked a plant to a polygraph's galvanic skin response leads—the part that measures changes in electrical conductivity. He said he was originally trying to see how long it took water to travel through the plant. Then he reported something more theatrical: when he merely considered burning a leaf, the pen jumped, as if the plant had reacted to his intention. He claimed the plant also reacted when brine shrimp were killed—dropped into boiling water. He proposed a paranormal idea he called "primary perception": that living cells can detect distant harm, even distant intent. In 1973, *The Secret Life of Plants* made Backster famous, although the scientific world remained skeptical.

But the deeper truth underneath Backster's story—the instinct that plants are thinking while they are growing (no AI needed)—turns out to be right. Passionflowers are locked in a long, intricate chess game with certain butterflies, especially those in the *Heliconius* family. The butterflies depend on Passionflower leaves as a nursery and a buffet; they lay their eggs there so the caterpillars can feed. In response, the plant arms itself. Some species load their leaves with toxic compounds that make the caterpillars sick. Others go further and grow tiny yellow nectaries or bumps on their leaves that look exactly like butterfly eggs. The *Heliconius*, being picky mothers, see the "eggs" and assume someone else has already checked in. They move on. The plant has faked them out with a handful of sugar and a perfect little lie.

Meanwhile, the flower keeps living up to its name. The scent comes from specialized cells on the petals and the corona filaments, exuding minuscule drops of fragrant oil that evaporate into the air—a mild, sweet, grassy perfume that's often overshadowed by the famous taste of the fruit. As summer rolls in and the first fruit ripens, the vines are still growing and still flowering.

Every bloom is a 24-hour event. The bud opens, offers up a pool of nectar, and waits for whatever winged visitor happens to drop in that day. The same "crown of thorns" that so moved the Jesuits is, for our carpenter bees and honeybees (*Apis mellifera*), simply a very chic landing pad.

The flowers are perfectly engineered for hummingbirds. Their long bills slip into the floral architecture like a key into a lock; as they drink, pollen dusts their heads and necks, turning them into accidental priests of cross-pollination. Some species, like *Passiflora quadrangularis* and *Passiflora maliformis*, take the night shift. They open after dark, casting a heavier, muskier sweetness into the air to lure moths and bats—including some that sleep under our Bathhouse—with a perfume that feels almost narcotic. Others are tuned to wasps and butterflies. Each species writes its own invitation, its own shape and scent, to suit the guest list.

And then there is the fruit. Most people meet Passionflower not as a vine, but as Passionfruit on a plate—wrinkled purple eggs full of golden pulp and black seeds. The scent is outrageous: tropical, tart, floral, like Mango

[1]

[2]

[3]

[1] Martin Johnson Heade traveled to Brazil, Nicaragua, and Colombia specifically to study hummingbirds in their natural habitat. He originally intended to publish a book titled *The Gems of Brazil*, but while the book never came to fruition, it resulted in some of the most iconic depictions of tropical flora and fauna in American art history. This one, *Passion Flowers with Three Hummingbirds*, was painted in 1875. Red Passionflowers (specifically the *Passiflora kermesina*) bloom on a vine in a lush South American jungle. [2] This mid-nineteenth-century illustration from Louis Van Houtte's *Flore des Serres et des Jardins de l'Europe* (1845–1883) captures the intricate beauty of the Passionflower. Beyond its striking, fringed corona, the work highlights the plant's distinctive climbing habit. Delicate, wiry tendrils emerge from the stem, acting as specialized "arms" that coil and "feel" in rotating spirals. [3] In this 1871 painting by Franz Ittenbach, the infant Christ is depicted holding a Passionflower, a choice rich with theological meaning. In Christian art, the parts of this flower represent the instruments of the Passion (the crown of thorns, the nails, and the wounds). By having the child hold it, the artist is foreshadowing his future sacrifice.

(*Mangifera indica*) and Pineapple (*Ananas comosus*) and Violet (*Viola*) all having a conversation at once. In perfumery, Passionfruit notes are used to make things feel more modern, more neon. In the kitchen they get spooned over pavlovas, into cocktails, on top of Yogurt, where the crunchy seeds do their best impression of caviar. It's easy to forget that all of that drama hangs, quite literally, from a plant that started as a little green thread under the soil.

For humans, Passionflower has been a companion for a different kind of work: calming us down. Indigenous communities across North and South America have used it for centuries—brewed as tea from leaves and flowers, or applied topically—to soften anxiety, calm the nerves, help coax sleep, and soothe burns, bites, and other everyday insults. Nineteenth-century Eclectic physicians in the United States adopted *Passiflora incarnata* (the Maypop) as a gentle sedative. Modern herbalists still turn to it for its quieting properties, thanks to a constellation of natural compounds, including certain flavonoids that appear, in lab studies and small clinical trials, to modulate GABA and support relaxation and sleep.

All of this—the climbing, the trickery, the perfume, the fruit, the chemistry—adds up to a plant that feels almost embarrassingly sophisticated. Computer scientist Alan Kay once said, "Some people worry that artificial intelligence will make us feel inferior, but then anybody in his right mind should have an inferiority complex every time he looks at a flower."

Imagine if Alan Kay had looked at this one. Amen.

[GROUNDING] : A MAP OF PLEASURE FROM THE GARDEN

THE VEGETABLE GARDEN

34°08' N / 118°12' W

LOS ANGELES, CALIFORNIA

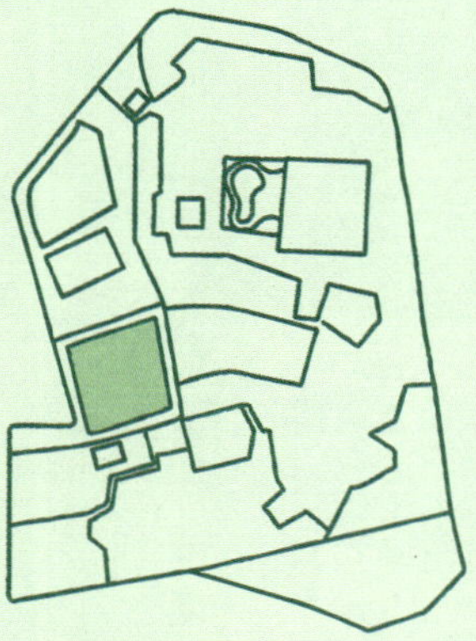

In Antarctica, your food arrives in boxes with barcodes on the side: frozen, canned, powdered, dehydrated, labeled "mixed vegetables" or "entrée, chicken, diced." On my trek across the continent, we watched giant boxes of supplies being pushed out of helicopters, sustenance for the people crossing the ice—freeze-dried reminders of things that grow on the other side of the world.

Here, you stop thinking about seasons because there are only two: light and dark. It's like someone has turned the saturation down on the world and forgotten to turn it back up. I've often said that trekking Antarctica was the greatest visual detox of my life—no color, no distractions, just a giant white desert to wipe the slate clean. But it was also a place without scent, almost nothing to inspire the nose. And then—if you are very lucky—you get to open the door to the greenhouse, and it all changes.

A Dutch bucket hydroponic system in the original greenhouse at the Amundsen-Scott South Pole Station, 1994.

At Amundsen-Scott South Pole Station they call it the South Pole Food Growth Chamber. It's a hydroponic greenhouse tucked inside one of the coldest, driest, most lifeless, most colorless places on Earth—a small, glowing box of humidity and chlorophyll floating in a sea of -70 degrees Fahrenheit. You step through the door from steel and linoleum into a different planet: warm, wet, bright, full of leaves and food. The smell is incredible—earthy, green, moist, like the inside of a garden glove or the breath of a compost pile.

The story started, fittingly, with someone who missed vegetables. In the late 1980s, Phil Sadler—a botanist who was also working as a heavy-machinery operator—was stationed at McMurdo Station, about 800 miles north of the South Pole. After one too many winters surviving on frozen Peas, he began to wonder why no one was growing anything fresh. He'd heard rumors of failed attempts in the 1950s—a lone Tomato plant on a windowsill or a few herbs under a desk lamp—but nothing had ever survived the long polar night. If hydroponics could sustain troops in the Pacific in the 1940s, he reasoned, it could surely survive Antarctica.

Sadler and a handful of volunteers scavenged scrap parts to piece a greenhouse together, clocking in for a second "night shift" only after their long 12-hour workdays were done. By 1992, the South Pole had its first volunteer-run "grow room." The enthusiasm around it eventually convinced the National Science Foundation to build a professional facility. They brought in the University of Arizona to design a state-of-the-art system, and Sadler's own company fabricated the mechanics. The South Pole Food Growth Chamber was fabricated, shipped in pieces, and assembled on site in 2004.

Phil Sadler inspecting Lettuce plants in the small prototype food-growth chamber.

On paper, its job is simple: grow fresh vegetables and herbs in a place where nothing grows. The air outside is too cold for anything to survive; the station sits at an altitude equivalent to 9,300 feet, with temperatures dropping below –100°F and months of total darkness. Supplies can only arrive in the brief austral summer; for eight or nine months of the year, the crew is entirely on its own. Frozen and dried food can keep people alive. But fresh food—especially anything leafy or green—is impossible to stockpile.

So inside this quiet room, plants are grown hydroponically: their roots in nutrient solution, not soil; their sun replaced by water-cooled lamps and LEDs; their weather controlled by sensors and climate computers. Lettuce, Kale, herbs, Cucumbers, Tomatoes, Peppers, Eggplants, Jalapeños, Basil, Cilantro, even Cantaloupes and Watermelons have been coaxed out of this room. The chamber can produce about 13 pounds of plant material a day—enough to put something fresh on almost every plate at the station in winter.

Food drop in Antarctica: Seeing supplies parachuted in while on my way to the South Pole in 2016.

Pepino Melons with different varieties of Squash from the garden, photographed by Hugh Davison.

But the real harvest is psychological. People wintering at the Pole talk about visiting the greenhouse the way others talk about church or pubs. It's the only humid, bright place in the station. It's where you go when you can't stand looking at another gray wall. It's a reminder that fresh food is medicine. Crews report better mood and health when they can eat something green that crackles between their teeth. Tending plants is self-care; the act of pruning, seeding, checking nutrient levels gives people a sense of agency and normality in a place where so much is out of their control.

When I visited, what struck me wasn't just the novelty—look, a Tomato at the South Pole—but how reverent people were around it. There is no such thing as a casual Tomato in that room. No such thing as a throwaway leaf of Lettuce. Everything is precious. When you've gone months without real food, you discover that a handful of Basil feels like a luxury. And the greatest luxury is the ability to grow it. You water the Cucumbers and remember that your hands are made for growing things that bring you analog joy in a world of tech that tries so hard to make us forget that.

Me in the hillside Veggie Garden at the Estate. Summer 2023.

NASA cares about this. The South Pole Food Growth Chamber was designed not just as a morale booster but as a test bed for space—a way of figuring out how to grow food in "ICE" environments: isolated, confined, extreme. The technology developed there—hydroponic delivery systems, water-cooled lights, remote monitoring—has fed directly into the Prototype Lunar Greenhouse in Arizona and plant-growth systems on the International Space Station. If we ever manage to grow Lettuce on Mars, it will owe a quiet debt to a room full of Kale at the bottom of the world.

So too in our own homes. The vegetable garden is the place we should all start. When I was a kid, it was the first thing my mother planted on our farm. I would watch the joy she got from tending to her veggies. There was a deep sense of achievement in watching them grow, which I see in everyone who turns a strip of grass in their backyard into a vegetable patch and becomes, in some small way, a vegetable farmer.

In South Central Los Angeles, my friend Ron Finley did this on the parkway. He started planting vegetables in the neglected strip of dirt between the sidewalk and the street and called it "gangsta gardening." He likes to say that growing your own food is like printing your own money—not because Lettuce will make you rich, but because it gives you a kind of freedom that supermarkets can't. In a neighborhood full of liquor stores, fast food, and dialysis clinics, he turned those skinny public verges into tiny farms: Kale, Collards, Sunflowers (*Helianthus annuus*), Tomatoes. His Ron Finley Project now teaches communities how to turn food deserts into food sanctuaries, one raised bed and stolen strip of land at a time. Gardening, he says, is his graffiti; instead of painting walls, he plants Carrots.

We once did a little collaboration together, selling seeds to raise money for his work. What I loved most wasn't the "project" part, it was the quiet subversion in it. A packet of seeds as a manifesto for living a good, curious life.

Activist and designer Ron Finley's urban garden in South LA, planted inside an empty swimming pool.

From there, the line to my friend Alice Waters is perfectly straight. She is the founder of the iconic Chez Panisse restaurant in Berkeley, California. Her influence inspired Michelle Obama's White House organic vegetable garden program. She has received a total of six James Beard Foundation Awards, and President Obama awarded her the National Humanities Medal. Alice has spent the better part of her life insisting that vegetables belong at the center of the table and at the center of education. In 1995 she started the Edible Schoolyard Project in Berkeley—taking a barren asphalt yard at a public middle school and turning it into a one-acre garden and kitchen classroom. There, kids grow Lettuce, Beans, and Broccoli, then go inside and cook what they've just pulled out of the ground. History, science, and politics are all taught through a bowl of soup and a bed of soil.

The Garden of the Villa Waldfried, painted around 1850. It captures the highly structured, ornamental gardening style popular among the European upper class during this era. This painting serves as a historical record of horticultural pride. During the mid-1800s, owning a diverse garden with a greenhouse was a status symbol, demonstrating the owner's wealth and their ability to "tame" nature into a productive paradise.

My partner, Harvey, with Martha Stewart at the end of summer 2025, in her vegetable garden in Bedford.

Alice has always argued that taste is a birthright, not a luxury. That if you give children a chance to grow and cook their own vegetables, they learn fractions and botany and citizenship at the same time. When I spoke with her for my last book, what stayed with me was her certainty that a simple school garden can change a child's idea of the world: that food doesn't come from packets, it comes from people and plants and place. And a vegetable garden reminds us all of this.

And then there is Martha.

Last summer Harvey and I visited Martha Stewart's home outside New York to see what might be the largest vegetable garden I've ever stood in. Martha has built an empire on sofas and saucepans, but walking around her property you realize the thing she is proudest of is the dirt.

Boy with a Basket of Fruit, created circa 1593 by the Italian Baroque master Michelangelo Merisi da Caravaggio. The painting depicts a young man holding luscious, ripe fruit, who is often identified as Caravaggio's friend and fellow painter Mario Minniti.

At her Bedford farm she's famously converted a donkey yard into perfectly gridded raised beds—long runs of Cabbage, Kale, Tomatoes, Beans, all grown in soil she talks about like jewelry. Her Cabbage patch is throwing heads that weigh eight to thirteen pounds, and she's beaming like a kid. Of all her accolades and all her success, that day she spoke more proudly about those Cabbages than about any magazine cover. It was like listening to someone show off their grandchildren.

So whether you're at the South Pole or in South Central, in a Berkeley schoolyard or a Bedford estate, the vegetable garden keeps doing the same job. It feeds. It heals. It gives us back a sense of control in a world that feels increasingly outsourced and prepackaged. Let the dirt under your fingernails be a sign of success.

Daylesford in our kitchen, with a late summer harvest.

INSIDE THE VEGETABLE GARDEN AT FLAMINGO ESTATE:

ARTICHOKE [*CYNARA CARDUNCULUS*]
BEANS [*PHASEOLUS VULGARIS*]
BEETS [*BETA VULGARIS*]
BROCCOLI [*BRASSICA OLERACEA*]
BRUSSELS SPROUTS [*BRASSICA OLERACEA*]
CABBAGE [*BRASSICA OLERACEA*]
CARROT [*DAUCUS CAROTA*]
CAULIFLOWER [*BRASSICA OLERACEA*]
COLLARD GREENS [*BRASSICA OLERACEA*]
CORN [*ZEA MAYS*]
CUCUMBER [*CUCUMIS SATIVUS*]
EGGPLANT [*SOLANUM MELONGENA*]
FENNEL [*FOENICULUM VULGARE*]
GARLIC [*ALLIUM SATIVUM*]
KALE [*BRASSICA OLERACEA*]
LEEK [*ALLIUM AMPELOPRASUM*]
LETTUCE [*LACTUCA SATIVA*]
MELON [*CUCUMIS MELO*]
ONION [*ALLIUM CEPA*]
PARSNIP [*PASTINACA SATIVA*]
PEAS [*PISUM SATIVUM*]
PEPPERS [*CAPSICUM ANNUUM*]
POTATO [*SOLANUM TUBEROSUM*]
RADICCHIO [*CICHORIUM INTYBUS*]
RADISH [*RAPHANUS SATIVUS*]
SHALLOTS [*ALLIUM CEPA*]
SPINACH [*SPINACIA OLERACEA*]
SQUASH [*CUCURBITA*]
SWEET POTATO [*IPOMOEA BATATAS*]
TOMATILLO [*PHYSALIS PHILADELPHICA*]
TOMATO [*SOLANUM LYCOPERSICUM*]
TURNIP [*BRASSICA RAPA*]
WATERMELON 'MOON AND STARS' [*CITRULLUS LANATUS*]
WATERMELON 'MOUNTAIN SWEET YELLOW' [*CITRULLUS LANATUS*]
ZUCCHINI [*CUCURBITA PEPO*]

[IX]
SEPTEMBER

FALL

DIRTY WORK

"September is the other January."

—GRETCHEN RUBIN

GARDEN TASKS:

- Scatter cover crops like Fava Beans, Clover, or Vetch in unused beds. ☐
- Start planting a garden of fall herbs: Chervil, Cilantro, and Dill. ☐
- Stop pruning woody herbs like Rosemary, Sage, and Thyme. ☐
- Divide and transplant perennials: Irises, Daylilies, and Agapanthus. ☐
- Plant fall color: Calendula, Viola, and Snapdragons. ☐
- Shop for spring bulbs. Start early Sweet Pea seeds for winter blooms. ☐
- Harvest last Figs, Guavas, and early Pomegranates before the birds do. ☐
- Begin Olive picking late in the month for curing or pressing. ☐
- Compost fallen fruit immediately to avoid wasps and fruit flies. ☐
- Mulch trees with compost but avoid fertilizer to let them harden off. ☐
- Prune trees lightly for the perfect shape once fruiting ends. ☐
- Add fallen Citrus leaves to the top of your compost pile. ☐
- Refresh tired soil with a healthy dose of compost and worm castings. ☐

TASK

MAKE A CORN HUSK DOLL ☐

Corn husk dolls are an old harvest craft—made wherever Corn was grown—often used as simple children's toys and as seasonal folk talismans that honor the Corn harvest and the spirit of the field. Soak dried Corn husks in warm water until soft and bendy, pat them dry, then bundle and tie the "head" with string; fold the husks down to form the body, add a thin strip for arms, and cinch at the neck and waist. Let them dry completely, then prop them on a shelf like a small, handmade guardian of the pantry.

TASK

GET COLORFUL WITH VEGETABLES

A wide variety of herbs and vegetables produce rich, unpredictable pigments: perfect for dying linen, paper, or wool. The magic in this technique is that because of the plant material, nothing comes out flat or identical.

These pieces were made by our friends Fran Gonzalez and Danica Roosevelt from Current Shapes Studio.

You can also dye straight from the kitchen:

- Beetroot for deep crimson-rose, Onion skins for gold to copper
- Red Cabbage for violet to teal depending on pH (add vinegar to push it pink/purple, baking soda to push it blue/green)
- Carrot tops and Marigold for warm yellows and olive greens
- Blackberries or Purple Basil for Lavender to mauve

Fix the color with a mordant—Vinegar is a simple helper, and alum is the classic fixative (especially for protein fibers like wool and silk)—then simmer your dye bath, soak your fabric or paper, and let the garden paint.

TASK MAKE A BUG SPRAY ☐

In a spray bottle, mix equal parts water and witch hazel (or vodka), add 30-50 drops total of Citronella, Eucalyptus, and Lavender essential oils, then shake hard and spray. Shake again before each use, avoid eyes, and patch test first (especially on kids or sensitive skin).

TASK WEAVE A BASKET ☐

September is the month when the garden starts giving you materials as much as it gives you food—prunings, dried stems, vines, leftovers—and basket weaving turns all of it into something useful. Gather long, flexible pieces like Grapevine, Willow, Wisteria, thin branches, or dried stems from herbs and flowers, soak anything brittle until it bends without snapping, then start with a simple base: cross a few sturdy sticks like a star and begin wrapping your flexible stems around and around, tightening as you go.

Don't worry about perfect; a garden basket should look handmade. When it feels solid, tuck the ends in, let it dry, and use it to carry harvest, hold flowers, or live on the table like proof that nothing in the garden is wasted.

SALT-BAKED LEEK-WRAPPED POTATOES

Salt Dough

1½ cups	fine kosher Salt
2½ cups	all-purpose flour
4 Tbsp	vegetable oil
1¼ cups	warm water
2 large	Leeks, pale green and white parts only, washed, trimmed, and cut down the center lengthwise
10 small–medium	Yukon Gold Potatoes
	Olive oil

1. Preheat oven to 375°F.
2. Mix together all salt dough ingredients (salt, flour, oil, and warm water) and knead to form a dough. Divide into 10 equal pieces. Cover and set aside.
3. Set a large pot of water over high heat to boil. Once boiling, add leeks and cook until tender. Remove and chill immediately in an ice bath.
4. Pull apart the leeks and, working with the flat strips, wrap each potato in 1–2 leaves.
5. Uncover dough and, using a piece at a time, roll out to ¼-inch thick. Place leek-wrapped potato in the center with any additional herbs you plan to use, and begin gathering the dough together around the potato, rolling between your hands to create a smooth surface. Repeat with remaining potatoes.
6. Set potatoes on a lined sheet tray and bake for 45 minutes, until the dough is hard.
7. Crack open to serve.

RECIPE

Zucchini Quiche with Caviar

PIE DOUGH FOR QUICHE

2½ cups	all-purpose flour
½ tsp	Salt
1 cup	butter, chilled, cut in cubes
1 large	egg
¼ cup	water, chilled
½ cup	cream, chilled

1. Whisk together flour and salt in a large bowl.
2. Toss in butter cubes and, using your thumbs and index fingers, work the butter in by pressing the cubes into the flour to form flattened pieces. Place the bowl in the fridge while you wash your hands and move on to the next step.
3. Whisk together the egg, water, and cream in a small bowl. Once mixed, pour the egg mixture over the flour. Use a spatula to mix and gather into a dough ball. Turn out the dough and wrap tightly in plastic wrap, leaving to rest in the refrigerator for 30 minutes.
4. Lightly flour a clean working surface.
5. Unwrap the dough, roll out to 2-inch thickness, and cut into 4 quarters. Stack the quarters and press down. Roll the stacked dough to 2-inch thickness. Repeat once more. Then wrap and chill for 30 minutes.
6. Unwrap dough onto a lightly floured working surface and roll out until you reach ⅕-inch thickness. Turn the dough as you roll and dust with flour as needed to prevent it from sticking to your work surface.
7. Cut the sheet of dough to fit your 9-inch tart tin and trim the edges. Chill again for 5 minutes, or until ready to use.

ZUCCHINI FILLING

4-5 small	Zucchini, sliced lengthwise on a mandoline to about 1 mm thick
½ tsp	kosher Salt
4 large	eggs
1 cup	whole milk
¾ cup	heavy cream
½ tsp	black Pepper
½ cup	Parmigiano-Reggiano, finely grated
To taste	caviar

1. Preheat oven to 375°F.
2. Working in batches, lay 5-6 slices of zucchini on top of each other and coil to form a zucchini rose. You can temporarily use a toothpick to hold the coil in place. Make 7-8 roses.
3. Arrange the zucchini roses into your unbaked prepared pie crust. Remove toothpicks if using, and lightly season with salt. Don't worry if the coils unfurl a little—this will help the egg custard mixture seep between the layers.
4. Whisk together the remaining ingredients (except the caviar) in a bowl and pour over zucchini until it just reaches the top of the crust.
5. Carefully set the quiche over a sheet pan and bake for 38-45 minutes, or until golden and set in the center.
6. Serve warm, topped with caviar, alongside a fresh green salad.

RECIPE

CHARRED CABBAGE ROLLS

CABBAGE ROLLS

1 large	Onion, small diced
2½ cups	mixed Mushrooms, roughly diced
4 cloves	Garlic, crushed and minced
½ cup	Walnuts, finely chopped
1½ tsp	Paprika
1 Tbsp	fresh Sage, finely chopped
1 Tbsp	fresh Dill, finely chopped
3 Tbsp	fresh Parsley, finely chopped
¾ tsp	Salt
To taste	Pepper
1 Tbsp	Lemon juice
⅔ cup	jasmine Rice, uncooked
1 large	egg, beaten
1 large	Savoy Cabbage, cored and blanched to separate leaves (outer leaves, core reserved)
2-3 cups	vegetable or mushroom broth

1. Heat a tablespoon of oil in a skillet over medium heat. When the oil begins to shimmer, add onions, mushrooms, garlic, and walnuts to sauté until softened and beginning to caramelize (about 2-3 minutes).

2. Add paprika, sage, dill, and parsley. Season with salt and pepper and stir to combine.

3. Turn off and remove from heat. Scoop mixture into a medium mixing bowl and leave to cool for 10 minutes.

4. Add the lemon juice, rice, and egg to the cooled mixture, stir to combine, and set aside.

5. Line a medium pot (3 qt) with reserved cabbage outer leaves and small core leaves and set aside.

6. Working with one cabbage leaf at a time, place 2-3 tablespoons of the mushroom mixture in the center of the leaf and firmly roll from the bottom up, tucking in the sides as you roll. Place cabbage rolls, seam side down, into the prepared pot. Repeat with remaining rolls and place them tightly side by side in the pot.

7. Set the cabbage roll-filled pot over medium heat and add broth. Season once again with salt and pepper, cover, and bring to a boil. Then turn down to a simmer and cook for 45 minutes, until cabbage and rice are tender.

YOGURT SAUCE

½ cup	Greek yogurt
1 clove	Garlic, crushed and minced
1 Tbsp	Lemon juice
1 pinch	Salt

Mix all ingredients in a small bowl and serve with hot cabbage rolls along with your favorite chili oil.

TASK

SMOKE THE HARVEST ☐

When the veggies become too heavy to carry, we light a fire. We invite our friend Burt Bakman—the obsessive pitmaster behind LA's iconic Slab and Trudy's Underground Barbecue—to turn his gaze from brisket to the vine. We forego the grill grates for something more primal, suspending whole Cabbages, strings of Peppers, and heavy Eggplants on wires above the coals. It is a slow, hypnotic way to cook, turning the vegetable patch into a smoking chandelier. As the vegetables spin gently in the heat, they soften and sweeten, drinking in the flavor of the wood. We eat them whole, pulled straight from the fire—charred, collapsing, and tasting of the earth they came from.

TASK ☐

Every beautiful, blooming garden deserves a mildly unsettling mascot. Here's how to make yours. Start with a simple frame: two wooden stakes lashed into a T-shape—this is your skeleton. Slide on an old shirt or jacket, then stuff it with Straw (classic), Hay, dried leaves, old rags, or shredded newspaper until it looks convincingly body-like. Dress it with personality: grandmother scarecrow, or hypebeast scarecrow—the kind that would spend their entire Sunday waiting outside the Stüssy store on La Brea. Give it a face (paint on burlap, buttons for eyes, creative liberties encouraged), then mount it in the garden like your property's slightly unhinged security guard.

JAN.
FEB.
MAR.
APR.
MAY.
JUN.
JUL.
AUG.
SEP.
OCT.
NOV.
DEC.

NOSE DIVE
[IX]

MANURE

SEP.

Finest pile of poop in Los Angeles. Flamingo Estate manure,
sold with our Mother's Day Harvest in 2022.

Farmer from the Eifel region of Germany
mucking out a cowshed, 1990.

Some years ago, we sold poop (literally) for Mother's Day. My thought was simple: "If your mother is 'the Shit,' give her some." It was a beautiful bag of fertilizer made from the finest goat and chicken manure at the Estate. I'll never forget the tantalizing smell that permeated the air as we packed those orders. It was the scent of fertility and open farmland, earthen and raw, intent on its mission to give it all back to the soil.

Biologically, this smell is a masterclass in paradox. Its primary drivers are indole and skatole—crystalline compounds derived from the breakdown of amino acids in the gut. In high concentrations, they scream "waste." Yet, nature loves a double agent: in minute amounts, these same molecules create the heady, narcotic sweetness of Jasmine and Orange blossom. It is a chemical reminder that the line between rot and bloom is thinner than we think.

Manure is the best natural fertilizer, but the nuance depends on the animal. Cow manure is grassy and fibrous. Horse manure is sweet and Hay-like, rich in p-cresol. The dry pellets of goats and sheep are earthy and mild. Chickens, however, don't hold back—their contribution is sharp with ammonia.

We mix this organic matter with Straw, which adds deep, animalic notes of musk. As the pile ages and breathes, actinobacteria get to work, breaking down the harsh volatiles and releasing geosmin—the damp, primal molecule responsible for the scent of rain on dry soil (Petrichor). The odor shifts from acrid to loamy, becoming the smell of life returning to the earth.

The word "manure" actually has nothing to do with excrement. Its roots are Latin for "hand" (*manus*) and "to work" (*operari*)—meaning "to cultivate." It is an ancient sign of care. Seven thousand years ago, humans likely noticed grass was thicker near dung piles and realized: this is good shit.

Here at the Estate, we give the goats and chickens the tastiest regenerative treats: Watermelon on hot days and root vegetables when it chills. The formula is simple: feed your animals great food, and soon enough you'll be eating great food yourself.

Calling manure "waste" is plainly wrong. It is nature at her most clever. The original thrifter, she takes what no one else wants and makes it holy. Infused with the sweet, rich smell of life at its most generous, it is, undoubtedly, the shit.

Nisi, one of our goats, munching on Sunflowers in the Goat Shed.

Group of male Chalkhill Blue butterflies (*Lysandra coridon*) feeding on minerals and salts from horse dung in the Picos de Europa Mountains, Spain.

A gathering of Green Bottle flies, feeding on cow dung, photographed by Bob Gibbons, South Africa, 2007.

October is the most forgiving, loving month in the garden. After the long, dry riot of summer, the air finally softens and the garden takes a deep, restorative inhale. The light turns honey-colored, signaling a time of renewal. The soil is still warm, ready for us to rebuild the beds, sow cool-weather greens, and wait for the first rain. But this golden shift isn't just in the sky—it is in the soil,

OCTOBER

This is the season of the Marigold. These bright orange blooms blaze across the Estate, becoming the beacon for both Diwali and Día de los Muertos. They serve as bridges between worlds, using their scent and neon color to guide the spirits of those we love back home. October is a time to honor the past while planting seeds for the future. It is a golden, sleepy kind of beauty that whispers: welcome home.

Before I fell in love with Marigolds in the garden, I fell in love with them at the movies. In *Monsoon Wedding* and a hundred Bollywood wedding scenes, the story doesn't really begin until someone strings the first Marigold garland. By the time the bride arrives, the whole world is stitched together in orange—doorways, pathways, staircases, even the steering wheel of the car—as if the only way to hold so much joy and chaos in one place is to tie it up with flowers. In *Dilwale Dulhania Le Jayenge*, in *Kabhi Khushi Kabhie Gham . . .* , in every delirious dance number where Aunties cry and Uncles drink too much, the backdrop is always the same: strings and strings of Marigold, like orange punctuation marks on the script.

Film still from the 2001 movie *Monsoon Wedding*, featuring Parvin Dabas as Hermant Rai on his wedding day, when Marigolds take center stage.

On film, you don't smell them, of course. You just know, without anyone saying it, that this is important. Someone is getting married. Someone is being blessed. Some god is being honored. Marigold becomes visual shorthand for *this is one of the days you will remember until you die.*

The smell of Marigold (and its strong, luminous color) is said to guide the departed back to the living, if only for a day. To leave no room for the wandering, the Marigold cannot be shy when exuding its perfume. So it puts on a show. Everything about its fragrance is complex and contrasting, proclaiming itself to the nose with sulfuric and green compounds that give it a sharp, living freshness—waking up the dead with notes reminiscent of life itself: soil, sun, and rain.

As Simon Barnes wrote in one of my favorite books, *The History of the World in 100 Plants*, one of the things that connects cultures is that we use flowers to mark the most important things in life: living and dying. Once a year in Mexico, on Día de los Muertos, millions of Marigolds (specifically the *Tagetes* species) take up the challenge of both. They light up the path for souls to visit their ofrendas, so the dead can be reunited with the living. Petals are scattered from the street to the altar like a bright, scented runway. The idea is simple and enormous: if you flood the world with Marigold—with its color and its smell—those you have lost will be able to find you again.

The celebration traces back to pre-Hispanic Aztec rituals tied to the goddess Mictecacíhuatl, the Lady of the Dead. The story goes that Mictecacíhuatl allowed spirits to travel back to Earth to reconnect with their family members. The musky, almost medicinal fragrance from Marigolds is said to lead souls from their burial place to their family homes. Throughout the years, this

Our tribute to Diwali at the Estate. Thousands of Marigolds in a giant ball, photographed by Hugh Davison, 2024.

tradition adopted Roman Catholic aspects from Spaniards who conquered Mexico. But all around the world, the Marigold is a symbol of this journey: a small, bright flower that offers itself as a guide between here and somewhere else.

Marigolds are not conventionally "pretty" in their aroma. In fact, at first whiff, they can be bitter and pungent, like crushed stems and rubber bands and something slightly sulfurous. But something interesting happens when you sit with the flower, letting more subtle aromatic molecules have their moment. Slowly, hints of Apple peel, Mango skin, and Citrus zest appear—fruity and vibrant and sharp. At its base, a warm, hay-like dryness sustains the ensemble, evoking notes of resin and earth. The final act that gives it aromatic gravity.

If you ask a French perfumer about Marigold, they probably won't think of graveyards or weddings first. They'll think of a difficult little oil called *Tagetes* (often distilled from *Tagetes minuta*). In the raw, it smells like crushed leaves, Green Apple peel, Citrus zest, and something slightly acrid, like a garden that's just been weeded in the heat. Used in tiny amounts, it does something no other ingredient can: it keeps a perfume honest. It cuts through sugar, holds Citrus together, and gives florals a spine. A drop too much and the whole formula smells like a freshly mown verge after rain. A drop in the right place and suddenly the perfume stands up straight.

Here at Flamingo, the Marigolds are a symbol of excitement. They explode in the garden, surging skyward with contagious enthusiasm, like they've just been told some very good news. I had fallen in love with the Marigold (*Tagetes erecta*) not in Mexico, but in India—where it appeared everywhere when people were at their most fragile and exuberant: at temples, at weddings, and in the homes and hearts of our friends. They were sometimes referred to as the "Flower of the Soul" because they were so loved by Lord Vishnu and Goddess Lakshmi, the ideal couple of Hindu mythology.

On one trip, we drove around India in a beautiful vintage car called a Hindustan Ambassador. Our driver was named Manjeet Singh, and he filled our days with laughter and stories. The car was not air-conditioned—and sounded like a sewing machine on the highway—but none of that mattered as we crisscrossed India, inhaling the Marigolds hanging from the mirror of our little vintage car. It was Manjeet who told me that Marigolds were considered "Gold Coins from God." Once he said it, I couldn't unsee it: each flower a small, minted sun, strung together into ropes of currency you could spend on the gods, on your family, on beauty itself.

In Jaipur, the Hindu morning prayers would echo from temples nearby, making the street dogs howl and stir me from bed. So Manjeet and I would drive to the flower market at sunrise and be met with an explosion of golden Marigolds and blossoms of deep magenta and bright yellows. I'll never forget the scent: a crushed, green aroma of leaf and soil that felt cool, alive, and damp—carrying a mist in the air from the fields where they had just been collected. I filled the entire trunk of our car with Marigolds, wrapped in sacks of bright turquoise fabric. Thousands and thousands of "Gold Coins from God" filling the car with color and scent. We sped off like Bonnie and Clyde with a car full of treasure.

Back at the Estate, the butterflies love them, as do chickens (farmers often add Marigolds to feed for more orange yolks). But pests detest them, especially *Tagetes patula*, which produces a cocktail of bioactive compounds that protects against nematodes, whiteflies, aphids, and certain beetles, while still attracting beneficial pollinators like bees and butterflies. Brilliantly, it's the same sharp, herbal, resinous scent that repels pests that gives the essential oil of *Tagetes* its distinct place in perfumery. It's that same compound mix—thiophenes and terpenes—that both wards off insects and gives a green, luminous character to fine fragrances. A bodyguard in the vegetable patch, and a magic wand in a perfumer's hand.

Our original Marigold seeds were given to us by the Marigold Society, a program started by a graduate of the UC Santa Cruz agriculture program to promote the growth of Marigolds and preserve the cultural uses of the flower. We make a special range of Marigold products each November when Día de los Muertos and Diwali, the Hindu Festival of Light, both collide on the calendar at the same time. The same flower that lines the road to the Cemetery in Oaxaca hangs in garlands over doorways in Jaipur and, for a few weeks at least, perfumes our bathroom sinks in Los Angeles.

Marigold garlands at a flower market in New Delhi, photographed by Phillip Huynh.

A recent study in plant neurobiology noted that Marigolds might be more living than we think. The plants respond to environmental stress (drought, salinity, heavy metals in the soil) using electrical signals. Tiny voltages pulse through stems and roots when the conditions change, triggering shifts in gene expression and leading to plant acclimatization. We asked Marigolds to guide the dead long before we knew they were carrying currents. Now scientists talk about those same plants running quiet diagnostics on their surroundings, adjusting themselves from the inside out.

The concept of "plant memory" is a fascinating and controversial topic. It's not memory in the human sense, with thoughts or recollections. Instead, it refers to a plant's ability to retain information from a past event and use that information to change its future behavior. A plant that has survived a drought might be more resilient to a subsequent drought. A plant that has been eaten by a particular insect might, over seasons, evolve to change its scent to a compound that repels it. In the case of Marigold, the very chemicals that make it smell of Green Apple and Rubber and sun-warmed leaves are part of a strategy: remember the attack, change the recipe, survive the next season.

This has led to debates in consciousness studies, a field that investigates the nature of consciousness and subjective experience. While no one claims a Marigold is "conscious" like an animal or human, these discoveries challenge the traditional view that complex behaviors and memory are exclusive to organisms with a brain and a nervous system. Instead, they suggest that complex information processing and adaptive behaviors are widespread in nature. The same flower we use as a spiritual satnav—laying down paths of petals for souls to follow—turns out to be running its own electricity, keeping track of droughts and poisons, fine-tuning its chemistry to stay alive. But we know this already, in a way. Anyone who has watched a Marigold lean toward the sun, close against the cold, or come back stronger after being cut down has seen a kind of stubborn intelligence at work.

In perfume, that intelligence reads as structure. Marigold (*Tagetes*) is rarely the star, never the pretty note in the advertising copy, but without it many compositions would collapse into syrup. It can make a Citrus accord feel like sunlight instead of Lemon cleaner. It can give a big white floral a touch of green that stops it from suffocating you with sweetness. It can pin a whole composition to the ground, the way a string of Marigolds pins a wild, emotional day to something physical and real.

The Marigold is a beacon of hope and joy; it reminds us to shine bright, even in dark times. Never was there such a smart and dutiful flower. It shows up for births and weddings and funerals. It guides souls and feeds chickens and protects Tomatoes. It gives French perfumers a way to keep their fragrances honest. It lets plant scientists argue about memory and consciousness. And in our garden at Flamingo Estate, it simply stands there in its orange frock, smelling of leaf and fruit and rain, doing its job with no fuss at all, like a very small sun that has decided to live among us.

→
Large harvest of Marigolds, also known as cempasúchil, for Día de los Muertos in Mexico. Photographed by Christine Chitnis.

Marigolds in a White Vase by British artist James Bolivar Manson, 1925.

[GROUNDING] : A MAP OF PLEASURE FROM THE GARDEN

THE LOVE GARDEN

34°08' N / 118°12' W LOS ANGELES, CALIFORNIA

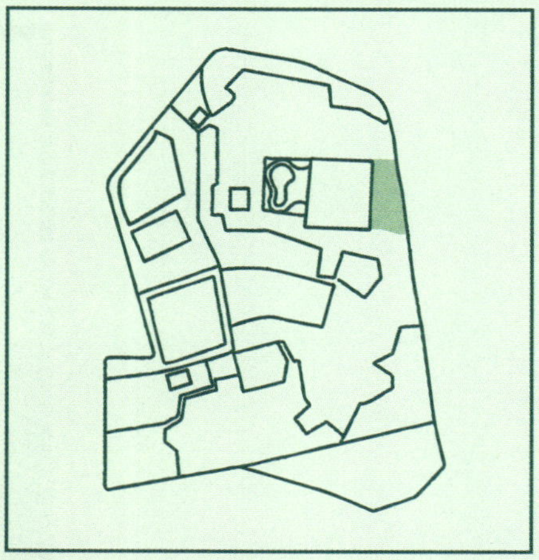

Shah Jahan ("King of the World") was the fifth Mughal Emperor of India, ruling from 1628 to 1658 at the height of the empire's wealth and confidence. He was a famously extravagant patron of horticulture, but by all accounts his greatest devotion was reserved for one person: his favorite wife, Mumtaz Mahal. She died in 1631, in her late thirties, giving birth to their fourteenth child. Historians say he shut himself away in grief, emerging with his hair turned white and a single, overwhelming project in mind—to build her a tomb and a garden so beautiful it would feel like paradise itself.

Those of you who have visited the Taj Mahal know it is often described as the world's greatest love letter. We have all seen its massive white walls and marble floors, but the building was never intended to be the star. Originally, it stood at the end of a true Mughal charbagh—a four-part paradise garden, closer to an orchard than a lawn. It was planted thickly with Citrus, Pomegranates, Mangoes, Dates, Mulberries, Roses, Jasmine, Lilies, Narcissus, and perfumed herbs underfoot. Shade, scent, and fruit were the point. The garden was meant to feel

Taj Mahal at Agra, 1905. Originally built in the seventeenth century with a lush "paradise garden" featuring dense fruit trees and Roses, the garden in this image reflects a British colonial makeover. By the time this photo was taken, the dense foliage of the Mughal era had been replaced by open, manicured lawns favored by British sensibilities.

like a cool, abundant oasis on the edge of a hot, dusty city—a literal foretaste of Paradise. And the famously white walls were there to reflect the green of the garden below.

Structurally, the garden followed the classic Persian-Islamic pattern: two main walkways and four water channels meeting at a central tank, those channels symbolizing the four rivers of Paradise—water, milk, wine, and Honey—flowing out from the central "Pool of Abundance." Each quadrant was further divided into sixteen smaller plots, like a living carpet laid out in plants.

But Shah Jahan did something more theatrical for his wife: he pushed the building back, onto the Yamuna riverbank, and let the entire garden become the focus. You weren't meant to rush straight to the marble. You were supposed to walk through a world of water and fruit and perfume first, so by the time you reached Mumtaz's tomb you had already been softened, cooled, and reminded of what all this grief was pointing toward: beauty and love, not just loss.

That original planting didn't survive intact. By the nineteenth century, after years of neglect and looting, the complex came under British control. The engineers who found it had a very different idea of what a "proper" garden should look like. The dense orchard was thinned and eventually replaced with the neater, elevated lawns and clipped flowerbeds you see now—more Victorian pleasure ground than Persian orchard. Straight

Emperor Shah Jahan, who built the iconic Taj Mahal for his wife, Mumtaz Mahal.

One of the earliest-known accurate depictions of the entire complex of the Taj Mahal was created between 1790 and 1810 using pen and opaque watercolor on paper by an unidentified Indian artist.

avenues of Cypress and tidy rectangles of grass took the place of the messy abundance of fruit and flowering shrubs. So when you look at those famous photographs—the long reflecting pool, the tight lawns, the postcard symmetry—you're seeing a kind of hybrid: Shah Jahan's geometry and water wearing a British lawn-and-border costume. Underneath the grass, the bones of the old orchard are still there. The love letter started out much juicier: more shade, more fruit, more scent, more actual Paradise. The building is the envelope; the garden is the real love note.

Over in Kashmir you can find another "love garden," Shalimar Bagh in Srinagar. Built on the shores of Dal Lake in 1619 by Emperor Jahangir for his wife Nur Jahan, it was literally nicknamed the "garden of love." Here the charbagh becomes a series of terraces and pavilions stepped down toward the water. If the Taj's garden is a love letter written for a dead wife, Shalimar in Kashmir is a love garden for a living one—a place for them to go walking, talking, flirting, and plotting in the cool air under fountains, Plane trees (*Platanus orientalis*), and fragrant blossom.

In Sissinghurst, England, Vita Sackville-West and her husband, Harold Nicolson, created a different kind of love garden around a ruined Elizabethan house in Kent. Their marriage was famously unconventional: deep affection, plus the freedom for each to pursue same-sex relationships. Harold laid out the bones—straight walks, brick walls, axes and vistas. Vita "painted" them with planting—Roses scrambling over towers, the White Garden, mixed borders in bruised plums and silvers. Sissinghurst is a garden built out of a complicated love that still held, a private language written in Yew (*Taxus baccata*) and old bricks and petals.

In Marrakesh, Yves Saint Laurent rescued the famous Jardin Majorelle as a love letter to the city and to his own life there. Together with his partner, Pierre Bergé, he restored and replanted the gardens, turned Jacques Majorelle's cobalt blue painting studio into a museum of Berber culture, and created

A view of Sissinghurst Castle Garden in Kent, England, 1949. The property was purchased as a ruin in the 1930s by Vita Sackville-West and Harold Nicolson, who transformed it into one of the world's most famous love gardens.

a "love gallery" of Yves's love-themed art. His ashes were scattered in the Rose Garden; the garden is his final resting place. In a similar way, Princess Diana was laid to rest in the grounds of her family's estate at Althorp, on a private tree-covered garden island in an ornamental lake—a landscape turned into a permanent act of remembrance.

Then there are the anonymous love gardens that never make it into history books but surface in newspapers and travel pieces. One widely reported story tells of an elderly farmer in rural Japan whose wife went blind and fell into depression. To coax her outside and give her something she could smell and

Moss Phlox lithograph by Edward Step, 1887.

feel, he began planting thousands of fragrant, vividly colored flowers—often described as shibazakura, or Moss Phlox (*Phlox subulata*)—around their house and former dairy fields. Over the years it became a literal sea of bloom—pink and purple waves so strong that strangers started visiting just to walk the paths—and his wife could "see" the garden through scent, touch, and the sound of visitors' voices.

All of these are love letters written in plants instead of ink. The Taj's orchard of Paradise, Shalimar's terraces, Sissinghurst's rooms, Majorelle's alleys, a Japanese field turned into a sea of color—each one is a reminder that sometimes the truest love letter is planted, not posted.

My love letter is for my beloved dogs, Freeway and Daylesford. They have been my constant companions for more than fifteen years, both of them rarely leaving my side, day or night. We have spent half of my adult life waking up and going to sleep together. Nobody has ever filled my heart with love more than the two of them.

As I write this book, Freeway has just been diagnosed with cancer. Reluctantly, and a little avoidantly, I have turned my mind to the possibility of a day without them running around my feet. I also want to find a place to bury and remember them, to soften the pain when it comes time to say goodbye—and to visit them every day.

For many years they have both started the day racing out the door next to my bedroom to pee. It's the same little piece of garden that I can see from my shower every morning, when my mind is clear and the sun is rising. This is also the part of the garden that is closest to the house, and therefore closest for me to protect. Since they are both golden Cocker Spaniels, I decided I would begin planting a yellow garden here—full of golden blooms that will remind me of them, and two large trees under which they will both rest.

Freeway and Daylesford in the Kitchen at Flamingo, photographed by Sean Hazen, winter 2024.

As I started to explore golden flowers, I realized there were so many that represent them both. For example, the mighty Golden Wattle (*Acacia pycnantha*) from my homeland, Australia. It is the national floral emblem, appearing on the Australian coat of arms; its colors inform our national sporting colors, and it's a kind of green-and-gold shorthand for the country itself. It bursts into bloom in late winter and early spring with clouds of tiny, fragrant yellow pom-poms—often after bushfires or drought—and so has come to symbolize resilience, unity, and renewal. For me, it's the perfect emblem for two small golden dogs who have seen me through every kind of weather and still bounce back wagging.

Freeway, Daylesford, and me, photographed by Chantal Anderson, 2024.

SUNFLOWERS (*Helianthus*)—Those big, brazen faces literally follow the sun through the sky. Across cultures they symbolize adoration, loyalty, and gratitude; one Sunflower is often said to stand for "my only love." They feel like the way a dog looks at you when you walk back into the room.

CALENDULA (*Calendula officinalis*)—The old Pot Marigold, with its simple golden Daisies, has been used in folk medicine for wounds and inflamed skin for centuries. Symbolically it stands for warmth, healing, and remembering.

CHRYSANTHEMUM (*Chrysanthemum × morifolium*)—The Chrysanthemum is one of those flowers that carries two truths at once. Across parts of Eastern Europe, it's a traditional flower of mourning—brought to cemeteries in autumn, laid on graves in dense, golden heads that last through cold weather. It's devotion that doesn't wilt easily.

And then, in Japan, the Chrysanthemum becomes something almost imperial: a symbol of longevity and renewal, the Imperial Seal of Japan (that crisp sunburst emblem), and the name of the country's highest national honor, the Supreme Order of the Chrysanthemum. Planted in this yellow corner, it feels right—formal, faithful, almost ceremonial—like a medal pinned to the earth that says: love matters.

IMMORTELLE (*Helichrysum*)—Also called Everlasting, it keeps its golden color even when dry and, in the language of flowers, symbolizes eternal love and remembrance. In Greek myth and Mediterranean folklore it decorates the crowns of gods and is hung as a good omen. A reminder that love doesn't end just because a body does.

ST JOHN'S WORT (*Hypericum perforatum*)—A bright, medicinal yellow, historically hung in houses and stables at midsummer to ward off evil and melancholy. It has always been a plant of protection and light against dark moods—exactly what dogs do without ever thinking about it.

When I think of Freeway and Daylesford resting under Wattles and ringed in Sunflowers, Calendulas, Marigolds, and Immortelles, it feels less like a cemetery and more like a continuation of their work: to bring warmth, protection, foolish joy, and a frankly unreasonable amount of loyalty into whatever patch of earth we're all in.

In the end, this little yellow corner at Flamingo Estate will be my own small Taj: not marble and minarets, but a few good trees and a crowd of flowers, planted so that two great loves have somewhere worthy to run in my mind, long after they're gone.

INSIDE THE LOVE GARDEN AT FLAMINGO ESTATE:

ANGEL'S TRUMPET [*BRUGMANSIA SUAVEOLENS 'DR. SEUSS'*]
APACHE BEGGARTICKS [*BIDENS FERULIFOLIA*]
BILLY BUTTONS [*CRASPEDIA GLOBOSA*]
BLACK-EYED SUSAN [*RUDBECKIA HIRTA*]
BLANKET FLOWER [*GAILLARDIA X GRANDIFLORA*]
BULBINE [*BULBINE FRUTESCENS*]
BUTTERWEED [*PACKERA GLABELLA*]
CALENDULA [*CALENDULA SP.*]
CALIFORNIA POPPY [*ESCHSCHOLZIA CALIFORNICA*]
CAT'S CLAW CREEPER [*DOLICHANDRA UNGUIS-CATI*]
CHANNEL ISLAND TREE POPPY [*DENDROMECON HARFORDII*]
CHRYSANTHEMUM [*CHRYSANTHEMUM × MORIFOLIUM*]
COREOPSIS [*COREOPSIS GRANDIFLORA*]
CUP OF GOLD VINE [*SOLANDRA MAXIMA*]
DAFFODIL [*NARCISSUS SP.*]
EVENING PRIMROSE [*OENOTHERA BIENNIS*]
FLANNEL BUSH [*FREMONTODENDRON CALIFORNICUM*]
FLOWERING QUINCE [*CHAENOMELES X SUPERBA 'LEMON LIME'*]
FRENCH MARIGOLD [*TAGETES PATULA*]
GOLDEN RAIN TREE [*KOELREUTERIA PANICULATA*]
GOLDENROD [*SOLIDAGO SP.*]
IMMORTELLE [*HELICHRYSUM ITALICUM*]
JAPANESE ROSE [*KERRIA JAPONICA*]
KANGAROO PAW [*ANIGOZANTHOS 'YELLOW GEM'*]
LANTANA [*LANTANA CAMARA*]
MADAGASCAR BUTTERFLY BUSH [*BUDDLEJA MADAGASCARIENSIS*]
MEXICAN MARIGOLD [*TAGETES ERECTA*]
PRICKLY PEAR [*OPUNTIA HUMIFUSA*]
ST. JOHN'S WORT [*HYPERICUM PERFORATUM*]
SUNFLOWER [*HELIANTHUS SP.*]
SWEET PEAS [*LATHYRUS ODORATUS*]
TIPU TREE [*TIPUANA TIPU*]
WATTLE [*ACACIA SP.*]
YARROW [*ACHILLEA MILLEFOLIUM*]
YELLOW AZALEA [*RHODODENDRON SP.*]
YELLOW JADE ORCHID TREE [*MAGNOLIA CHAMPACA*]
YELLOW TRUMPET TREE [*HANDROANTHUS CHRYSOTRICHUS*]
ZINNIA [*ZINNIA ELEGANS*]

[4]

[2]

[1]

[3]

[5]

[1] Shalimar Gardens in Lahore, Pakistan, 1996. Constructed in 1642 during the reign of the fifth Mughal Emperor, Shah Jahan, to symbolize an earthly utopia.

[2] The gardens at Sissinghurst are famous for a series of intimate "garden rooms" enclosed by hedges—a safe place for secret love.

[3] Shalimar Bagh seen from the shore of Dal Lake in Kashmir, India, 1780.

[4] Annual blooming of Moss Phlox at Hitsujiyama Park in Chichibu, Japan, 2008.

[5] Jardin Majorelle in Marrakesh, featuring the iconic blue building and red pathways—two signature elements that inspired the gardens at Flamingo.

[X]
OCTOBER
FALL

DIRTY WORK

"I wonder if leaves feel lonely when they see their neighbors falling."

—JOHN MUIR

GARDEN TASKS:

- Plant Peas and Fava Beans along fences or trellises to fix nitrogen and feed the soil. ☐
- Sow Lettuce every two weeks for continuous harvest through winter. ☐
- Direct-seed Cilantro, Parsley, and Dill—cooler nights bring out their flavor. ☐
- Plant California natives now so roots establish before spring. ☐
- Cut back spent summer herbs (Rosemary, Sage, Thyme) to shape and encourage fresh growth. ☐
- Thin and pinch Sweet Peas when at 4-6 inches tall to encourage branching and good airflow. ☐
- Top-dress beds with compost and mulch after planting to retain moisture. ☐
- Citrus: fruit is sizing up—feed lightly with compost and water deeply every two weeks. ☐
- Harvest fall Chilies and string them into a ristra for preserving and festive decor. ☐
- Olives: continue harvesting; rinse and cure for winter. ☐
- Pomegranates: Pick before rain splits them. ☐
- Guava and Persimmon: Harvest as they soften. ☐
- Prune dead wood only; save structural pruning for winter dormancy. ☐
- Mulch beneath trees with leaves, straw, or shredded bark to protect roots from cool nights. ☐
- Sow wildflowers: California Poppy, Tidy Tips, Clarkia, and Larkspur for early spring color. ☐

TASK

EAT SUNNIEST SIDE UP ☐

If you keep hens, treat their eggs like a living color study. The yolk gets its glow from what they eat—carotenoids in particular—so you can "turn up the saturation" by letting them snack on unsprayed Marigold petals, dark leafy greens, Carrot tops, Pumpkin, Squash, and Sweet Potato. And yes, a few spices can shift things, too: a pinch of Turmeric or Paprika mixed into their feed can deepen color and add a subtle savory warmth to the eggs (go light—think seasoning, not curry night). Keep their normal feed as the base, introduce new treats slowly, and then crack an egg each week and watch the palette change.

TASK

Host a Diwali Dinner

Diwali is the Festival of Lights. It symbolizes the spiritual victory of light over darkness. My friend Varsha Mathur creates the best Diwali menu in Los Angeles—passed down from her grandmother in Jaipur. Let the Marigolds light the way, and fill the table with trays of Cardamom and Pistachio sweets (Mithai), spicy Samosas, Saffron-laced rice, ghee (clarified butter)-laden curries and winter tandoori vegetables, like Eggplants, Carrots, and Squash. There are no rules; this is about joy (Varsha also makes the greatest chicken tenders in the world, and always surprises me with them). Only invite people who shine bright.

TASK

LOVE THE THREE SISTERS

A milpa—often called the Three Sisters—is what happens when plants decide to love each other. Corn grows tall and steady and offers its stalk as a living trellis. Beans climb that stalk and, as legumes, help pull nitrogen into the soil—feeding the whole little family instead of demanding more from it. Squash stays low and spreads wide, shading the ground like a protective skirt: it holds moisture, cools the soil, and makes it harder for weeds to move in. Together they're structure, nourishment, and shelter—three sisters with different gifts, thriving because they're planted close enough to lean on one another. Plant the Corn first in a small block, add Beans once the Corn is up, and tuck Squash around the edges to seal it all in. This is a spring activity, but begin sourcing your seeds now.

TASK

RAISE CHICKENS

If you're going to keep chickens, feed them like you're trying to make the best eggs of your life. Start with a quality layer feed as the base, then upgrade with the good stuff from the garden: kitchen scraps and greens, Marigold petals for deeper golden yolks, herbs like Oregano and Thyme for a sturdy flock, and seasonal treats like Pumpkin, Squash, berries, and Watermelon. Give them grit and oyster shell, keep fresh water always available, and let them scratch and forage as much as possible—happy hens make better eggs, and better eggs make better breakfasts.

TASK

MAKE WATTLE SOLID PERFUME

Pick a bowl of fresh Wattle blooms, then spread a thin layer of odorless fat (vegetable shortening or deodorized Coconut oil) in a shallow dish and press the flowers gently into the surface like you're tucking them into bed. Cover, let it sit 24 hours, then lift out the spent blooms and replace with fresh—repeat for 4–7 days (longer if you want it louder) until the fat smells like warm, honeyed-yellow spring. Scrape into a small jar or tin and dab onto wrists and collarbones. Patch test first.

TASK

MAKE A MARIGOLD ALTAR

OFRENDA

On the Day of the Dead (Día de los Muertos), to build an ofrenda is to build a bridge. You are creating a beacon for the spirits of loved ones to find their way home, guided by the scent and color of the earth. While traditions vary from region to region, the main thing is to do it with love. The most critical element is the Marigold (Cempasúchil). Its pungent scent and neon-orange petals act as a spiritual GPS. Finally, place the photos of those you miss at the very center, surrounded by their favorite earthly pleasures and some candles.

TASK

Take a Golden Shower

Hang a small bundle of Mountain Marigolds (*Tagetes lemmonii*) or Calendula (*Calendula officinalis*) in your shower, up high and out of the direct spray, and let the steam do the work. Every hot rinse becomes instant aromatherapy—sunny, herbal, and mood-lifting—like bathing inside a warm yellow field.

RECIPE

LOVER'S MARIGOLD PASTA

My grandmother always baked a lasagna when we were having a bad day. It's forever been my favorite comfort food. This is Chef Sandy's Marigold update of my grandma's classic.

PASTA SHEETS:

- 3 cups all-purpose flour
- 4 large eggs
- 1 pinch Salt
- Semolina flour for dusting
- 1 bunch small Sage leaves, picked

[1] Measure 3 cups of all-purpose flour onto a clean working surface and create a mound.

[2] Make a well in the center of the mound and crack in 4 eggs with a pinch of salt.

[3] Using a fork, carefully whisk the eggs to break the yolks and mix while using your free hand to gently push in a little flour at a time. Continue until it is no longer easy to use the fork and using both hands, incorporate the remaining flour into the dough.

[4] Knead by pushing down with the heel of your hand and turning the dough each time. Continue for 7-10 minutes.

[5] Wrap the pasta dough in plastic wrap and leave to rest for 30 minutes.

[6] Working with ¼ of the dough at a time, leaving the rest covered so it doesn't dry out, roll out the dough on the widest setting of a pasta roller, 3-4 times, each time folding it onto itself.

[7] Continue rolling the dough through; however, each subsequent time, turn the dial to a thinner setting until you reach setting 5 or 6. Repeat with remaining quarters.

[8] Cut the pasta sheets down to squares. Dust with semolina, cover, and set aside until ready to cook.

MARIGOLD SQUASH SAUCE:

- 1 Tbsp butter
- 1 Tbsp Olive oil
- 1 small white Onion, diced
- 2 cups roasted Butternut Squash, peeled and cut into small cubes
- 2 cloves Garlic, sliced
- ¾ cup heavy cream
- ¼ cup orange Marigold petals, washed and dried
- ¼ cup Parmigiano-Reggiano, grated
- Salt and Pepper to taste

[1] In a saucepan set over medium heat, add butter and olive oil to melt.

[2] Once the butter has melted, add the onions and butternut squash and sauté for 3-4 minutes until softened and caramelized.

[3] Stir in garlic and continue to cook until fragrant.

[4] Add cream, marigold petals, and Parmigiano, leaving to simmer for 1 minute. Season with salt and pepper to taste.

[5] Turn off heat and use an immersion blender to create a creamy luscious sauce. Reheat on the stove before plating.

ROASTED SQUASH:

[1] Toss in olive oil and season with salt and pepper.
[2] Roast on a sheet pan in a 375°F oven until the flesh is softened and the outside is caramelized.
[3] Keep warm until plating.

ASSEMBLY:

- Roasted Hazelnut halves
- Optional: fresh ricotta
- Fresh Marigold petals
- Fresh herbs: Dill, Parsley, and Basil are all welcome!
- 1 bunch small Sage leaves, picked
- Fresh Lemon juice

[1] Bring a pot of well-salted water to a boil.
[2] Place in 8 sheets of pasta (enough for 2 servings). The pasta will float to the top when it is ready.
[3] Toss cooked pasta in olive oil and on a plate begin to assemble the layers, starting with warm sauce and roasted squash, then pasta, more warm sauce, hazelnuts, and more roasted squash. You can add fresh ricotta to the layers if you like!
[4] Garnish with fresh marigold petals and fresh herbs, finish with a squeeze of fresh lemon juice, and serve hot and immediately!

UPSIDE DOWN PINEAPPLE CAKE

RECIPE

INGREDIENTS:

- 5 Tbsp unsalted butter, melted
- ½ cup light brown sugar
- 7 canned Pineapple rings
- 12 maraschino Cherries
- 1¼ cups all-purpose flour
- 1 tsp baking powder
- ¼ tsp baking soda
- ¼ tsp Salt
- 1 cup granulated sugar
- 5 Tbsp Olive oil
- ½ cup buttermilk
- ¼ cup Pineapple juice, reserved from the can
- 1 egg, room temperature
- 2 tsp Vanilla extract

PREPARATION:

[1] Preheat oven to 350°F.

[2] Melt butter and pour into a parchment-lined 9-inch cake pan.

[3] Sprinkle brown sugar on top of the butter evenly across the pan.

[4] Arrange pineapple rings on the brown sugar and butter mixture and fill the holes with the maraschino cherries. Set aside.

[5] Sift flour, baking powder, baking soda, salt, and granulated sugar into a large mixing bowl.

[6] In a separate bowl, whisk together olive oil, buttermilk, pineapple juice, egg, and vanilla.

[7] Pour wet ingredients into dry and use a spatula to mix. Do not overmix!

[8] Pour cake mixture over pineapple rings.

[9] Bake for 40 minutes, or until a cake tester comes out clean.

NOSE DIVE
[X]

MUSK

The smell of my dogs is something I hold holy. I wake to Freeway and Daylesford—inhaling a warm note that says: *you're here, it's morning, let's begin*. I bury my nose in their fur and floppy ears as much as I can. Together we carry food down to the goats, where we are met by the same scent. Warm fur and wet soil, coming together in a perfect musky combination.

In the fragrance world, "musk" gets tossed around constantly. But the original musk—the raw material—is in almost none of what we wear today. The story of musk is in many ways the story of modern perfumery. And like any good story, it starts with an animal.

High in the Himalayas, the male musk deer produces an aromatic secretion from a gland often called the "musk pod." Its scent is warm, sweet, and deeply sensual. This is what perfumers call animalic: skin-like, living, intimate. In nature, it marks territory and lingers so mates (or rivals) can find it days, sometimes weeks, later. On human skin, it does something similar: it clings, it fixes, and it releases slowly.

That power made musk one of the most prized materials in perfumery, but also the most overhunted. Demand was so high that the musk deer was pushed to the brink of extinction. Perfumers needed a solution, so "noses" went searching for musk's shadow everywhere. They found musk-like warmth in plants: Labdanum resin from the Rock Rose offered a leathery amber scent; Ambrette Seed, a Hibiscus cousin, provided a softer version. Angelica root was a close match.

OCT.

But the revolution arrived in the early twentieth century via Croatian-Swiss chemist Leopold Ruzicka. He discovered the molecular structure of natural deer musk and successfully recreated it synthetically. This ethical breakthrough earned him the 1939 Nobel Prize in Chemistry and birthed modern perfumery.

Chanel N°5 was among the first to use this synthetic version. Today, synthetic musk is the backbone of many fine

Musk Deer, And Birds Of Paradise by William Daniell (1769-1837). The central figure is a musk deer, known for the valuable musk pods found in the males. In this painting, you can see the deer's characteristic lack of antlers and its somewhat arched back.

The Thibetian Musk, 1835.

A Pet Dog by John Thomas, around 1870.

OCT.

A Terrier by British artist John Fitz Marshall.

fragrances and nearly all functional scents, from laundry detergent to lotion. It softens sharp edges, blends ingredients, and adds longevity.

Maybe that's why musk still lands the same way: as comfort. Familiarity. A quiet sense of being held. It brings us back to that feeling of warm fur and skin—a reminder from our animal friends that we are not alone.

Freeway visiting the goats and chickens near the Vegetable Garden.

November is the garden's witching hour. The air turns heavy with smoke—fireplaces, crushed herbs, cured Tobacco—signaling the move from autumn's bright harvest into the garden's deeper, shadowed wisdom. Citrus begins to glow: Meyer Lemons, Mandarins, early Oranges. Olives finish their harvest, and Pomegranates and Persimmons beg to be picked before the first storm clouds arrive. The garden makes its skeletal shift toward winter, dropping leaves as a signal to rest.

NOVEMBER

We mulch deeply and feed with compost, allowing the pace to slow. This is a month for "checking in"—honoring the "teacher plants" that have guided human consciousness for millennia. At dusk, Brugmansia turns on its opulent perfume, a fairy-tale flower that reminds us of the magic hidden in the dark. November asks us to follow the smoke, cross the portal, and find the treasures waiting in the garden's quiet, dreaming soil.

Hypnos (Greek for "sleep"), by German photographer Wilhelm von Gloeden, in Taormina, Sicily, circa 1900. Gloeden's work was pioneering for its use of classical Mediterranean motifs and its exploration of dark magic.

Often called "Angel's Trumpet," Brugmansia might as well be the mermaid's trumpet—so prolific is its scent and its history of dark seduction, leading many to their death. It is a fairy-tale flower in the most literal sense: a beautiful thing that hides a curse.

The trope of a witch disguising herself as a beautiful woman is a classic element in fairy tales. The most famous example is *Snow White*, where the Evil Queen, a powerful sorceress, is consumed by jealousy over Snow White's beauty. To enact her plan to kill the princess, she brews a potent poison. She then transforms herself into a seemingly harmless peddler woman, approaches Snow White without arousing suspicion, and offers her the perfect, poisoned Apple. One bite, and Snow White falls into a death-like sleep.

Nowhere does art imitate life more than under the beautiful trumpet flowers of Brugmansia. She is one of the most beautiful plants in the garden, with a scent unlike any other I have ever smelled. Yet she contains potent hallucinogenic compounds, including scopolamine, hyoscyamine, and atropine. These are tropane alkaloids; they act as powerful anticholinergics, blocking acetylcholine, a crucial neurotransmitter responsible for nerve transmission. That blockade can produce delirium, terrifying hallucinations, disorientation, and amnesia. In toxicology literature, trips from Brugmansia and her cousin Datura are described as "terrifying rather than pleasurable," often involving complete loss of contact with reality.

Nevertheless, the white trumpet flowers of Brugmansia have always been among my favorites, and I have ached to craft a candle with their fragrance. But every part of the living plant is exceptionally poisonous—seeds, leaves, flowers, sap—and the alkaloid content changes with season and moisture, making "safe" dosage essentially impossible to know. So you should never use real Brugmansia for anything you intend to eat, drink, smoke, or apply to the skin. Or should you? At least in stories.

Brugmansia on our terrace by John Reagan, winter 2025.

During the 1850s, Samuel Bond was employed as a paymaster at the gold mines of Marmato in New Granada, now known as Colombia. In 1853 he wrote to Sir William

Jackson Hooker, director of Kew Gardens, describing the plants of the region. Among them was a Brugmansia that residents called *tonga*, reputed to grant a form of "second sight." Officials had outlawed its use because large amounts could cause insanity or death, yet the ban was often disregarded by Indigenous people searching for fortune. Many believed that, in the right dose, the plant could sharpen awareness and reveal buried treasure and hidden mines. A tantalizing promise of wealth, only shown to those willing to step into another dimension.

The stories about Brugmansia almost always frame it as a gateway to the spirit world. The flowering trumpet can reveal truths or grant access to another realm. Its qualities—the powerful psychoactive compounds and the profound, hallucinogenic visions they produce—were not seen as side effects but as proof that spirits were present. It was a doorway, not a drug.

In Ecuador, the Jivaro peoples (Shuar and Achuar) of the Amazon are famously known for their use of Brugmansia in shamanic rituals for divination, healing, and social justice. They believed that the plant's spirit, often personified as a powerful ancestor, would guide them through visions to find the root of a problem or the location of a missing person.

Various Indigenous groups in the Colombian Amazon and along the Andean highlands, such as the Kofan and Inga peoples, have a long history of using Brugmansia (often referred to as *toé*) in their spiritual practices to gain wisdom. In nearby Peru, *Brugmansia suaveolens* is considered one of the strongest and most dangerous "teacher plants"—reserved for experienced shamans, never for casual experimentation.

Shamans praise the plant for its wisdom and its ability to guide them through complex spiritual journeys, but there is a strict code around its preparation and use. The hallucinations can be protracted, disorienting, and physically punishing; the shaman's role is to steer the traveler through the storm. In this way, Brugmansia contradicts the cliché of "folk medicine"—its pharmacopeia is as disciplined and rule-bound as in any clinic.

It has also been used as a potent tool of social control. In some Andean communities, if a child was misbehaving or a young person strayed from the tribe's values, a shaman might administer a tiny, carefully controlled dose. The resulting hallucinatory experience was meant to be terrifying—a spiritual journey to the underworld where they would face the spirits of their ancestors and be corrected. This was seen as a way of reconnecting them with the tribe's moral code; the terror itself was a kind of medicine, a memory no one wanted to repeat.

Shadow stories persist into the present. In Colombia and elsewhere, scopolamine—derived from Brugmansia and related Nightshade plants—has become notorious as "Devil's Breath," a tasteless drug used in crime to render victims confused, compliant, and amnesic. These are not romantic visionary journeys but chemical kidnappings of free will, a grotesque misuse of a compound that also, in tiny patches behind the ear, quietly prevents motion sickness on cruise ships.

Legend says if you sleep under a Brugmansia, you can't wake up because the angels will come for you. More likely, it's the effect of breathing in too much heavy scent in still, humid air—but the warning is sound. Acting on the autonomic nervous system, the chemicals in the plant are capable of severe damage to the heart, eyes, and digestive organs, and the volume of alkaloid toxins in mature flowers is potentially enough to kill a person. Yet in a clinical environment, carefully controlled doses have positive effects: scopolamine is used to treat nausea and depression; atropine is life-saving in certain heart and nerve-gas emergencies; related compounds help in Parkinson's treatment and during surgery.

All this danger, wrapped in one of the most extraordinary scents in the garden.

What makes Brugmansia so seductive? To begin with, the fragrance will knock you out with wonder. Chandler Burr, a perfume critic, once described it as a "liquid, narcotic-heavy floral," a note that feels more like atmosphere than smell. Gardeners say the yellow cultivar 'Charles Grimaldi' "smells like one of the most expensive perfumes you could buy." The *Los Angeles Times* described Angel's Trumpet as "virtually impossible to resist."

Many personal accounts from gardeners mention that the scent is almost imperceptible in the early day, becoming overwhelmingly

A Sicilian boy holding Brugmansia potion, Wilhelm von Gloeden, circa 1900.

A portrait of two Jivaro (Shuar) women from the Amazon basin, captured in the early twentieth century. The image showcases ceremonial attire, including intricate beadwork, woven belts, and feathered ornaments. Brugmansia was used in these ceremonies, often administered by shamans to bridge the gap between the physical and spirit worlds. Young Shuar boys traditionally drank an infusion of the plant during a several-day journey to a waterfall. This rite of passage was intended to induce visions of ancestral spirits that would provide them with power and protection.

A Jivaroan family on the banks of the Marañón river, eastern Ecuador, 1901. Beyond ceremonial use, Brugmansia was a domestic fixture of these settlements, often cultivated in household gardens as a living bridge between the family and the spirit world. While women curated the botanical knowledge for healing, the entire community participated in the spiritual landscape where plants like Maikua provided a vital sense of protection and ancestral continuity.

powerful as the sun sets. The transition is gradual and masterfully accomplished. At first light, the Brugmansia seems to be still recovering from the night's exhalation—fresh, green, almost silent. By midday, the scent turns a touch waxy, with a pollen-like warmth and a faint creaminess.

In the early evening, things begin to get interesting. The flower seems to awaken, turning on its party mode with a honeyed scent that's creamy, increasingly floral, and faintly vanillic, often with an Orange blossom or Ylang-Ylang brightness. By nightfall, the show is in full swing.

Brugmansia's midnight act is one of the most complex in the floral realm. It's when the flower is at its most magnificent, and an opulent, narcotic, hypnotically sweet cloud covers the air. At this time, the entire garden seems to quiet just to let her talk—and she does so with rich radiance, a creaminess that glows, a warmth and a spice that beckons everyone to listen. Just before dawn, the Brugmansia delivers a deep, musky encore, softly fading away to a scent of sweet hay, ready to reset the cycle.

At Flamingo Estate, Brugmansia crowns the night-pollinating garden. We also have one on the dinner terrace, and by sunset, its scent has crawled into every corner of the house, seducing us forward. This is the only way one can enjoy Brugmansia in perfume because there is no commercial absolute or essential oil. The flowers yield almost no usable volatile oil, and any attempt at solvent extraction would bring along the toxic alkaloids. Extraction is not just impractical; it's dangerous. Instead, perfumers attempt to recreate its accords inspired by its scent profile—halos of Jasmine, Ylang-Ylang, Tuberose, Orange Blossom, Vanilla, and musk—which, as you might imagine, never come close to the real thing. Angel's Trumpet is always a ghost.

For the night-active visitors—hawk moths, perhaps bats—the strong, sweet, musky aroma is a beacon through the dark. By waiting until evening to exude their most opulent fragrance, the plants avoid wasting energy and pollen on daytime pollinators like bees, who are not well suited for these large pendant trumpets. They save their seduction for the suitors who can actually handle the architecture.

There is another twist to Brugmansia's story. All seven known species are now listed as Extinct in the Wild by the IUCN Red List. They once grew along the Andes from Venezuela to northern Chile and in parts of Brazil; now they survive only in gardens, courtyards, pots, and as "escaped" populations outside their original range. Botanists suspect that the wild plants depended on now-extinct megafauna to disperse their seeds; when the animals disappeared, the plants did too—except where humans kept them alive for their beauty and their power. It is strange to stand under such abundant flowers and realize you're looking at an extinct wild genus, being sustained by our mixed motives: ornament, curiosity, and the occasional desire to step across the border of the self.

An exquisite 1870 illustration by Louis van Houtte, capturing the "bloody" red hues of the high-altitude *Brugmansia sanguinea*. Once a prized exotic import for European greenhouses, this plant is now considered extinct in the wild and exists only through human cultivation.

A few years ago, Esther Perel, renowned psychotherapist and author, came for dinner at the Estate. We sat on the terrace, under the Brugmansia, and talked about seduction while the flowers turned their volume up for the night. Her most well-known concept is the paradox of intimacy and desire. She argues that the very things that create a sense of security and intimacy in a relationship—predictability, comfort, and emotional fusion—are often the things that kill sexual desire and eroticism.

Perel asserts that seduction thrives on a degree of mystery and separateness. When

Brugmansia on the dinner terrace of Flamingo, painted by John Reagan, winter 2025.

two people become too emotionally fused and their lives completely merge, the "space" for seduction disappears. In order for a partner to remain an object of desire, they must remain a bit of a mystery—a separate individual with their own world. That distance is what allows for the creative act of seduction to take place, bridging the gap between two independent beings.

For Perel, seduction isn't a one-time event but a continuous practice. It's about how you greet your partner at the end of the day, how you talk to them, and how you show them that you're still interested and curious about who they are. This kind of daily seduction is what keeps the flame of desire alive, long after the initial sparks of a relationship have faded.

The Brugmansia opens its trumpet flowers every evening to seduce. Over time, those flowers have been interpreted as many things—medicine, doorway, poison, subject of Frida Kahlo's erotic paintings, folk remedy for pain, urban legend, and police warning. But with every opening flower, with every nightly act of wondrous scent, we're reminded that we too have the power to turn on our own magic—to remain a little mysterious, a little dangerous in the best possible way, and to cast our own hypnotic spell for the ones we love, without ever touching the poison.

Hanging yellow Brugmansia down by the pool at the Estate.

[GROUNDING] : A MAP OF PLEASURE FROM THE GARDEN

THE DRUG GARDEN

34°08' N / 118°12' W LOS ANGELES, CALIFORNIA

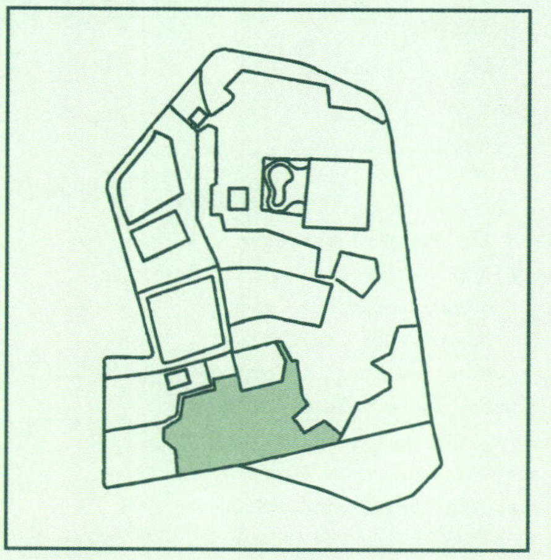

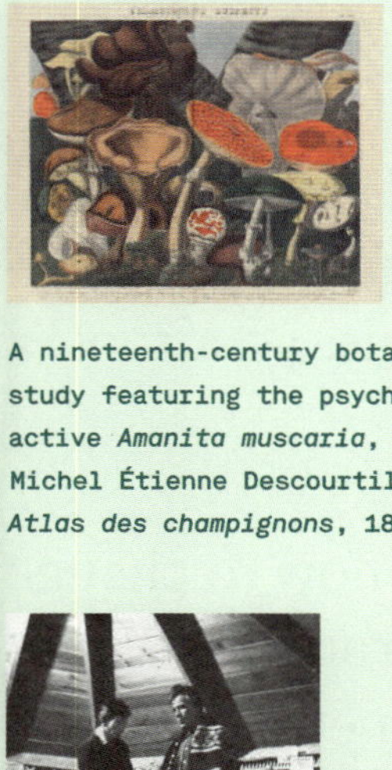

A nineteenth-century botanical study featuring the psychoactive *Amanita muscaria*, from Michel Étienne Descourtilz's *Atlas des champignons*, 1827.

A Roadman (priest) conducting a Native American Church Peyote ceremony inside a traditional hogan near Piñon, Arizona, 1954.

← *The Drug Garden* painted by John Reagan, 2025.

I never once smoked pot as a teenager. In fact, it wasn't until I was in my thirties that I smoked anything at all. My mother always drew a straight line from Marijuana to slackers, and from there it was a short ride to joining a gang, a neck tattoo, and prison. Any kind of drug was a crime.

Somehow, I also never smoked cigarettes. For all the vices and bad behaviors I managed to collect, Tobacco was (thankfully) never one of them. But I had my share of other habits, and in recent years I've done a lot of self-work—much of it with gratitude to my friend Elise Loehnen, who encouraged me to crack myself open and look honestly at my patterns.

To do so, I took some trips without ever leaving home. I skipped the nicotine and went straight to psychedelics.

We tend to think of "tripping" as chaotic and destructive. But if you look at the Native American Church, for example, using Peyote (*Lophophora williamsii*) as a sacrament—as a tool

The myth of Santa Claus sprouts from the *Amanita muscaria* mushroom. A red-and-white psychedelic mushroom used by Sámi shamans in Lapland who delivered the fungi through chimneys when snow blocked doors. The tales of "flying" reindeer came from shamans observing the erratic behavior of reindeer after they ingested the fungi.

A botanical watercolor of the psychoactive *Amanita muscaria* (Fly Agaric), painted by British artist and illustrator Beatrix Potter, 1892. Long before she created Peter Rabbit, Potter was a dedicated amateur mycologist (someone who studies fungi).

In Lewis Carroll's *Alice's Adventures in Wonderland*, this scene is one of the most famous literary nods to altered states of consciousness. Alice encounters the hookah-smoking Caterpillar atop a mushroom that grants the power of size alteration—a scene widely interpreted as a Victorian literary exploration of psychoactive experiences. Illustration by Sir John Tenniel, 1865.

→
Psilocybin from the Estate, photographed by Hugh Davison, winter 2025.

for healing rather than escape—you see something very different. Drug use in many Indigenous cultures isn't a dark secret; it is structured, communal, and in some ways deeply healthy. It is not a way to check out, but a way to check in.

My own psychedelic use was done with a therapist, who held my hand literally and figuratively. I would encourage you to work with a professional if you're embarking on this kind of work. Over a series of sessions, he took me on a journey with psilocybin, MDMA, and ketamine. I found the experience transformative. Alongside regular therapy, my anxiety and negative inner dialogue quieted to a whisper.

I explained to my friends that psilocybin therapy felt like finding money in a pocket that I had forgotten about. After those investigations into the shadow, I could see things more clearly. I had deep forgiveness for other people. I had a renewed appreciation for my own flaws. I came out of those sessions clear and oddly happy—less at war with myself.

When we talk about a "Drug Garden" at Flamingo Estate, we are careful not to look at it through a Western lens of prohibition and shame, but through an ancient lens: as a tool, a fragrance, and a doorway.

All of this has taught me that plants know how to change the air around us, and the thoughts that move through it. Sometimes they do it to heal. Sometimes to warn. Sometimes to pull us a little closer to one another, or to whatever we imagine is just beyond the garden wall.

I'm grateful to have ended up here, surrounded by this unruly group of leaves, resins, flowers, and smokes that I now think of as friends and healers.

In the end, my mother was right—I did join a gang after all.

[1]

[2]

[2] The evil witch offers Snow White a poison Apple in Disney's 1937 film. Long before this film, the trope of the witch began with Mandrake. In the 1400s, this herb was the primary ingredient in "flying ointment"—a potent salve that induced vivid hallucinations of soaring through the night. The iconic trope of a witch on a broomstick was born from this chemical reality: the stick was the Mandrake branch, and the "flight" was the psychedelic effect.

[1] A Belle Époque advertisement for Absinthe Vichet, circa 1900, capturing the euphoric and ethereal mood associated with the potent, Wormwood-infused spirit known as the Green Fairy. By the turn of the century, absinthe had become the quintessential drink of the French social classes, so central to daily life that 5:00 p.m. was widely known as "L'Heure Verte" (The Green Hour). Its immense popularity eventually led to a moral panic. Opponents claimed it caused "absinthism"—a supposed syndrome of hallucinations and violent behavior—leading to its ban in the US and much of Europe by 1915.

[4]

[3]

[3] The Stacking Room of the Opium Factory at Patna, India, circa 1850. Indian workers are shown meticulously arranging thousands of Opium "cakes" on floor-to-ceiling racks. These cakes were standardized balls of Opium, wrapped in dried Poppy petals, destined primarily for the Chinese market during the height of the Opium trade.

[4] This image is a detail of a Huichol yarn painting. The Huichol, or Wixárika, people of Mexico create these colorful artworks using yarn and beads as offerings to their gods and to reflect their spiritual relationships with nature deities and ancestors. The art often depicts sacred designs and symbols related to their life and rituals, such as the Peyote pilgrimage.

[5]

[5] The "Just Say No" campaign was a hallmark of 1980s American social policy, primarily spearheaded by First Lady Nancy Reagan as a centerpiece of the "War on Drugs." Modern critics often view it as an oversimplification of a complex medical and social crisis. By framing drug use as a simple moral "choice," it arguably contributed to the stigmatization and mass incarceration of users rather than fostering a public health-based approach to addiction. It did little to address the root causes of drug abuse, such as poverty, mental health, or systemic issues.

[6]

[6] *The perfect joint*, by Hugh Davison, 2025.

[7]

[7] *The Smoker* by Flemish artist Joos van Craesbeeck. In 1635, Tobacco was still a relatively new and potent import to Europe. Craesbeeck captures the intoxicating effect of the smoke—the wide eyes and gaping mouth suggest a head rush or a sensory shock.

[8]

[8] Close-up studies of the Opium Poppy (*Papaver somniferum*) showing the flower bud (left) and the seed capsules or pods (center/right) at various stages of maturity, magnified to reveal their architectural structure. They were originally published by Karl Blossfeldt in his landmark 1928 photobook, *Art Forms in Nature*.

THE SCENTS OF VICE

Less controversial, at least these days. It is something we have grown here for a long time—but not to smoke. We originally grew it for its oil, to use in our soaps.

MARIJUANA has a double life. The smell people complain about in a stairwell is only one chapter of a much longer, more interesting story. On the plant, before anyone touches it, Cannabis smells green and resinous—closer to a Tomato vine or a crushed Nettle than to "weed." The moment you move into a cured flower, the scent profile shifts. A properly cured bud smells like a pantry full of terpenes. There is always a core of warm, slightly dank herbal resin—like Hops, Bay Leaf, and Sage all sharing one jar—but around that core, you can have almost any accent: fruit, forest, funk, spice. It contains animalic qualities that share ground with musk, oud, and leather. Then there is the smoke, which drops into the familiar sweet-burnt zone: toasted herbs, hashish, tar, and bonfire.

TOBACCO (*Nicotiana tabacum*) also suffers from a bad reputation. Fresh Tobacco leaves don't smell like smoke at all. They smell green and slightly bitter. But the curing barn is where the magic happens. As the leaves are air-cured, starches convert to sugars and resins concentrate. The air in a good curing shed smells like warm straw, molasses, dried Raisins, Figs, and Dates.

This is the note perfumers chase. In 1919, Ernest Daltroff created Tabac Blond for Caron, a tribute to the "flapper girls" of the roaring twenties—women who wore trousers, challenged gender norms, and smoked. It was a sensation: leather, Tobacco, and florals. To this day, a touch of Tobacco Absolute makes a fragrance feel grown-up and warm. It is one of my favorite scents in our apothecary—smelling like my grandfather's office: fruit, leather, and Cedar shavings.

THE VISIONARIES

Beyond the recreational, there are the plants that demand reverence. These are the "teacher plants." They are not for parties; they are for portals.

MAGIC MUSHROOMS (*Psilocybe spp.*) are more than 200 species of fungi containing psilocybin. These intelligent organisms share one goal: to alter the conscious mind. One of the tools used to identify whether you have magic in your hands is smell. "Gold Caps" carry a scent of earth and musk; "Wavy Caps" are reminiscent of freshly ground flour. "Liberty Caps" smell of wet grass and moss, while "Blue Angels" carry the scent of their coastal habitat: clean, brisk, and slightly salty.

PEYOTE (*Lophophora williamsii*) is a small, spineless cactus and is perhaps the most sacred plant of the North American deserts. For millennia, Indigenous peoples have used it as a sacrament, believing its consumption allows the individual to commune with the Divine and find medicine for spiritual imbalance. It can take ten to thirty years for a Peyote button to mature. Only then will it flower, before ripening into the fleshy fruit containing mescaline. Because of this, it is a plant that demands protection as much as it offers it.

DIVINER'S SAGE (*Salvia divinorum*), also known as "Sage of the Seers," is known to open portals. Its scent is reminiscent of the soft, loamy soil of the Oaxacan cloud forest where it grows. For generations, Mazatec shamans have used it for divination and healing. The active ingredient, salvinorin A, is one of the most potent naturally occurring hallucinogens, and it is one of the few that is not an alkaloid.

IBOGA (*Tabernanthe iboga*) is Indigenous to forests of the Congo Basin. Its flowers are white trumpets with pink speckles, but the power lies in the root bark. It contains ibogaine, a potent psychoactive. In small doses, hunters use it as a stimulant to stay motionless for hours. In large doses, it is the heart of the Bwiti initiation rite. Men eat the grated root and enter a days-long trance, facing a "waking dream" of anxiety and memory to connect with ancestors. It is a terrifying, physically punishing ordeal, but it is currently being studied for a miraculous side effect: ibogaine seems to reset the brain's opioid receptors, helping addicts break free from crippling heroin and fentanyl dependence without withdrawal.

MANDRAKE (*Mandragora officinarum*) is one of the most misunderstood residents of the garden. Contrary to the misconception that it is a fictional plant invented for Harry Potter, the Mandrake is quite real, and the bizarre superstitions surrounding it have a firm scientific basis. Its heavy, bifurcated roots often split to resemble human legs, leading to the ancient belief that the plant was a semi-sentient being that would shriek when pulled from the earth, killing anyone who heard it.

The reality is almost as strange. Mandrake is the feistiest member of the Nightshade family, a cousin to Brugmansia that contains a potent cocktail of tropane alkaloids. In the Middle Ages, these chemicals were the primary ingredient in "flying ointment"—a hallucinogenic salve pounded together with animal grease. When absorbed through the skin, the alkaloid hyoscine imparts a vivid sensation of weightlessness and aerial motion. This is precisely where the image of the witch flying on a broomstick was born; the stick was a symbolic Mandrake branch, and the "flight" was a chemical journey taken without ever leaving the ground.

During the Inquisition, merely possessing a Mandrake root was enough to have a woman declared a heretic; it was viewed as an instrument of the Devil, allegedly germinated from the shadow of the gallows. In 1431, the accusations against Joan of Arc were even bolstered by the claim that she carried a Mandrake root in her pocket. Yet, beneath the dark folklore lies a history of profound mercy. It was the world's original anesthetic. As early as the first century, a Greek physician used Mandrake wine to knock patients into a deep, death-like sleep for surgery—a medical breakthrough that predated modern anesthesia by nearly two thousand years.

THE POISONS & THE POTIONS

Finally, there are the plants that walk the razor's edge between medicine, magic, and death.

WORMWOOD (*Artemisia absinthium*) is a silver-leafed shrub that gives off a strong, Sage-like scent when crushed. Its bitter compounds were originally used to expel intestinal worms (hence the name). But in the eighteenth century, it was distilled into the emerald-green liqueur known as absinthe. It became the muse of the Bohemian crowd—Oscar Wilde, Picasso, and Van Gogh all swore by the "Green Fairy." While it was blamed for Van Gogh's madness and eventually banned, we now know it was likely the cheap alcohol, not the Wormwood, that caused the damage. Today, the plant has been rehabilitated: in the 1970s, Chinese scientists extracted artemisinin from a related Sweet Wormwood (*Artemisia annua*), creating the world's most effective treatment for malaria and winning a Nobel Prize.

In the mountains around the Black Sea and the Himalayas, certain RHODODENDRON (*Rhododendron ponticum*) produce nectar laced with grayanotoxins. Bees turn it into "mad honey"—a dark, reddish Honey that can make the body flip its switch. I saw it being harvested when I was climbing to Mt. Everest Base Camp and heard stories of its local use as a recreational drug and a sexual stimulant. In large doses, it has also been a weapon. In 65 BC, the Persian King Mithridates VI, pursued by the Roman army, left pots of this on the roadside. The Roman soldiers ate it greedily, fell into a stupor of hallucinations and low blood pressure, and were easily killed.

The OPIUM POPPY (*Papaver somniferum*) is another plant that carries two lives in the same body. It is stunning in the field—papery petals, a sculptural seed pod, a delicate, almost careless beauty. Chemically, it is a factory for alkaloids that medicine cannot imagine living without: morphine, codeine, thebaine—molecules that taught us how to treat pain, suppress cough, quiet the nervous system, and also how easily relief can become dependence. To speak about the Poppy honestly, you have to hold both truths: the compassion of pain relief and the devastation of misuse.

THE SMOKE GARDEN

At Flamingo, we have an area we call the Smoke Garden—an ongoing experiment in the way plants burn. Broadly, I think of them in four uses: Temple, Tonic, Travel, and Taste.

[SMOKE AS TEMPLE]

→ These are the classic "church resins," meant for Gods first and humans second.

FRANKINCENSE (*Boswellia spp.*) bleeds as pale resin from desert trees. On a hot coal, it smells of Lemon, Pine, and Honey. When the bark of the MYRRH (*Commiphora myrrha*) tree cracks, the tears come. Darker and more bitter than Frankincense, it smells of licorice, earth, and balsamic vinegar. It is one of the oldest aromatics in human history, used to embalm pharaohs and bless altars. For thousands of years, SANDALWOOD (*Santalum album*) has been shaved into powder and burned to calm the mind. It is the "It Girl" of perfumery; creamy and milky with no sharp edges, anchoring nearly half of all modern perfumes. The bright, milky resin of Central America, burned COPAL (*Bursera spp.*) is used on altars for Día de los Muertos.

[SMOKE AS TONIC]

→ Plants burned like spiritual brooms to scrub a space.

WHITE SAGE (*Salvia apiana*) is sacred to Southern California tribes. A dense, camphorous smoke that clears the air. PALO SANTO (*Bursera graveolens*) is the South American "Holy Wood." Burns with quick bursts of Citrus, Mint, and Coconut. MUGWORT (*Artemisia vulgaris*) is used in European folk magic for protection, and in Chinese medicine as moxa to warm acupuncture points.

[SMOKE AS TRAVEL]

→ The trance plants, whose smoke is for crossing thresholds.

The aroma from TOBACCO (*Nicotiana tabacum*) evokes mystery, sensuality, and centuries of history. Yet at its core, it remains one of the most sacred spiritual plants in American Indian tradition, to be deeply respected. CANNABIS (*Cannabis sativa*) was used for at least 4,000 years in funerary and shamanic rituals. A single whiff evokes something primal. From sacred, to illegal, to valued medicine—its role as a boundary crosser remains.

[SMOKE AS TASTE]

→ The kitchen herbs that move from pot to coal.

When tossed on a fire, BAY LEAF (*Laurus nobilis*) smells like a Mediterranean hillside. ROSEMARY (*Rosmarinus officinalis*) cleans a room with the scent of Pine needles and hot stone. CLOVES (*Syzygium aromaticum*) & STAR ANISE (*Illicium verum*) smell like Christmas and spice markets—warm, medicinal, and festive.

[XI]
NOVEMBER

WINTER

DIRTY WORK

"In November, the earth is growing quiet. It is making its bed, a Winter bed for flowers and small creatures."

—CYNTHIA RYLANT

GARDEN TASKS:

- [ ] Citrus season begins as Meyer Lemons and Oranges start to color. Harvest as needed.
- [ ] Mulch under Citrus and Guava, and lightly feed Citrus with compost or worm castings.
- [ ] Finish Olive harvest and start curing or pressing.
- [ ] Pick remaining Pomegranates and Persimmons before rain splits or they soften.
- [ ] Prune lightly only; cut back Cane Berries.
- [ ] Clean up fallen leaves and fruit to prevent fungal issues.
- [ ] Tend cool-season veg (Kale, Spinach, Fennel, Broccoli, Cauliflower) and thin seedlings.
- [ ] Succession sow Lettuces, Arugula, and Radishes every two weeks; plant Garlic and Shallots.
- [ ] Sow winter herbs: Parsley, Chervil, Cilantro, Dill.
- [ ] Plant bulbs and Wildflowers and sow Sweet Peas for spring bloom.
- [ ] Roses: remove diseased leaves and give a light prune before dormancy.
- [ ] Divide and replant perennials; cut back Salvias, Gaura, and grasses to reset.
- [ ] Feed ornamentals with compost only; stop fertilizing for the season.
- [ ] Plant Strawberries; enjoy Sasanqua Camellias as they begin blooming.
- [ ] Apply dormant disease sprays to fruit trees.
- [ ] Order seed and plant catalogs for winter dreaming.

TASK

PLANT A COVER CROP

When the garden beds go quiet in winter, don't leave them naked—plant a cover crop. Scatter seeds of Clover (*Trifolium spp.*), Vetch (*Vicia spp.*), Peas (*Pisum sativum*), Oats (*Avena sativa*), or Rye (*Secale cereale*), water them in, and let them grow into a soft green blanket that protects soil from erosion, keeps weeds from moving in, and holds moisture through the cold months.

The real magic is underground: Legumes like Clover, Vetch, and Peas help pull nitrogen into the system, ensuring your beds have more nutrients waiting when it's time to plant again.

When spring comes, cut it down and leave it to rot back into the bed like a gift—green manure, future fertility.

The Real Magic Is Underground

TASK

ROLL A PERFECT JOINT

This is the kind of thing they should've taught in school. We like to blend our Marijuana buds with other flowers and herbs to enhance flavor and effect, or to help the Cannabis burn more slowly. Raspberry leaf (*Rubus idaeus*), Mullein (*Verbascum thapsus*), Rose petals (*Rosa spp.*), Peppermint (*Mentha x piperita*), and Passionflower (*Passiflora incarnata*) are among our favorites. Lavender (*Lavandula spp.*) and Chamomile (*Matricaria recutita*) can amplify the relaxing qualities of certain strains thanks to shared terpenes; Lavender also helps smooth out the harshness of the smoke. Damiana (*Turnera diffusa*) is known to lift the mood and promote relaxation with a mild, creative euphoria. When combined, they become a smoky arrangement designed to let your mind bloom.

TASK

MAGIC MUSHROOM TEA

Start with 1 cup of water and 1–2 grams of dried Magic Mushrooms (chopped). Bring water to a gentle simmer and steep Chamomile until the tea turns soft gold, then sweeten with Honey for a floral, calming finish. If you want it more "summer magic," add 1 tablespoon fresh Orange zest, a handful of Blueberries, and let them infuse for a minute before you drink—soothing, and quietly dreamy.

TASK

Get Grandma's Silver Out

If you are going to have a party, make it classy.

TASK

GET WITCHY

The image of a witch flying on a broomstick took hold in the Middle Ages, when Mandrake was a key ingredient in "flying ointment"—a hallucinogenic salve said to create a vivid sensation of flight. The "broom" was often symbolic: a branch as a handle, and a chemical journey taken without ever leaving the ground.

To honor the witches in your life, November is the perfect time to make a broom, when branches are bare and easy to gather.

Go outside and find a straight, sturdy stick about as long as your arm (fallen is better than cut) and let it be your handle.

Gather your "bristles": thin, bendy twigs, tough grasses, or the dried stems of herbs like Lavender, Rosemary, or Sage—after you've used the leaves in the kitchen. Make a bundle about as thick as your wrist.

November Is the Perfect Time to Make a Broom

Fan the bristles around one end of the handle like a skirt, then tie them on tightly with twine, wrapping again and again until it feels solid. Trim the ends if you want it neat, or leave it a little wild.

Hang the broom upside down overnight to set, then sweep the porch, the kitchen, or the bad mood right out the door.

RECIPE

WHOLE ROAST COFFEE CHICKEN

☐

INGREDIENTS:

Roast Chicken

1	whole chicken (about 5 pounds)
1½ Tbsp	kosher Salt
1-2 Tbsp	Olive oil
1 head	Garlic, cut in half
1 bunch	fresh Thyme
1 bunch	fresh Oregano
1	yellow Onion, cut into wedges
3	Yukon Gold Potatoes, quartered
1 dash	black Pepper, freshly cracked
½ cup	chicken stock

Coffee Gravy

½ cup	cold-brew Coffee
¼ cup	tamari
⅓ cup	Maple syrup
1 cup	chicken stock
1 cup	butter, chilled & cubed
1 tsp	Salt, or more to taste
½ tsp	freshly cracked Pepper

METHOD:

ROAST CHICKEN:
Preheat oven to 350°F.
Pat chicken completely dry and generously salt and oil the chicken both inside the cavity and all over the skin.
Place garlic and herbs into the cavity of the chicken and tie the legs together. Set aside.
Add onions and potatoes to the bottom of the roasting pan. Add salt, olive oil, and freshly cracked black pepper, and toss well. Add the chicken stock to the bottom of the pan.
Place chicken, breast side up, on top of the potatoes and onions, and roast for 35 minutes. Turn temperature up to 410°F without opening the oven door and continue roasting the chicken for another 40 minutes.
Remove chicken and allow it to rest for 20 minutes before carving.

COFFEE GRAVY:
Add the coffee, tamari, maple syrup, and chicken stock to a saucepan and cook over medium heat until the mixture reduces to ½ cup.
Swirl cold butter cubes into the reduced sauce, one cube at a time, moving the pan to emulsify the butter into the sauce.
Once you've added all the butter, add salt and pepper to taste.
Pour the sauce into a gravy boat to serve with the chicken.

RECIPE

CHOCOLATE CAKE WITH CANNABIS

☐

INGREDIENTS:

Cannabutter

7 grams	ground Cannabis (decarboxylated)
1 cup	unsalted butter
1 cup	Water

Chocolate Cake

2 cups	all-purpose flour
2 cups	sugar
$\frac{3}{4}$ cup	unsweetened cocoa powder
2 tsp	baking powder
$1\frac{1}{2}$ tsp	baking soda
$1\frac{1}{2}$ tsp	kosher Salt
1 cup	buttermilk
$\frac{1}{2}$ cup	Olive oil
2	large eggs
2 tsp	Vanilla extract
1 cup	boiling water

Chocolate Cannabuttercream

$1\frac{1}{2}$ cups	butter, softened
$\frac{1}{2}$ cup	cannabutter, room temperature
1 cup	unsweetened cocoa powder
4 cups	powdered sugar
$\frac{1}{2}$ cup	milk
1 tsp	fine kosher Salt
2 tsp	Vanilla extract

METHOD:

CANNABUTTER:

Preheat your oven to 240°F, then spread your finely ground cannabis evenly on a baking sheet.

Bake for 35-40 minutes, stirring occasionally to evenly dry. The cannabis should be dry and crumbly.

Add butter and water to a saucepan set over low heat and warm until the butter has melted.

Add the decarboxylated cannabis to the melted butter. Simmer for 2-3 hours, stirring occasionally and keeping at a gentle simmer.

Strain and store in an airtight container in the refrigerator.

CHOCOLATE CAKE:

Preheat the oven to 350°F.

Mix all dry ingredients in a large mixing bowl and set aside.

Mix all wet ingredients in a medium mixing bowl and set aside.

Add wet ingredients into dry ingredients and stir to combine.

Pour batter evenly into three 7-inch lined cake tins and bake cakes on the middle rack of your oven for 40 minutes, or until a cake tester comes out clean. Leave to cool completely on a rack before assembling.

CHOCOLATE CANNABUTTERCREAM:

Add butter and cannabutter to the bowl of a stand mixer with a whisk attachment and beat on high for 5 minutes, until the butter is fluffy and light.

Turn the mixer down to low and add cocoa powder and powdered sugar a spoonful at a time, adding more only when the last has fully incorporated.

Add milk, salt, and vanilla, and turn the mixer up to high to beat until the buttercream is light and aerated.

ASSEMBLY:

Place one cooled cake on the bottom of a serving plate, top with chocolate cannabuttercream, and repeat for remaining layers. Continue to frost the sides of the cake until the entire cake has been covered in buttercream. Serve with a cold glass of milk.

Psilocybin Ghee

Chef Ella Murphy's ghee is made as a slow infusion, using clarified butter as a nourishing base that carries flavor and compounds gently through the body. The mushrooms are finely ground and infused at low heat, allowing them to integrate evenly into the fat rather than stand apart. Warm spices like Cinnamon, Cardamom, Clove, Ginger, and Vanilla add depth and softness, supporting digestion and lending a familiar, comforting quality to the ghee.

INGREDIENTS

1 pound	unsalted butter
4 grams	dried Psilocybin Mushrooms, finely ground
1	Cinnamon stick, lightly crushed
1	Vanilla bean, split lengthwise
2 Tbsp	fresh Ginger, thinly sliced
3	Cardamom pods, lightly crushed
2	whole Cloves

30 SERVINGS

METHOD

[STEP 01]

- Melt the butter in a heavy-bottomed saucepan over very low heat, uncovered and without stirring. As the butter melts and separates, skim off the white foam that rises to the surface. Once the milk solids have settled at the bottom and the butterfat is clear and golden, remove the pan from the heat and strain through a fine mesh sieve or cheesecloth.
- The yield should be approximately 1¾ cups of ghee.
- Allow the ghee to cool slightly so it remains warm but not hot.

[STEP 02]

- Return it to the saucepan or transfer it to a double boiler set over the lowest possible heat.
- Add the ground mushrooms, cinnamon stick, vanilla bean, ginger, cardamom pods, and cloves.
- Keep the heat very low and allow the mixture to infuse for 60 to 90 minutes, stirring gently every 10 to 15 minutes. The ghee should not simmer or bubble at any point.

[STEP 03]

- Remove the ghee from the heat and let it cool slightly, then strain through cheesecloth or a nut-milk bag into a clean, clear glass container, pressing gently to extract as much ghee as possible.
- If using vanilla extract instead of a vanilla bean, stir it in while the ghee is still warm. Mix well and allow the ghee to cool completely and solidify.

[STEP 04]

- Store the ghee in an airtight clear glass container. It will keep for several weeks at room temperature or up to 3 months refrigerated. Always label clearly with contents and date, and use a clean, dry spoon for each serving.
- Eat by the spoonful, spread on toast, stir into hot chocolate.

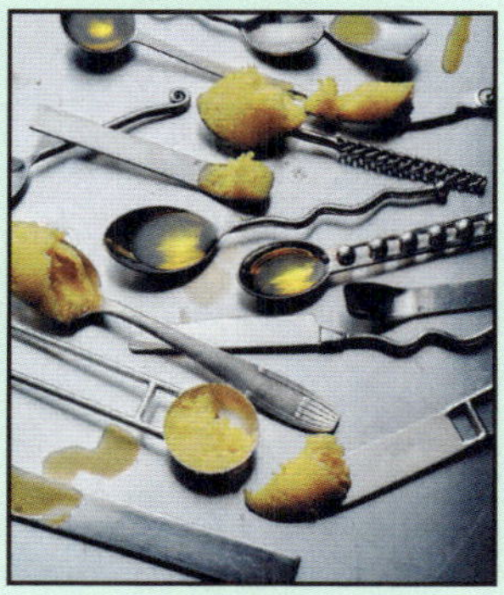

JAN.

FEB.

MAR.

APR.

MAY.

JUN.

JUL.

AUG.

SEP.

OCT.

NOV.

DEC.

NOSE DIVE
[XI]

FUNK

Meet funk: Sour. Metallic. Stinky. Strong.

Back in the 1600s, the word “funk” was created to describe a strong, pungent smell. Think Roquefort Cheese, fermented Cacao, Périgord Black Truffle.

By the mid-twentieth century, “funk” evolved to describe something earthy, raw, and emotionally potent. Funky music borrowed from the language of smell to describe the powerful, visceral quality of something soulful and complicated.

NOV.

Something that has lived, fermented, and evolved. Absolutely impossible to ignore.

Funk is an in-your-face-here-I-am kind of smell. It is far more interesting than anything considered perfect. In food, funky smells are the byproduct of microbial metabolism.

It communicates ripeness, spoilage, or nutrient availability.

Above all, funk challenges.

The world of luxury scents and gourmet foods know this—choosing funk as their poster child when it comes to smells and tastes. Fine Cheeses, Truffles, and aged Wines lead with sour, sulfuric, even pungent notes. They crinkle the nose and instigate conversation, even discussion. Yet when balanced properly, these funky assets are interpreted as refined, interesting, deeply pleasurable.

Chefs play with the universe of funk by creating combinations and perfecting proportions. Picture Blue Cheese with a slice of Pear and a sip of Port Wine. Once all three mix in tongue and nose, everything comes into balance. It's the same with master perfumers, who know that a drop of aged ambergris, castoreum, or hyraceum—some of the most bizarre, yet prized raw materials in perfumery that come from animal secretions and excretions—add an indispensable depth and sensuality to compositions. Funky. Slightly dirty. Completely spellbinding. If used well, it's what takes a fragrance to a level of absolute mastery. Chanel Cuir de Russie, Yves Saint Laurent Kouros, or Hermès Eau des Merveilles. All completely and utterly reliant on just a touch of it to confuse, then seduce.

And it's got layers. There's ocean funk, which is brined and salty and intimate with the smell of Seaweed. Resinous funk settles in oud and aged sap and old woods like Cedar. Certain tropical fruits, like Durian, smell slightly fermented—funky in a sweet-gone-wild kind of way. Then we have funk from the soil—the Truffles and the mushrooms—and the damp, rich must that comes from organic decay. And then, at the throne of it, Cheese. The world of Cheese is a playground of funk made incarnate. The funkier the Cheese, the more microbial chaos happening within.

Urgent in its need to express it all, funk is like the cool extravagant aunt who's always a bit too much. Life of the party, a little chaotic, and no doubt the favorite.

Get your funk on.

The Pope of Gastronomy: legendary French chef Paul Bocuse displays a prized, stinky Black Truffle, wearing the prestigious Meilleur Ouvrier de France collar.

December is warmth—moving from the outside in, starting in the Spice Garden and settling in the heat of a roaring kitchen oven. This is the month of roasting: Garlic sizzling, Potatoes browning, Pumpkin seeds crackling—heat as reassurance that a feast is on its way. We celebrate by hanging Hoshigaki, watching Hachiya Persimmons turn into deep amber candy. We mull wine with Apples, Pears, Citrus, and Cloves. The year's final harvest becomes our holiday decor: we craft

DECEMBER

wreaths from smoked Citrus, Bay, and Clove, and stud Oranges into fragrant Pomanders. While the rest of the garden goes dormant, the Torch Aloes deliver fiery, succulent spikes like orange fireworks across the Estate. As Daffodils and Narcissus poke through the soil, we keep the earth warm around them, mulching deeply with fallen leaves and straw to insulate their roots. Everything and everyone is tucked in, toasty, and ready for the year to come.

A Pepper tree in the Flamingo Garden, painted by John Reagan, winter 2025.

On January 16, 1982, Spago opened on the Sunset Strip in West Hollywood and Los Angeles got a new star. It was Wolfgang Puck's original paparazzi-hungry restaurant, the place where the city finally admitted that food was part of celebrity. On opening night, eighteen Rolls-Royces jammed the little parking lot. Inside, the room was dressed in pale pink and beige, with a "see-and-be-seen" exhibition kitchen designed by Barbara Lazaroff glowing like a television set.

The signature bite that night was the now-legendary Smoked Salmon "Jewish Pizza"—a crackle of crisp dough spread with crème fraîche, scattered with Chives and Red Onion, and crowned with Caviar. Regulars in those early years included Sidney Poitier, Michael Caine, Sean Connery, Billy Wilder, Jack Nicholson, and Warren Beatty, huddled at a center round; Champagne flowed and Jewish Pizzas came and went in stacks, and everyone pretended this was just a regular dinner.

Around town, the rest of the cast assembled:

At Chasen's in West Hollywood, the room was still all red-leather booths and clubby service, its most famous dish a thick, buttery Chili so beloved that Elizabeth Taylor had quarts of it flown to the set of *Cleopatra* in Rome. Ronald Reagan proposed to Nancy there, then kept coming back from the Governor's Mansion and the White House; Oscars after-parties turned the place into a second awards show.

Mr Chow in Beverly Hills was white-lacquered and glossy, a dining room as much about art as about Peking Duck—Andy Warhol, Jean-Michel Basquiat, Jack Nicholson, and Lana Turner all passing through at one time or another. Keith Haring painted the owner, Michael Chow, as three wriggling Green Prawns in a bowl of Noodles, and the actual Green Prawns on the menu—violently colored, almost cartoonish—were said to be Haring's favorite dish.

Le Dome, co-owned for a time by Elton John, sat on the end of the strip like a lit shell—a chic French stage set wrapped around its famous circular bar. The gossip columns listed regulars like Sylvester Stallone, Richard Gere, Gregory Peck, Liza Minnelli, Diana Ross, Sting, Julio Iglesias, agents and rock stars turning Seafood and Steak au Poivre into props for their own performances.

Down in Santa Monica, Chinois on Main opened in 1983, Puck's East-meets-West landmark, quickly dubbed the epicenter of LA's social scene. Goldie Hawn, Robert Redford, Robert De Niro, and Mick Jagger ate Shanghai Lobster with curry and shatter-crisp Spinach, whole catfish, Goose Liver with Mango. The room was always packed with producers and musicians squeezed into too-small chairs.

The original Spago Hollywood (8795 Sunset Blvd), featuring its iconic *Eyes* mural. This was the epicenter of celebrity power dining before the legendary location closed its doors in 2001.

And threaded through this whole world, almost like a running joke, was California Pink Peppercorn. Everywhere you looked there were these tiny blush-colored bullets—on risotto, on fish, on pasta, hiding in Pepper mills—the "spice of the eighties," as one restaurateur called it, an edible emblem of nouvelle cuisine's obsession with lightness and color.

In Ciro's Pomodoro, next to the Beverly Center, food critic Barbara Hansen singled out a plate of Pink Peppercorn Pasta with Roasted Bell Peppers, Shrimp, and Blueberry Vinaigrette. "How's that for trendy?" she wrote, admiring and amused at the same time. At Chinois, a review described seared Scallops "topped with a confetti of Pink Peppercorns" in a Beurre-Rose-style Sauce of Red Wine and Onions. At Patina, on Melrose Avenue in Hollywood, you could order Lobster Risotto with Pink Peppercorn Sauce. Over on Beverly Boulevard, Café Blanc sent out Chilean Sea Bass topped with Orange Rind and Pink Peppercorns.

It was the perfect spice for that decade in Los Angeles. On a white plate under a halogen spotlight, the little Peppercorn did everything at once. It was a color accent, a texture, a fragrant scent. Chefs loved how it behaved graphically: tiny round dots positioned just so along the edge of a sauce, a constellation you were not quite sure if you were meant to eat or just

Mr Chow, 1986, Acrylic on canvas, Keith Haring artwork © Keith Haring Foundation.

Restaurateur Mr. Chow watches a noodle chef in his restaurant, New York, New York, December 9, 1983.

admire. In magazines, you'd see it perched on Scallops, hiding in a sauce for Lobster, freckling a disc of fresh Goat Cheese like a blush. It had the same energy as Memphis furniture and shoulder pads on *Dynasty*—decorative, confident, a little ridiculous.

And here's the '80s plot twist: Pink Peppercorn was not really Pepper at all, which made it even *more* eighties. It isn't a seed from the Pepper vine, but the dried berry of the California Pepper tree, *Schinus molle*—a Cashew cousin from the Andes Mountains that was first planted along mission roads and dusty Los Angeles streets for shade. Long before it found its way into Pepper mills in Beverly Hills, it had been standing outside hardware stores and bakeries, shaking its feathery leaves over parked cars, dropping clusters of rosy berries onto cracked sidewalks. A street tree, doing municipal work, then suddenly upgraded to celebrity status—invited into the best dining rooms in town and sprinkled over plates for movie stars.

It fit the era perfectly because it was slightly fake and slightly dangerous. A Pepper that was not Pepper. A berry from the Cashew family—cousin to Mango—dressed up as fine seasoning. Then came the rumors: headaches, swollen eyelids, upset stomachs. Articles appeared warning that Pink Peppercorn might behave like Poison Ivy when eaten. Doctors and regulators noticed that *Schinus* sat in the same family tree as allergens and irritants. The US Food and Drug Administration got nervous and banned imports. Overnight, those pretty pink dots disappeared. Chefs quietly retired their jars, moved on to balsamic vinegar and sun-dried Tomatoes. Pink Peppercorn went from overnight status symbol to a has-been.

[LEFT] Su Huntley's 1980 painting of Le Dôme's menu. [RIGHT] Diana Ross and Hollywood agent Irving Paul "Swifty" Lazar. They were attending Lazar's annual Oscar party at Spago's restaurant in Hollywood, California, on April 11, 1988.

That rise and fall is very Los Angeles. A face in the crowd, plucked from obscurity, put under lights, then dropped just as fast. A street tree whose berries were seen briefly as fashionable, then left to stain the pavement again.

If you walk through certain neighborhoods in Los Angeles in December, you will still see those berries hanging in grape-like clusters—translucent pink and coral, each one the size of a Peppercorn, weighing down the tips of the branches. When a car rolls over the ones that have fallen into the gutter, they crack and release their remarkable scent. On a warm winter afternoon at Flamingo Estate, when the air is dry and the light is thin, I've stepped out of the house and realized the pathway smells of the Pink Peppercorn because of the trees we have here: sweet, peppery, resinous, caught between spice and perfume.

A classic early 1900s postcard showcasing the legendary Pepper Tree Walk on Marengo Avenue in Pasadena. Planted in the late nineteenth century, these Pepper trees created a sprawling natural canopy that became a primary tourist attraction for early Southern California visitors.

The first impression is bright and crisp—a Peppery spark that feels less like heat and more like electricity. There is Citrus in it: Grapefruit zest, a twist of Lemon rind, that little sting you get when you peel an Orange and the oils spray up into your face. Underneath is a gentle sweetness, almost like Rose petals left in a warm room. There is something floral, but not soft; something woody, but not heavy. Juniper, maybe, and Angelica root. It is spice, but it is also already a finished, perfect fragrance.

In perfume, Pink Pepper from the California Pepper tree has become a kind of bridge. It sits between Citrus, flower, and wood and speaks all three languages. It's bright enough to stand with Lime, Grapefruit, and Bergamot in the top of a perfume, pushing their light further, making them feel more modern, less polite. It's rosy and fruity enough to flirt with Rose and Geranium in the heart, giving them a little neon edge, stopping them from collapsing into nostalgia. And there is that dry, woody, almost smoky thread running underneath that nods to Cedar, Vetiver, and the darker resins waiting in the base. At Flamingo Estate, we think of Pink Pepper as the thing that switches the lights on. You will find it in our Jasmine and Damask Body Wash and Hand Soap, keeping them from smelling too "old lady." It's inside our Jasmine candle for the same reason, to give the scent some electricity, some star power.

The tree itself has had a much longer, stranger life than its brief '80s stardom suggests. Before it became the California Pepper tree, *Schinus molle* was simply Mulli in the high valleys of Peru. The Quechua used its berries to brew Chicha de Molle, a fermented drink that tasted of spice and sun. They chewed the resin as a kind of chewing gum, burned the leaves in ritual smoke to cleanse and bless, used the bark and berries as antiseptic for wounds and aching joints. The tree was a pharmacy, pantry, and an altar.

Sometime in the nineteenth century, seeds and saplings began to travel north on ships—carried by missionaries, sea captains, and hopeful settlers. In California, the Pepper tree thrived. It liked the dry heat and the thin, stony soils. It liked being ignored. By the 1880s there were avenues of them in Los Angeles and San Diego, lacing the air with their faint Peppery smell whenever someone brushed against a branch. They were planted at missions and ranchos, in schoolyards and plazas, in front of courthouses and motels. Their feathery leaves and weeping silhouettes became part of the city's visual vocabulary long before Palm trees took over the postcards.

So when French chefs and food editors in the 1980s went searching for something new to scatter on their plates, Pink Pepper was ready. Dried and packed in little glass jars, its berries left the tree for a second time and flew back across the ocean, this time as garnish. They appeared in Pepper mills on white tablecloths, rattling against Black and Green Peppercorns. They landed on Carpaccio and Goat Cheese, floated in Cream sauces, sat like tiny ornaments on Strawberry Tarts. Then came the panic, the FDA letters, the quiet vanishing—and the California Pepper tree was left once more to do its quiet work in the background.

What I love now is that Pink Pepper has found its way into perfume instead of trying to dominate the plate. It has slipped out of the restaurant and into the bottle. If the 1980s made it a visual symbol—those perfect dots against white porcelain—then modern perfumery has rescued its smell from that decade and given it back its depth. Now, instead of sitting on Kiwi and Sea Bass, it sits on Jasmine and Damask Rose.

Since the early 2000s, Pink Pepper has quietly gone from curiosity to almost standard equipment in modern perfumery—showing up in something like one in every fourteen new fragrances (which is huge for a single spice note). Its use in fragrances is growing at 7 percent annual growth, which is faster than overall perfume market growth. An industry trend report literally called Pink Pepper "the note of the future" and "a clear marker of something modern and youthful."

We love a good celebrity comeback.

Jean-Michel Basquiat, Michael Chow, Basquiat's Mother, and Two Waiters, 1986, Black and White Print 8 × 10 inches. Image and Artwork © 2026 The Andy Warhol Foundation for the Visual Arts, Inc. / Licensed by ARS

[GROUNDING] : A MAP OF PLEASURE FROM THE GARDEN

THE SPICE GARDEN

34°08' N / 118°12' W LOS ANGELES, CALIFORNIA

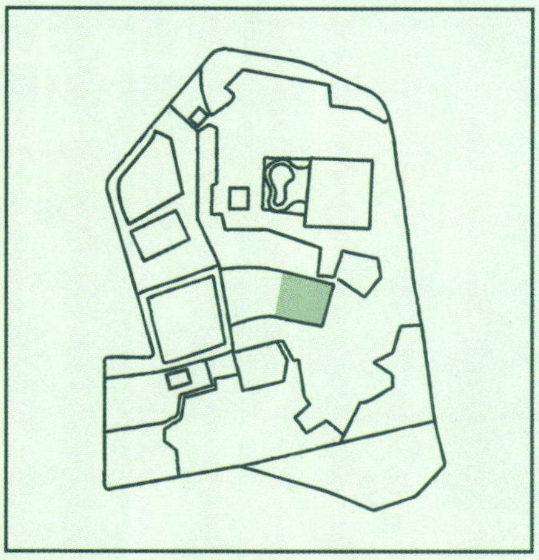

Fresh Mint from the Flamingo Garden, photographed by Phillip Huynh in 2023.

When I was in high school, I worked in a Thai restaurant called Eazy Peezy. It sat in Main Beach, just next to Surfers Paradise—a glossy beach town full of high-rise hotels, surf shops, and kids with cleaner sneakers than mine. We didn't live anywhere near there. Our farm was more than an hour away, so after work I'd climb into my car and make the long drive past Sugar Cane fields and orchards.

My job was to chop. Vegetables, herbs, spices—anything that might end up in the wok. The kitchen was small and hot, and I stood shoulder to shoulder with the chef. When an order came in—say, green curry—a ticket would slam onto the counter and I had about sixty seconds to get everything into a small metal bowl. Chiles, Galangal, Lemongrass, Garlic, Thai Basil. I would slide the bowl to him and he'd slam it into the pan with a hiss of oil.

He was a fiery taskmaster—forever shouting over the roar of the burners, telling me to move faster and learn every recipe by heart so my hands could work before my brain even caught up. I was expected to know which curry needed Makrut Lime

Cooking Thai in the kitchen, and then later in Thailand learning about food and spices in my early twenties.

leaves, which one took Holy Basil, which one began with Ginger instead of Galangal. There was no time for guessing.

The kitchen was open to the dining room, so the patrons could see everything. This mortified me. All the fancy kids from my school would come in with their glossy parents for expensive Thai dinners, and there I'd be—hair smelling of fish sauce, hands stained yellow from Turmeric—chopping their vegetables. One night a family from school pointed and laughed as they walked past the line. I can still feel the burn of that shame in my cheeks. For years afterward, that feeling was rocket fuel. I wanted a life where no one could laugh at me behind a plate of pad thai.

Time, of course, is always the great judge of these things. Looking back now, my nights at Eazy Peezy were a kind of apprenticeship. I learned how to make tom yum goong, khao

An eighteenth-century botanical illustration of a Cinnamon tree (*Cinnamomum verum*), from *Die Welt in Bildern*, a historical illustrated work published in Vienna.

Hand-colored lithograph of Garlic (*Allium sativum*) by David Blair from Robert Bentley and Henry Trimen's *Medicinal Plants*, London, 1880.

soi, and green curry with my eyes closed. I learned how to prep an entire dish in under a minute, and how to slice a Chile so fine it looked like red thread. But more importantly, I learned the art of spice—how a pinch of the right thing can turn a simple pot of Coconut milk into a drum solo.

At home, our food was classic Australian English—meat and mashed Potatoes. If there were spices in the house, they lived in the back of the cupboard: a dusty jar of Cinnamon that came out once a year at Christmas. We never thought of spices as the main event, and certainly never as perfume.

The Thai kitchen changed that forever. I learned that Galangal is Ginger's wilder cousin—harder, more citrusy, with a Pine-like, slightly floral smell that hits you in the back of the throat. That Lemongrass is bright and green and lemony, but with something almost minty humming underneath. That Makrut Lime leaves, when you tear them in half, release a fragrance so sharp and clean it's like someone opened a window in your head. I fell madly in love with Thai Basil and Holy Basil (still my favorite scent on Earth) and Cilantro, which I could eat by the handful like salad.

I would drive home late at night with all those smells clinging to me—Chile and Garlic on my fingers, Coconut and Lime in my hair. I didn't know it then, but those shifts were my first lessons in perfume, in how smell can guide you long before language arrives.

Recently, Harvey and I were invited by the Prime Minister of Thailand to speak about the way Thailand can increase its "soft power" by investing in its farms and ingredients. We were on television with the Prime Minister and presented to government officials, promoting the idea of bringing the same gravitas to Thai spices that Italy has brought to Parmesan and Japan to Kobe beef. These ingredients are treasures.

Heirloom Garlic arranged in a kitchen garland, photographed by Hugh Davison at the Estate kitchen, 2024. The ultimate flavor amplifier, we cook with it constantly—and occasionally hang it at the front gate to keep the energy vampires away.

From Tod Browning's iconic 1931 film *Dracula*, in which Count Dracula prepares to make Mina his next victim. Girl, where was your Garlic???

Botanical illustration of the Saffron crocus (*Crocus sativus*) from *La Botanique* by Jean-Jacques Rousseau, published in Paris, 1822.

Today at Flamingo, the Spice Garden sits in a prime position—the sunniest part of the property, at the bottom of the big brick staircase. It's the first place the morning light hits and the last place the evening heat lets go. We grow Cinnamon (*Cinnamomum verum*), Saffron (*Crocus sativus*), Clove (*Syzygium aromaticum*), Garlic (*Allium sativum*), Fennel (*Foeniculum vulgare*), Cumin (*Cuminum cyminum*), California Nutmeg (*Torreya californica*), Black Pepper (*Piper nigrum*), Pink Pepper (*Schinus molle*), Celery Seed (*Apium graveolens*), Cardamom (*Elettaria cardamomum*), Ginger (*Zingiber officinale*), Turmeric (*Curcuma longa*), Curry Leaf (*Murraya koenigii*), Mustard (*Sinapis alba*), Jalapeños (*Capsicum annuum*), and more.

In 1637, these jars of spice represented the pinnacle of aristocratic luxury, more valuable than gold. Paolo Antonio Barbieri's *The Spice Shop* captures the era when a handful of Peppercorns or a stick of Cinnamon was a global status symbol.

CINNAMON is the best example. Its power lives in the bark—peeled, dried, rolled into quills—and a single pinch can light up a whole kitchen like a match. It's heat and sweetness, perfume and warning, proportion as destiny.

NUTMEG, too, looks innocent until you grate it: warm, woody, peppery, sweet—and in high doses, strangely mind-altering, as if the seed has its own mischievous secret.

CARDAMOM is minty-honeyed brightness with a green, camphorous edge—the "Queen of Spices," elegant but unmistakable, the kind of note that makes coffee feel dressed.

CLOVE is warmth with a dark, medicinal polish; you smell it and your nervous system sits up straighter.

Then there are the spices that behave like lightning. MUSTARD is one—a tiny seed that becomes a nose-clearing fire the moment it's crushed and activated. JALAPEÑOS are another. Brush past the plants and you get that faint metallic green note—the smell that inspired our Highland Park Jalapeño Candle—but bite one and your body floods itself with endorphins, turning pain into a kind of pleasure. Los Angeles understands this paradox better than most cities: heat as medicine, thrill as nourishment.

And SAFFRON—Saffron is devotion. A spice so hard-won it feels almost religious: threads lifted by hand from flowers that bloom briefly, once a year, and carry a scent like warm hay, leather, and sunlight trapped in cloth.

When the wind picks up in the Spice Garden you can smell TURMERIC—grounding, musky, earthy, like fresh soil and late afternoon sunshine.

CURRY LEAF, crushed between your fingers, is its own sensory spell: first a flash of Mandarin and Lime, then toasted spice and warm Pepper.

The spice market on the grounds of the Royal Palace in Tehran, circa 1890.

A vendor navigates the streets of Caracas, Venezuela, in 1937 with a massive haul of Garlic—the essential spice that powered the city's kitchens and markets.

Standing there, you realize spices are not "background." They are small, concentrated forces—bark, seed, pod, stigma—designed to survive, to persuade, to protect, to seduce.

On hot days, standing there feels like being back in that Thai kitchen—only now the sky is bigger, the birds are louder, and I'm the one writing the recipes. A chorus of bees works the flowers. The soil is alive with worms and mycelium. Every leaf, every seed head, is some small act of rebellion against blandness.

I have enormous gratitude for that grumpy old Thai chef now. For the long drives, the burned fingertips, the nights I wanted to hide when my classmates walked in. In their own way, they all seasoned my life. They gave me my first real understanding of flavor, of smell, of courage.

They gave my life some spice.

INSIDE THE SPICE GARDEN AT FLAMINGO ESTATE:

ALLSPICE [*PIMENTA DIOICA*]

BAY LEAF [*LAURUS NOBILIS*]

BLACK PEPPER [*PIPER NIGRUM*]

CALIFORNIA NUTMEG [*TORREYA CALIFORNICA*]

CARDAMOM [*ELETTARIA CARDAMOMUM*]

CELERY SEED [*APIUM GRAVEOLENS*]

CHILE / JALAPEÑO [*CAPSICUM ANNUUM*]

CILANTRO [*CORIANDRUM SATIVUM*]

CINNAMON [*CINNAMOMUM CASSIA / VERUM*]

CLOVE [*SYZYGIUM AROMATICUM*]

CUMIN [*CUMINUM CYMINUM*]

CURRY LEAF [*MURRAYA KOENIGII*]

FENNEL [*FOENICULUM VULGARE*]

GALANGAL [*ALPINIA OFFICINARUM*]

GARLIC [*ALLIUM SATIVUM*]

GINGER [*ZINGIBER OFFICINALE*]

HOLY BASIL [*TULSI OCIMUM TENUIFLORUM*]

LEMONGRASS [*CYMBOPOGON CITRATUS*]

MAKRUT LIME [*CITRUS HYSTRIX*]

MORINGA [*MORINGA OLEIFERA*]

MUSTARD [*SINAPIS ALBA*]

PAPRIKA [*CAPSICUM ANNUUM*]

PINK PEPPER [*SCHINUS MOLLE*]

ROSELLE [*HIBISCUS SABDARIFFA*]

SAFFRON [*CROCUS SATIVUS*]

STAR ANISE [*ILLICIUM VERUM*]

THAI BASIL [*OCIMUM BASILICUM VAR. THYRSIFLORA*]

TURMERIC [*CURCUMA LONGA*]

[1]

[2]

[3]

[4]

[1] The "waffle gardens" surrounding the Indian Pueblo of Zuni, photographed in 1873 as part of the US government's Geographical and Geological Explorations West of the 100th Meridian, show how the Zuni people used sunken, grid-like plots to grow vegetables such as Peppers in arid environments.

[2] Pepper plant (*Capsicum annuum*) by Franz Anton von Scheidl in 1776.

[3] Harvesting Garlic as recommended in the fifteenth-century medieval health handbook, *Taccuinum Sanitatis*.

[4] Vintage souvenir postcard from 1948 with strings of red Chili Peppers, known as ristras, hanging to dry in the autumn sun. The practice of drying Chili Peppers is a traditional method of preservation in the American Southwest, particularly in New Mexico.

[XII]
DECEMBER

WINTER

DIRTY WORK

"Rest is not idleness."

—JOHN LUBBOCK

GARDEN TASKS:

- [ ] Mulch deeply under trees with leaves, compost, or straw to insulate roots and hold moisture.
- [ ] Collect fallen leaves for compost or use them as mulch—free minerals for the soil.
- [ ] Harvest cool-season vegetables: Kale, Chard, Spinach, Arugula, Fennel, Carrots, Beets, Peas.
- [ ] Succession sow Lettuce, Radish, Cilantro for steady winter picking.
- [ ] Feed leafy greens every few weeks with diluted compost tea or fish emulsion.
- [ ] Protect seedlings from slugs and snails after rain; keep beds tidy and mulched between rows.
- [ ] Cut back tender herbs (Mint, Parsley, Chervil) to encourage compact growth.
- [ ] Plant Garlic, Onions, and Shallots if you haven't yet—last call before the solstice.
- [ ] Enjoy winter bloomers: Camellias, Narcissus, Hellebores—top-dress with compost.
- [ ] Plant winter color: Violas, Pansies, Stock, Calendula; sow Sweet Peas if you haven't yet.
- [ ] Plant Ranunculus, Anemones, and Freesia bulbs to root quietly through the cold.
- [ ] Cut back spent Salvias and grasses, but leave some seed heads for birds.
- [ ] Turn compost and add a little nitrogen (kitchen scraps and green clippings) to keep it cooking.
- [ ] Repair trellises, edging, and irrigation while the garden rests.
- [ ] Clean and oil tools so they're ready when spring arrives.

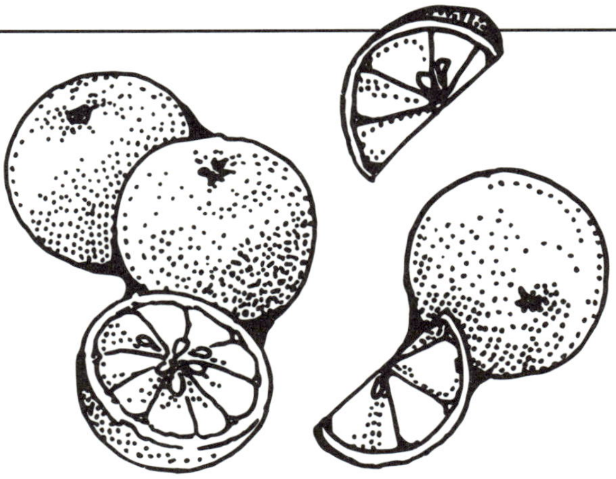

TASK SMOKE YOUR ORNAMENTS ☐

Skip the plastic and glass, and make ornaments that actually perfume the room. Slice Citrus (Oranges, Lemons, Mandarins) into thin rounds, then dry them in a low oven until leathery. Set up a smoker—or DIY one with a pot, foil, wood chips, and a rack—and smoke the slices for 1-2 hours over something mild and sweet like Apple or Cherry wood. For extra magic, toss in a few Cinnamon sticks or Star Anise.

TASK MULL SOME WINE ☐

Heat your favorite red wine with sliced Apples, Pears, Citrus, Cinnamon, Cloves, Star Anise, and a bit of sweetener (we prefer Honey or Cane Sugar). Add brandy, or don't. Simmer gently (don't boil) until your kitchen and living room smell incredible. Serve hot.

TASK

CREATE A FAMILY SPICE BLEND

My mother and I were traveling through Greece, and I had an unforgettable meal with the family of one of the farmers. They made the pasta by hand, then finished it with a very special family spice blend. I asked what it was, and they refused to tell me. The blend was a secret recipe—handed down from one generation to the next. They'll gift it to friends, but they never reveal the ingredients.

I love the idea of every family having its own proprietary spice blend—something a grandmother passes down to the grandkids and everyone remembers. It's the kind of thing that makes pasta taste incredible on a cold night. To start your own, experiment with the bold, concentrated forces of the garden: Fennel, Cumin, Garlic, or the sharp, citrusy spark of Pink Pepper.

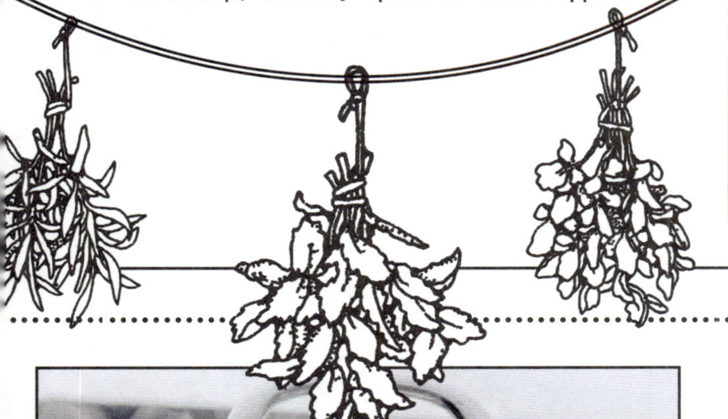

TASK

BOTTLE YOUR OWN CHRISTMAS TREE

A few years ago we made an essential oil from hundreds of discarded Christmas trees. If you don't have a fancy alembic still to steam-distill it, you can do a simple version at home.

Chop up the needles and tuck them into a large pot with a little water. Set a small heatproof bowl in the center to catch the drips, then cover the pot with the lid upside down and pile ice on top. As the water simmers gently, steam rises through the needles, carrying their oils. The vapor hits the cold lid, condenses, and drips into the bowl.

Let it go for 30-60 minutes, refreshing the ice as needed. Carefully remove the bowl and skim off the oil (it will float on top). The leftover Pine water is a fragrant hydrosol for linens, floors, or a quick room mist—and the rest of the tree can go straight into the compost.

TASK

HANG HOSHIGAKI

☐

Hoshigaki is Japan's way of turning a Persimmon into a piece of candy. Traditionally made in the countryside each autumn, it's simply Hachiya Persimmons, air, time, and hands. You peel the fruit but leave the stems on, tie a string around each one, and dip them quickly in boiling water to sterilize.

Then they're hung in a dry, warm, breezy spot—a sunny window or under the eaves—and left to dry. After about a week, you begin to gently massage each Persimmon every day so it shrinks and softens, and the sugars migrate to the surface. Over 4-6 weeks they turn from bright orange to a deep, translucent amber, and a natural white "frost" of sugar blooms on the skin. They're ready when they're firm but pliable, chewy, and intensely caramel-sweet. Properly made, Hoshigaki will keep for a year . . . but in my experience, they never last that long.

TASK

☐

Plant a Real Holiday Tree

My mother and I planted a Mango tree (*Mangifera indica*) on my first Christmas at Flamingo Estate. Now it's my official Christmas tree. Every year we decorate it like a shrine—lights, ribbons, the whole ceremony—and every time it sprouts another Mango, I think about my parents, the holidays, and how this is the only tree that gifts me back.

If you don't have a Mango, pick any living tree you can commit to—Citrus, Olive, Bay, Fig—plant it or claim one in the yard, decorate it for the season, and let it become a tradition that grows instead of gets thrown away.

TASK ☐

Make a Wish

A Wishing Tree is our Thanksgiving gesture. Gather your end-of-year thank-yous and your please-let-this-happens, write them down on small scraps of paper, and tie them to a tree with string or ribbon. Then walk away and let the wind do the rest—shaking them loose, spinning them around, and filling the air with gratitude and intention.

TASK

MAKE A WREATH

☐

We like to smoke Citrus and combine it with Clove and Bay Leaves, but there are no rules—and it doesn't even need to be circular. Gather whatever the garden is giving (branches, leaves, herbs, dried flowers), tie it into a shape that feels good with twine, and hang it on the door. The important thing is that it tells everyone, before they even knock, that this is a happy home.

TASK

HANG CLOVE & ORANGE POMANDERS

☐

Take a firm Orange and use a toothpick to poke small holes all over the skin, then press whole Cloves into the holes. For extra fragrance, roll the Orange in Cinnamon or Nutmeg. Let it dry in a cool, airy spot for a week or two. Once ready, hang it near a window, on your Christmas tree, or the old-school way—around your neck or belt.

RECIPE

MEAT PIE

MEAT FILLING:

- 1½ lb ground beef
- Salt and Pepper, to taste
- 1 medium yellow Onion, small diced
- 1 large Carrot, diced
- 2 stalks of Celery, diced
- 3 cloves Garlic, minced
- 1 Tbsp Tomato paste
- ½ Tbsp dried Oregano
- 1 tsp dashi powder
- 1½ Tbsp sherry vinegar
- 1 Tbsp cornstarch
- 2 cups chicken stock
- ½ cup frozen Peas

[1] Set a heavy-bottomed pot with 2 tablespoons of oil over medium-high heat.

[2] Sear and brown the ground beef, breaking up the mince and seasoning with salt and pepper. Remove and set aside.

[3] In the same pot, add the onions, carrots, celery, and garlic. Sauté until softened (about 3–4 minutes).

[4] Add the tomato paste, stirring to cook for 1 minute. Turn heat down to medium.

[5] Add the oregano, dashi powder, sherry vinegar, cornstarch, and beef plus all its juices to the pot, stirring to combine.

[6] Pour in the chicken stock, bring to a simmer, and season once more before turning the heat to low. Leave to simmer for 30 minutes, until reduced by a third. Turn off heat, stir in frozen peas, and set aside.

PIE DOUGH:

- 2½ cups all-purpose flour
- ½ tsp Salt
- 1 cup butter, chilled and cut into cubes
- 1 large egg
- ¼ cup water, chilled
- ½ cup cream, chilled

[1] Gently whisk flour and salt in a large bowl.

[2] Add the butter cubes and, using your thumbs and index fingers, work in the butter, pressing it into the flour to form flattened pieces. Place the bowl in the fridge while you wash your hands and prepare the next step.

[3] Whisk together the egg, water, and cream in a small bowl. Once mixed, pour the egg mixture over the flour. Use a spatula to mix and gather into a dough ball. Turn out the dough and wrap tightly in plastic wrap, leaving to rest in the refrigerator for 30 minutes.

[4] Unwrap the dough, roll out to 2-inch thickness, and cut into 4 quarters. Stack the 4 quarters and press down. Roll the stacked dough to 1-inch thick, wrap, and chill.

ASSEMBLY:

- A small bowl of water
- 2 eggs and 1 egg yolk, beaten, for egg wash

[1] Preheat the oven to 415°F.

[2] Lightly flour a clean work surface, unwrap the dough, and dust with flour.

[3] Roll the dough out until you reach ⅕-inch thickness. Turn the dough as you roll and dust as needed to prevent it from sticking to your work surface.

[4] Use a ring mold or a knife to cut out 5-inch rounds or squares (whichever you prefer!). You should get 12 total.

[5] Place ⅓ cup of meat filling in the center of half of your cutouts, wet the edges of the dough with a little water, and adhere the top cutouts.

[6] Use a fork to crimp or pinch and fold to secure the edges of the pie. Repeat this process with the remaining pies.

[7] Brush the tops of the pies with egg wash and refrigerate for 15 minutes before baking.

[8] Bake for 20 minutes, or until golden and crisp. Serve hot with ketchup!

RECIPE

COCONUT CURRY SQUASH BOWL

☐

RED CURRY PASTE:

- 16 dried Chile de Árbol Chiles, seeds removed and soaked in warm water
- 2 Tbsp Lemongrass, pale tender stem only (heartier outer leaves removed)
- 1 Tbsp Galangal, peeled and grated
- 4 cloves Garlic
- ½ tsp toasted Coriander
- ½ tsp toasted Cumin
- ½ tsp Turmeric powder
- 1 Tbsp chopped Cilantro root and stems
- 2 small red Shallots, peeled and roughly chopped
- 1 tsp Lime zest
- ½ Tbsp Lime juice
- 1 tsp neutral oil
- ¼ cup reserved Chile soaking water

[1] In a food processor, combine all ingredients and process into a smooth paste. You can also use a mortar and pestle to pound the ingredients into a paste.

PINK PEPPERCORN AND PEPITA CROUTONS:

- 3-4 slices of sourdough bread, cut or ripped into small bite-sized pieces
- 4 Tbsp fresh Pink Peppercorns
- 2 Tbsp untoasted Pepitas
- Olive oil
- Salt, to taste

[1] Preheat oven to 375°F.

[2] Toss bread, peppercorns, and pepitas in a bowl with a generous amount of olive oil, seasoning with salt to taste.

[3] Bake for 15-20 minutes, tossing intermittently, until golden and fragrant.

COCONUT CURRY SOUP:

- 2 Tbsp Olive oil
- 2 Yukon Gold Potatoes, peeled and roughly diced
- 2 medium Carrots, peeled and roughly diced
- 1 cup Butternut Squash (or any Winter Squash of your liking), peeled and diced
- 1 yellow Onion, peeled and diced
- 2 cans Coconut milk
- 3 Tbsp red curry paste
- 1 cup vegetable broth
- Salt, to taste

[1] Set a heavy-bottomed pot over medium-high heat with 2 tablespoons of olive oil.

[2] Add potatoes, carrots, squash, and onions; sauté for 3 minutes, until they begin to soften.

[3] Add coconut milk, curry paste, and vegetable broth, stirring to combine.

[4] Bring to a boil, then turn down to a simmer. Season to taste and continue to cook for 30 minutes. All the vegetables should be fork-tender.

[5] Remove from heat and, using an immersion blender, blend until smooth.

[6] Serve hot in hollowed-out roasted squash bowls, topped with pink peppercorn and pepita croutons.

RECIPE

SANDY'S GINGERBREAD COOKIES

GINGERBREAD:

- $2\frac{1}{4}$ cups all-purpose flour
- 2 tsp ground Cinnamon
- 2 tsp ground Ginger
- 1 tsp baking soda
- $\frac{1}{2}$ tsp fine Sea Salt
- $\frac{1}{4}$ tsp ground Cloves
- $\frac{1}{2}$ cup unsalted butter, room temperature
- $\frac{2}{3}$ cup packed dark brown sugar
- $\frac{1}{3}$ cup unsulphured blackstrap molasses
- 1 large egg yolk
- 1 tsp Vanilla extract
- 1 Tbsp milk

PREPARATION:

- Mix together all the dry ingredients in a medium bowl and set aside.
- In the bowl of a stand mixer with a paddle attachment, on medium speed, cream together butter and sugar.
- Add molasses, egg yolk, and vanilla; continue to mix until combined.
- Turn the mixer down to low and spoon in the dry ingredients until completely incorporated. Add milk to soften the dough.
- Scoop out the dough, wrap in plastic wrap, and rest in the fridge for 15 minutes.
- Preheat oven to 350°F.
- Lightly flour a clean work surface and unwrap the dough.
- Roll out dough to $\frac{1}{4}$-inch thickness. Cut out shapes to your liking (geometric shapes or gingerbread men) and transfer onto a parchment-lined sheet tray.
- Bake for 9–10 minutes, until the edges are set and the center is still soft. For a crispier cookie, you can bake for an extra 3 minutes.
- Cool completely on a wire rack before decorating.

SUGAR ICING:

- 1 cup confectioners' sugar
- 2 tsp light corn syrup
- $\frac{1}{4}$ tsp Vanilla extract
- 1 Tbsp milk
- Food coloring: we used red, yellow, black, white, and green

PREPARATION:

- Sift the sugar, then mix in the corn syrup and vanilla extract.
- Add milk, 1 tsp at a time, to reach a thickness similar to Manuka honey.
- Divide into 5 small bowls (one for each color) and add food coloring a little at a time until you reach your desired color.
- Transfer icing into separate piping bags, and happy decorating!

NOSE DIVE
[XII]

ROASTING

There is nothing as comforting as the smell of Garlic sizzling, Potatoes roasting, Pumpkin seeds crackling in heat. The very heat that releases buttery and caramelized smells is what warms us, and we get intimate with the world by being there, and breathing it in.

When food goes through the alchemy of heat, it comes out transformed. In the process, flying molecules get released into the air and signal to our system that energy and sustenance is on the way. Stirring the appetite awake with the sweet, toasted smells of sugar and carbs jumping out to meet us. So, our brains prepare and anticipate. Releasing dopamine and stimulating the opioid system, which triggers warm feelings.

Upon smelling roasted vegetables and baked bread, we experience a wild sense of euphoria and comfort. Food is coming. Life will continue. We are safe. These familiar aromas can reduce activity in the hypothalamic-pituitary-adrenal (HPA) axis, lowering stress hormones like cortisol.

It's impossible to capture the full aromatic immensity of food transforming in heat. But to try, we can focus on one process we know well: the smell of food "browning." This magical smell is due to the Maillard Reaction, and it happens when amino acids from proteins meet sugars at high heat. Well above 300°F, hundreds of new aromatic compounds are produced. Among them, pyrazines, which are nutty and popcorn-like. Furans, sweet and caramel-like. And thiophenes, mostly savory and meaty.

When coming into direct contact with flame and smoke, things get intense. Grilling and charring releases smoky, woody aromas that can be both spicy and sweet. Oils and fats fall on hot coals and instantly combust, releasing the classic barbecue smell we can recognize with our eyes closed. Sugars are burning and caramelizing, edges are blackening, and plant fibers release an ashy, earthen scent.

1950s catalog showcasing the "modern" luxury of a glass-door oven, designed to take the guesswork out of Sunday dinner and holiday baking.

[PAGE 400] *Woman Basting a Roast* by H. Armstrong Roberts, circa 1969.

DEC.

Frying is a world of its own, perhaps the most complex of them all, releasing smells that occur from fat undergoing lipid oxidation–a.k.a., oil molecules flying into the air. This process produces molecules such as aldehydes, which are buttery and warm. Ketones, mostly creamy and rich. And lactones, redolent of sweet Coconut. Of course, the fat here matters. If we're frying with Olive oil, the scent will be mostly grassy. Peanut oil, nutty. Ghee, rich and buttery. The most legendary of them all—crispy-fried-chicken-esque—is an aldehyde called 2,4-decadienal. We know. We love it. There is nothing like it.

Someone once said that the smells of frying bacon and coffee were enough to make a man forget his troubles. Science proves it.

Illustration of roast pork from *The Complete Cook* by Nell Heaton, 1947.

CREDITS

INTRO

Sean Hazen, 8
Jeffrey Blackler / Alamy, 9
Glasshouse Images / Alamy, 10
Library of Congress, 11
Jeremy Liebman, 12, 21
Christian Högstedt, 14
Adrian Gaut, 15-17
Hugh Davison, 18, 23
Pia Riverola, 22-23

JANUARY

Hugh Davison, 24, 26, 29, 34, 39, 40, 43-48, 54
Gado Images / Alamy, 27
Abbas / Magnum Photos, 28
Wade Watson/WWD/Penske Media via Getty Images, 29
Album / Alamy, 30
Dania Maxwell / © 2023, Los Angeles Times, 31
Valentino Del Toro, 31
Sean Hazen, 32-33, 41
Historic Images / Alamy, 36
Jeremy Kost, 37
Well/BOT / Alamy, 38
Phillip Huynh, 40
© 2011 Dorann Weber / Getty Images, 40
Courtesy of White Buffalo Land Trust, 40
© Purix Verlag Volker Christen / Bridgeman Images, 41
Pia Riverola, 41, 50
Drew Escrivá, 45
The MET, Henry L. Phillips Collection, Bequest of Henry L. Phillips, 1939, 52
Hegel Holidays Water Glass poses on an umbrella. Painting by Rene Magritte (1898-1967) 1958 Sun. 59, 5×50 cm Private collection, Magritte, Rene (1898-1967) / Private Collection / Luisa Ricciarini / Bridgeman Images Artwork © 2026 C. Herscovici / Artists Rights Society (ARS), New York, 53
2nd May 2020, No. 2 by David Hockney, 54
John Von Pamer, 55

FEBRUARY

Hugh Davison, 56, 62, 71-72, 76-81
Phillip Huynh, 58, 71
University of Southern California Libraries / California Historical Society, 59, 64, 66, 71, 74
May Gibbs © The Northcott Society and Cerebral Palsy Alliance 2026, 60
Penta Springs Limited / Alamy, 63
Sepia Times/Universal Images Group via Getty Images, 64
NB/FS / Alamy, 65
Local History Collection, Orange Public Library & History Center, Orange, CA, 69
UC Riverside, Library, Special Collections and University Archives, 69
Workman and Temple Family Homestead Museum, City of Industry, California, 71
Pia Riverola, 71, 74, 82, 84, 86
Dick Whittington Photography Collection, USC Digital Library, University of Southern California, 71
Sean Hazen, 71
Drew Escrivá, 84, 86
Francois Halard, 84, 86

MARCH

Hugh Davison, 88, 93-94, 107-109, 112-113, 118
Bonnie Schiffman Photography / Getty Images, 90
Barry King / Alamy 91
Graeme Harris, All Rights Reserved 2026 / Bridgeman Images, 92
Touring Club Italiano / UIG / Bridgeman Image, 95
Drew Escrivá, 96, 102
Pierre Blanchard / Stefano Bianchetti / Bridgeman Images, 98
Pictorial Press Ltd / Alamy, 100
Buzz Pictures / Alamy, 100
WALT DISNEY PICTURES / RGR Collection / Alamy, 100
Maximum Film / Alamy, 100
Lebrecht Music & Arts / Alamy, 100-101
RGR Collection / Alamy, 101
Pictorial Press Ltd / Alamy, 101
UCL Art Museum, University College London, UK© UCL Art Museum, University College London/Bridgeman Images, 101
PVDE. All rights reserved 2026 / Bridgeman Images, 101
Jimson Weed, 1936-37 (oil on linen), O'Keeffe, Georgia (1887-1986) / Indianapolis Museum of Art at Newfields, USA / Photo © Indianapolis Museum of Art / Gift of Eli Lilly and Company / Bridgeman Images Artwork: © 2026 Georgia O'Keeffe Museum / Artists Rights Society (ARS), New York, 103
Sean Hazen, 107
Jude Liana, 111
Peter Rae / Fairfax Media via Getty Images, 114
Agencja Fotograficzna Caro / Alamy, 119

APRIL

Christian Högstedt, 120
Hugh Davison, 122, 133, 138, 140-145, 149, 151
Florilegius / Bridgeman Images, 124
National Archives, Sir Henry Wellcome Collection, 124
Biblioteca Capitolare, Verona, Italy / Bridgeman Images, 125
O. Vaering / Bridgeman Images, 127
George Catlin, Bull Dance, Mandan O-kee-pa Ceremony, 1832, oil on canvas, Smithsonian American Art Museum, 128
Paul HANNY / Gamma-Rapho via Getty Images, 130
Courtesy of Swann Auction Galleries Bridgeman Images, 132
Science Photo Library / Alamy, 134
University of Southern California Libraries / California Historical Society, 134
imageBROKER.com / Alamy, 134, 136
Mention Naturallis Biodiversity Center, 135
Dick Whittington Photography Collection, USC Digital Library, University of Southern California, 135-136,
Culture Club/Getty Images, 136
ART Collection / Alamy, 136
JBP/AIC/Bridgeman Images, 136
Prismatic Pictures / Bridgeman Images, 136
Public Domain / NYC Public Library, 137
Bookend / Alamy, 137
Pia Riverola, 139
Lordprice Collection / Alamy, 146
Look and Learn/Bridgeman Images, 151
SSPL/UIG/Bridgeman Images, 151
Keystone View Company/FPG/Archive Photos/ Getty Images, 151
Keystone-France/Gamma-Rapho via Getty Images, 151
Rolls Press/Popperfoto via Getty Images/ Getty Images, 151
Calle Hesslefors/ullstein bild via Getty Images, 151
Christopher Pillitz / Alamy / Alamy, 151
George Rose/Getty Images, 151
Reg Speller/Fox Photos/Getty Images, 151
Mary Evans/Bridgeman Images, 151
Gravure Francaise / Alamy, 151
Trinity Mirror / Mirrorpix / Alamy, 151
Allan Cash Picture Library / Alamy, 151
Lordprice Collection / Alamy, 151
Ewing Galloway / Alamy, 151

MAY

Hugh Davison, 152, 154, 160, 169-174
The Nature Notes / Alamy, 156
Kim Landy / Getty Images, 157
San Diego Historical Society Negative Collection, 158
Valley Times Collection / Los Angeles Public Library, 158
Look and Learn / Elgar Collection / Bridgeman Images, 162
ARTGEN / Alamy, 163
Clement Prioli, All rights reserved 2026 / Bridgeman Images, 163
Pia Riverola, 169
Lebrecht Music & Arts / Alamy, 176
Staff/Mirrorpix via Getty Images, 179

JUNE

Hugh Davison, 180, 182, 188, 190, 193, 197-199
Markus Volk / Alamy, 184
BG/OLOU / Alamy, 184
Arclumiva / Alamy, 185

Pia Riverola, 186
Phillip Huynh, 188
Adriano Bacchella / Cuboimages / Bridgeman Images, 189
Prismatic Pictures / Bridgeman Images, 191
Aaron Curry, 192
Bridgeman Images, 194
A. Dagli Orti / © NPL - DeA Picture Library/Bridgeman Images, 195
Past Pix/SSPL/UIG/Bridgeman Images, 200
Copyright "Ed Ruscha," 202

JULY

Hugh Davison, 204, 210-213, 220-225, 229, 231-235, 239
Paul Souders / Getty Images, 214
Penta Springs Limited / Alamy, 217
Craig P. Burrows, 219
MeijiShowa / Alamy, 230
New York Public Library / Public Domain, 230
Jack Bool, 232
Sean Hazen, 236, 241
mauritius images GmbH / Alamy, 238
Pia Riverola, 240-241

AUGUST

Hugh Davison, 242, 248, 257, 261-262, 264-267
Ken Done, 244-245
Lebrecht Music & Arts / Alamy, 246-247
FPG / Archive Photos / Getty Images, 249
Leslie Kirchhoff, 250
The Advertising Archives/Bridgeman Images, 252
ClassicStock / Alamy, 253
Smithsonian Libraries / Public Domain, 253
State Library of Florida, 253
Mary Evans / Bridgeman Images, 254
Pictures Now / Alamy, 254
Pia Riverola, 256, 271
Drew Escrivá, 257
Andy Warhol, Campbell's Soup I: Tomato, 1968 / Image and Artwork © 2026 The Andy Warhol Foundation for the Visual Arts, Inc. / Licensed by ARS, 258
Alfred Stanley Johnson / The History Center, Mansfield PA, 259
JJs / Alamy, 259
Phillip Huynh, 263
Hulton-Deutsch Collection / CORBIS / Corbis via Getty Images, 268
CSU Archives/Everett Collection / Bridgeman Images, 271
© Patrizia Laporta, All Rights Reserved 2026 / Bridgeman Images, 272
© SUDA ISSEI Works, image courtesy of Akio Nagasawa Gallery, 273

SEPTEMBER

Hugh Davison, 274, 276, 280, 285-286, 291-298, 302
Martin Johnson Heade, 279
Chronicle / Alamy, 279
Franz Ittenbach, 279
Richard Christiansen, 284, 289
Elizabeth Weinberg / AUGUST, 287
CCI/Bridgeman Images, 288
Caravaggio, 290
Drew Escrivá, 299
Roger Bamber / Alamy, 300
Sueddeutsche Zeitung Photo / Alamy, 303
Sean Hazen, 304
Bob Gibbons / Alamy, 305
Nature Picture Library / Alamy, 305

OCTOBER

Hugh Davison, 306, 308, 310, 314, 326-327, 329-333
PictureLux / The Hollywood Archive / Alamy, 309
Phillip Huynh, 311
James Bolivar Manson / Christie's Images / Bridgeman Images, 312
Christine Chitnis, 313
Library of Congress, 316
Private Collection/Bridgeman Images, 317
Arthur M. Sackler Gallery, Smithsonian Institution, USANational Museum of Asian Art, Smithsonian Institution / Bridgeman Images, 318
Malindine / Popperfoto via Getty Images, 319
Penta Springs Limited / Alamy, 320
Sean Hazen, 321
Chantal Anderson, 321
John von Pamer, 322
Florilegius / Alamy, 322
Koichi Kamoshida / Getty Images, 324
Public Domain/Flikr - uh_simon, 324
Public Domain/Flikr - Charlie Dave, 324
Koichi Kamoshida / Getty Images, 325
Pia Riverola, 328
Drew Escrivá, 334
Art Collection 2 / Alamy, 337
Chronicle / Alamy, 337
The Picture Art Collection / Alamy, 337
John Fitz Marshall © Christopher Wood Gallery, London, UK / Bridgeman Images, 338
Richard Christiansen, 339

NOVEMBER

Hugh Davison, 340, 343, 348, 350, 353, 355, 359-365
The Picture Art Collection / Alamy, 342
Baron Wilhelm von Gloeden / FM Archive / Alamy, 345
George Rinhart / Corbis via Getty Images, 346
Smithsonian Institution, Bureau of American Ethnology, 346
Drew Escrivá, 349
Carl Iwasaki / Getty Images, 351
Well / BOT / Alamy, 352
Mary Evans / Bridgeman Images, 352
Shawshots / Alamy, 354
Pictorial Press Ltd / Alamy, 354
CPA Media Pte Ltd / Alamy, 354
John Mitchell / Alamy, 354
Prismatic Pictures / Bridgeman Images, 355
Joos Van Craesbeeck, 355
Karl Blossfeldt, 355
US National Library of Medicine / Public Domain, 356
USDA Library / Public Domain, 357
Keystone-France/Gamma-Keystone via Getty Images, 366
Image Professionals GmbH / Alamy, 368
Laperruque / Alamy, 368
Paul Dronsfield / Alamy, 368
Connect Images / Alamy, 369
Carlos Gutiérrez Herrero / Alamy, 369
Photo by Jean-Pierre Fizet / Sygma via Getty Images, 369
Homer Sykes / Alamy, 371

DECEMBER

Hugh Davison, 372, 374, 382, 386, 392-399
RLFE Pix / Alamy, 375
Keith Haring artwork © Keith Haring Foundation, 376
Allan Tannenbaum / Getty Images, 377
Su Huntley, 378
Jim Smeal / Ron Galella Collection via Getty Images, 379
Courtesy of the Gerth Archives and Special Collections, CSU Dominguez Hills, 380
Andy Warhol, photo, Jean-Michel Basquiat, Basquiat's Mother, Michael Chow and Friends 1984 / Image and Artwork © 2026 The Andy Warhol Foundation for the Visual Arts, Inc. / Licensed by ARS, 381
Phillip Huynh, 383
Florilegius / Alamy, 385
piemags / Alamy, 385
Culture Club / Getty Images, 387
Luisa Ricciarini / Bridgeman Images, 388
Private Collection © Look and Learn / Bridgeman Images, 389
Keystone-France/Gamma-Keystone via Getty Images, 389
Heritage Images / Alamy, 391
piemags / DCM / Alamy, 391
H. ARMSTRONG ROBERTS / Alamy, 400
© GraphicaArtis / Bridgeman Images, 403
© Look and Learn / Bridgeman Images, 404

NOTES